THE
DRAGONS' DEN
GUIDE TO
ASSESSING YOUR
BUSINESS
CONCEPT

FOREWORD BY DIANNE BUCKNER

THE
DRAGONS' DEN
GUIDE TO
ASSESSING YOUR
BUSINESS
CONCEPT

THE PRODUCERS OF CBC's DRAGONS' DEN WITH JOHN VYGE

John Wiley & Sons Canada, Ltd.

Library and Archives Canada Cataloguing in Publication Data

The Producers of CBC's Dragon's Den
    The Dragons' Den guide to assessing your business concept / The Producers of CBC's Dragon's Den, John Vyge.
Includes index.
Issued also in electronic format.
ISBN 978-1-118298-80-0
    1. Business planning. 2. Small business—Planning.
3. Marketing research. 4. Dragons' Den (Television program).
I. Vyge, John, 1966- I. Title. II. Title: Assessing your business concept.
HD30.28.V94 2012   658.4'012   C2012-903030-9
978-1-118-31387-9 (ebk); 978-1-118-31385-5 (ebk); 978-1-118-31386-2 (ebk)

Production Credits
Typesetting: Laserwords
Printer: Dickinson

Editorial Credits
Executive editor: Don Loney
Managing editor: Alison Maclean
Production editor:
    Jeremy Hanson-Finger

John Wiley & Sons Canada, Ltd.
6045 Freemont Blvd.
Mississauga, Ontario
L5R 4J3

Printed in the United States of America

1 2 3 4 5 DP 16 15 14 13 12

Partner Credits
Sony Pictures Television:
Lindsay Pearl
    Director of Consumer Product
        Licensing
    Formats, International
        Distribution
Lisa O' Connell
    Product & Brand Manager of
        Consumer Product Licensing
    Formats, International
        Distribution

CBC's Dragons' Den:
Karen Bower
Dianne Buckner
Molly Duignan
Sandra Kleinfeld
Keri Snider
Marc Thompson
Tracie Tighe

SONY
PICTURES
TELEVISION

CONTENTS

FOREWORD
By Dianne Buckner

Everyone loves it when entrepreneurs get a deal with one of the multi-millionaires on *Dragons' Den*. The people pitching for investment are thrilled of course—their dream of building or expanding their business is taking a big step forward. The Dragons themselves love investing and getting a piece of a potentially hot money-maker. And those of us on the production team are delighted, knowing that when the show is eventually broadcast, viewers will share the joy as well! It's wonderful to watch success in the making.

But for every deal that gets done in the Den, there are dozens of others that get flamed. The Dragons have little patience for entrepreneurs who arrive with no business plan, no realistic sense of the value of their company, and no clue about how they're going to capture even just one percent of a multi-billion-dollar industry (as they so often claim they will do).

John Vyge has done an amazing job of distilling the lessons learned from *Dragons' Den* as well as from larger world of business in *The Dragons' Den Guide to Assessing Your Business Concept*.

This book is designed to help would-be entrepreneurs understand what it takes to launch a successful product or service. John breaks down one case study after another into "Ten Success Factors." The business concepts that built well-known companies such a Netflix, Tim Hortons, ReMax, Bacardi Rum, and Mattel are examined alongside dozens of the pitches that have been featured on CBC's hit television show!

How did 19-year-old Ben Gulak, the inventor of a battery-powered unicycle called the Uno, manage to get all five Dragons to invest? What was it about Marissa McTasney of Moxie Trades, creator of a new line of work-wear for women, that so intrigued one of the Dragons? Why did Trudie Wiseman and Jamie Bailey of Canadian Recycle Plastic Products walk out of the Den with a deal?

Sometimes it seems there's an element of magic to what occurs in the Den, when the right idea is presented by the right person at the right time. It can appear that there's an indescribable mix of qualities and circumstances at work, a mysterious kind of chemistry that convinces the Dragons the opportunity in front of them is irresistible.

But as John Vyge shows, there's no random type of "magic" at work. In fact, the process of building a successful business can be described very clearly, as you'll see in this book. John lays out the series of simple steps that every entrepreneur can take, in order to develop their business. He covers off the type of research that can be done to ensure there's a market for your idea, and how to define your value proposition. I would bet that even just the exercise of coming up with that definition will make a reader's business plan that much better. How can you size up your competition, or your costs? What's the right approach to take to branding? To your actual launch? All of these questions and much more are answered by reading the book in your hands.

You want to be prepared, because the fact is that along with the many happy deals done on *Dragons' Den*, we've also heard far too many heart-breaking stories of people who've sacrificed their marriages, their homes, and their savings in pursuit of an idea that just didn't have potential. There's no need for that. Look at the Dragons' own personal stories. None came from especially privileged backgrounds, yet through their own hard work and ingenuity, they've all achieved fame and fortune, and the sense of satisfaction that comes from creating something new and of value to many. It's a dream that *can* be a reality.

So get to it! You have the tools. And once the revenue from your business is growing steadily, you may even be ready to face the Dragons—and be one of the special breed that leave the *Dragons' Den* with a deal!

Part I

The DNA of Your Business Concept

Screen your business concept to ensure that it adheres to the 10 Dragons' Den Success Factors for a scalable growth business.

CHAPTER 1

WHY WOULD THE WORLD CARE ABOUT YOUR IDEA?

"You guys are super impressive. I feel good about the future of this country knowing that it's in the hands of entrepreneurs like you. You guys will make a difference in our country because you're innovative and you're entrepreneurial."
—Dragon to Pitchers

Success Factor #1: Focus on a Singular Pain Point

Solve a yet-to-be-solved burning problem that nothing on the market currently addresses, or addresses poorly. Figure out the root cause of the problem, and use it to design and build a solution in the form of a product or service.

If you want to grow a business quickly, you need to target the customer's *nerve centre*—a singular problem that has not been adequately solved by other competing brands. If you can kill your customer's pain, the market will rush to your product or service. If you want a company with scalable growth potential, you need to isolate a standalone problem or identify a problem with all other competing brands, and then present your product or service as the solution to the customer's needs. And scalability is essential if you want to attract investors.

Great businesses are inspired by an unsolved problem, market void, or issue that is currently not being addressed by anything on the market. Moxie Trades Work Wear clearly illustrates this concept because its founder, Marissa McTasney, built an entire business after discovering a surprising lack of work wear for women.

Moxie Trades Work Wear

Pitcher: Marissa McTasney, Season 3, Episode 4

Focus: How a Problem Inspires a Business

"I was looking to find my passion. I left my corporate job to learn how to build a house. I went to the store and I said, 'Where are the pink work boots?' and the store manager said, 'I get asked [that] all the time.' What I discovered is, there's this huge market that's been untapped. I think I'm on to something."
—Pitcher to Dragons

PRODUCT DESCRIPTION

Work wear for female contractors, carpenters, and factory workers.

DRAGONS' DEN BY THE NUMBERS

- **The Ask:** $600,000 for 49% of the business.
- **50%:** The percentage of boots sold by Moxie Trades that are pink.
- **$600,000:** The amount of revenue the Pitcher had generated before the show.
- **75%:** The percentage of the business requested by the Dragons in exchange for $600,000, an offer that was turned down by the Pitcher.

Pitcher Marissa McTasney of Moxie Trades standing in front of her key clientele, female construction and factory workers.

THE WARM-UP: SINGULAR PAIN POINT DEFINED

A pain point is a yet-to-be-solved problem that your product or service addresses. A singular pain point is the highest-priority problem that you want your brand to solve. The purpose of focusing your product or service solution on a singular pain point is to have your product or service become the preferred choice of the customer or client. This might be done by developing a completely new product or service, but it could also be achieved by introducing a new price point, or by adding value to an existing product by adding a service or training component, or by identifying a need your target market didn't even know it had.

The process of identifying pain points involves:

- **Survey Techniques:** Methods of discovering problems people have with current solutions available in the market. These include one-on-one interviews, workshops, prototype reviews, observation, and surveys.
- **User Stories:** One-sentence summaries of problems that people would like addressed by your product or service.
- **Pain Point Prioritization:** A shortlist of yet-to-be-solved problems that your product or service addresses.

Survey Techniques

An entrepreneur like you who is looking to invent the next blockbuster product or service shouldn't start with a prototype, a revenue model, or a value proposition. Rather, you should start with a consumer who has a specific problem that has been unsolvable up until now. Try to find out everything about the problem before you devise your solution because there might be no room for error. Not having a conversation with potential customers in advance of formulating a solution should be inconceivable to you, given the valuable information you can glean from a simple conversation or a more detailed assessment. When launching your business concept, some of the ways to have that conversation with a potential customer are:

- **One-on-One Interviews:** Speak to potential customers to find out how they are addressing the underlying need that your product or service addresses. Interviews can also confirm that the underlying need exists.
- **Workshops and Focus Groups:** Conduct group interviews to stimulate discussion about the underlying need.

- **Prototype Reviews:** Conduct walk-throughs or demos of your product or service, and ask potential customers to give you feedback on how well (or not) it solves the current need.
- **Observation:** Observe people using your and competitors' products or services.
- **Surveys:** Email questionnaires asking people to identify what annoys them with current "solutions" or gaps in the marketplace. Consider hiring your college-age children and friends to conduct preliminary surveys. With sufficient resources, you can even hire a market research firm to do the work for you (more about this in Part IV, Chapter 22 on Target Market Analysis).
- **User Stories:** Refine your findings into one-sentence summaries of problems that people would like addressed by your product or service. Or use the questions below to start a conversation with your customer.

User Stories

One of the most powerful market research tools for discovering pain points is a **user story**. A user story is a *single-sentence* statement of what a potential customer would do with a product or service like yours if he or she had total design freedom. It should not be confused with a case study, which is a multi-sentence summary of how someone has successfully used a product or service. One of the best formats for writing up a single-sentence user story was devised by Mike Cohn[1]:

> "As a [customer] . . . I want [What is the customer trying to achieve?] . . . so that I can [What is the benefit you are expecting?]."

You can gather user stories by talking to potential customers and showing them a working prototype. If you talk to them, they'll identify a whole host of problems they have, which you can then use to revise and refine your product or service into a true painkiller. Separate the nice-to-haves from the need-to-haves and focus on the latter. If you are bootstrapping your business, be sure to keep your prototype costs to a minimum. Although every product or service type will vary, you should be spending hundreds of dollars, not thousands. Of course, the amount you spend depends on the complexity of what you are trying to achieve, so if you have investment capital behind you, your budget might be higher than that of someone starting out of a garage. Cost guidelines depend on your industry, which you will research later (discussed in Part IV, Chapter 20). Just be sure to keep enough capital in reserve to rebuild your prototype several times if the first iteration doesn't meet your target customers' needs.

User Story Examples

User stories should follow a three-part format so that they reveal pain points. To illustrate, here are three examples of user stories that could lead to products or services that resolve them:

- "As a stay-at-home mom, I want to be able to search through my monthly expenses for cheaper alternatives, so that I can **cut my monthly spending**." Mint.com may have been created using a user story like this.
- "As a busy working professional, I want to be alerted when my Social Insurance Number is being used to open up an account without my permission, so that I can **keep someone from stealing my identity**." LifeLock.com, a wildly popular identity theft protection service in the United States, might have been created using a user story like this.
- "As a business traveller, I want to be able to access hundreds of books in digital format while sitting on a plane, so that I **don't have to carry print versions** of the books I want to read." The iPad may have been created using a user story like this.

Pain Point Prioritization

While assessing your business concept and its market using this book, you may uncover all kinds of problems with current marketing offerings. But if you try to solve too many problems with your product or service, your solution may become unfocused and unmemorable. As you'll discover in Chapter 16, part of becoming attractive to customers is defining the problem-solving mission behind your product or service. That's not to say that your offering shouldn't solve many different problems, but when you're launching a business, your resources are most likely limited and they should stay focused. For now, try to prioritize the problems you wish to solve by its:

- **Value to the Customer:** If you solve this problem for the customer, will it mean enough to the customer for them to buy your product or service?
- **Your Ability to Charge for It:** Will you be able to charge the customer a premium in order to solve this problem for them?

> **Dragon Lore**
>
> Pain points are the nerve centre of your customers. The more burning the problem, the more likely a customer will rush to buy your product or service.

When it comes to pain points, nothing leads to more dissatisfaction than a dirty diaper. But filling landfills with throwaway diapers is not exactly cost-conscious or ecologically conscious. One company, AppleCheeks Diapers, was featured on *Dragons' Den* because it addressed a clear market void—the need for a cloth diaper system for ecologically conscious parents who are tired of throwaway diapers that end up in landfills.

AppleCheeks Diapers

Pitchers: Amy Appleton and Ilana Grostern, Season 6, Episode 13

Focus: Define the Singular Pain Point

A product that meets a need among cost-conscious and environmentally aware parents.

BACKGROUND

Amy Appleton and Ilana Grostern are two moms from Lachine, Quebec, who have developed a cloth diaper to suit modern parents. Made of bamboo and organic cotton, the diapers retail for $20 apiece.

PROBLEM STATEMENT

Environmentally conscious parents want to use cloth diapers but aren't fond of getting their hands dirty. Cost-conscious parents can achieve savings over purchasing disposable diapers.

PROPOSED SOLUTION

The diaper consists of an outer pant, an absorbent insert, and a flushable lining. The lining can be dropped into the toilet without needing to touch the deposit. The outer pant and insert are then put into the wash, where the agitation of the washing machine pulls the insert out, so again there's no need to touch any of the dirty parts.

BUSINESS CASE

- **Revenue Model:** The diapers are currently being sold online and in boutiques.
- **The Ask:** $100,000 for 15% of the ownership.
- **Company Valuation:** $667,000.
- **Proof-of-Concept:** The business generated $500,000 in sales last year and gross profit margins of 45%.

DRAGONS' DEAL

Amy and Ilana are looking for money to take their company to the next level. They are testing samples that have been manufactured overseas with a view to bringing the retail price down and getting into the big box stores, while increasing their margins. A couple of Dragons made bids, and the moms accepted $100,000 for 25% of the company.

DEAL SYNERGIES

One Dragon has connections to the big box stores that can help the company expand their distribution, while the other offers marketing expertise.

AppleCheeks reusable cloth diapers, being pitched in the Dragons' Den by Pitchers Amy Appleton and Ilana Grostern.

No company represents Canadian entrepreneurial success more than Tim Hortons. It's a cultural icon and it's a true inspiration for any entrepreneur who's looking to get into retail or any other business space for that matter. The following case study shows how the Tim Hortons business model adheres to the 10 Dragons' Den Success Factors.

A Real-World Case Study: Tim Hortons

"It was chaotic to say the least . . . By golly, I borrowed ten thousand from the credit union and I had to learn in a hurry."[2]
   —Ron Joyce, co-founder of Tim Hortons

Canada is the donut store capital of the world, with more donut stores per person than anywhere else in the world. Ron Joyce and the late NHL hockey player Tim Horton must have been able to see into the future back in the 1960s, because today the cultural icon has more than 4,000 locations worldwide and counting. Co-founder Ron Joyce, who became franchisee of "Tim Horton Donuts" store #1, became a full partner of Tim Hortons and turned the franchising concept into a multi-billion-dollar part of the Canadian psyche.

BACKTESTING TIM HORTONS

Looking back at the Tim Hortons business model, we can backtest it to see if it meets each of the Dragons' Den Success Factors:

SUCCESS FACTOR #1: FOCUS ON A SINGULAR PAIN POINT

People were tired of stale coffee and donuts made in an unclean environment.

SUCCESS FACTOR #2: BUILD A PROTOTYPE

Drive-through franchise store #1 was a converted, boarded-up gas station on Ottawa Street in Hamilton, Ontario. Tim Hortons still stands there today.

SUCCESS FACTOR #3: DEFINE THE VALUE PROPOSITION

No-frills, always-fresh product made in a clean environment.

SUCCESS FACTOR #4: ESTABLISH A REPEAT REVENUE MODEL

According to some figures, 40% of Tim Hortons' customers come four times a week and 10% come 10 times a week.[3]

SUCCESS FACTOR #5: TARGET A DISRUPTABLE MARKET

Coffee drinkers who were looking for a cleaner, fresher coffee-and-donut environment than the mom-and-pop donut shops they were frequenting before.

SUCCESS FACTOR #6: BUILD A LEAN FEATURE SET

No sandwiches. No soup. No croissants. When the first Tim Hortons store opened, it served just two products: coffee and donuts.[4]

SUCCESS FACTOR #7: COLLABORATE WITH STRATEGIC PARTNERS

Tim Horton, who brought experience owning a coffee-and-donut shop, later became a full partner with Ron Joyce, who brought franchising experience, having owned a Dairy Queen franchise.

SUCCESS FACTOR #8: FIND A CATALYST FOR GROWTH

The word of mouth generated by the "always fresh" value proposition is a viral marketing bonanza for the business.

SUCCESS FACTOR #9: SCALABILITY

Franchising allows for rapid expansion because franchisees bring much-needed capital and human resources to get each new store off the ground in a timely manner.

SUCCESS FACTOR #10: DEVELOP A BUSINESS MODEL

A restaurant franchise business model with repeat revenue coming from ongoing operator fees.

Self-Help Workshop: How to Focus on a Singular Pain Point

Develop a list of pain points that your customers have with brands that compete with your product. Identify any current gaps in the marketplace.

1. Create a list of **questions** that you want answered by potential users of your product or service. Questions to ask potential customers might include:
   - What issues do you have with existing solutions to this problem?
   - What type of product or service would be an ideal solution to this problem?

2. Conduct **one-on-one interviews.**

   Set up one-on-one interviews with potential users of your product or service.

3. Hold **group workshops** (multi-person) and **focus groups.**

   Hold group brainstorming sessions to determine potential problems with existing solutions by asking attendees such questions as:
   - What are you trying to achieve?
   - What is the result you are expecting?
   - How do you currently address the underlying problem?

4. Conduct **prototype reviews.**

   Ask a group of potential customers to use and/or test your product or service and tell you how they feel about it. There are three ways to build a mock-up of your product or service:
   - **Prototype:** Create a fully functional version of your product or sample of your service, if your budget allows. Ask your potential customers to test it. Observe how they use it, and what questions they ask. Measure results where possible. For example, if your invention promises to solve a problem in a given amount of time, then time each of your product or service testers to prove it.
   - **Mock-Up:** If budget is an issue, create a mock-up of your product that allows people to grasp what it is you are selling.
   - **Paper or Digital Prototype:** If you have absolutely no budget available to produce a prototype, draw one on paper.

5. **Observe.**

   Observe people interacting with existing solutions to the underlying problem that your product or service addresses. Analyze how people currently solve the problem.

6. Conduct **surveys.**

   Send out surveys to potential buyers of your product or service.

7. Write up **user stories.**

   Format all responses into one-sentence stories of how a prospective customer might use your product or service:

   "As a [*customer*] . . . I want [*What is the customer trying to achieve?*] . . . so that I can [*What is the benefit you are expecting?*]."

   Your answers, when organized in single-sentence user-story formats, will result in valuable information that can be used to refine your business concept.[5]

8. Develop your list of user stories into a **prioritized shortlist** of pain points.

9. What is the **overriding pain** that is addressed and solved by your product or service, and what is its root cause?

10. Write your **problem statement**.
    What is the *highest and best use* for your product or service?

When an entrepreneur learns to focus on the customer's needs first, and not just a product that he or she has come up with, the path to a scalable growth business becomes more flexible. The entrepreneur will be more free to evolve the original product into something the customer is willing to pay for.

As you'll see in the next chapter, you can use the customer's needs to refine your business idea over time into something the customer truly wants.

Chapter 2

Build an Evolutionary Prototype

"Failure is a good part of what builds the character of an entrepreneur. I think you need some."
—Dragon to Pitcher

> ## Success Factor #2: Build a Prototype
>
> Put a rudimentary version of your product or service idea together as fast and as cheaply as possible. Your prototype should be detailed enough that a potential customer or investor can understand exactly what your product or service is, how it works, and what problem it solves. It should also be low cost so that you can build another one if the original isn't the complete solution to the customer's pain point or needs modification.

Every now and then, a novel product or service hits the market, and everyone starts talking about it. We all can point to examples—Groupon, Facebook, the iPad—and we become riveted by the new entry to the market, like the reaction to a black swan appearing in a lake full of white swans. In his groundbreaking book, *The Black Swan: The Impact of the Highly Improbable,* author Nassim Taleb writes about this phenomenon, referring to unexpected events in history that change the expectations and mindsets of scores of observers in an instant.[1] If you want to be a hit in the marketplace, become the black swan in your product or service category.

A key step toward becoming the black swan of your industry is to hold off on the business-planning process until you have a working prototype in hand. Budding entrepreneur Max Schellenberg knew this when he created his prototype for a reversible, customizable zipper shoe called the MaxReverse shoe and then brought it to *Dragons' Den.*

MaxReverse Shoes

Pitcher: Max Schellenberg, Season 6, Web Pitch

Focus: A Prototype in Action

"Right now the prototype is actually being made in China. I want to build myself an empire. I wanted to do so much that I wanted to make a game so I could do it all—because I thought I couldn't do it in real life."
—Pitcher to Dragons

PRODUCT DESCRIPTION

The world's first reversible shoe.

DRAGONS' DEN BY THE NUMBERS

- **The Ask:** $50,000 for 30% of the business.
- **$7.50:** The cost to make each MaxReverse shoe in China.
- **$50,000:** The amount of capital offered to MaxReverse by one Dragon, which the entrepreneur accepted.
- **6,000:** The number of units of MaxReverse shoes that will have to be ordered on its first run with the manufacturer.

MaxReverse Shoes being demonstrated in the Dragons' Den by Max Schellenberg.

THE WARM-UP: EVOLUTIONARY PROTOTYPE DEFINED

In your quest for a market that fits your product or service, you will need a rudimentary model of your product or service to show to prospective customers, investors, and other interested parties. The purpose of a prototype is to have something tangible in your hands to demonstrate that your business concept is sound, will have a demand, and is something people would be willing to pay for. And your prototype should evolve over time as you learn from your interactions with the market. Two key reasons to build your prototype are:

- **Verification:** To verify that your product or service works as intended.
- **Validation:** To validate that your product or service does what people would be willing to pay you for.

The process of prototyping involves:

- **Step 1:** *Mock-Up:* Create a representative version of your product or service out of paper or modelling clay (for products), or, for a service, put sticky notes on a whiteboard to describe the steps in the process, to show user interfaces with the product.
- **Step 2:** *Exploratory Prototype:* A one-feature-at-a-time approach that results in a working prototype you can use to test a specific feature. Create a working, partial-feature throwaway version of your product or service to test individual features of your product or service.
- **Step 3:** *Evolutionary Prototype:* Create a working, full-feature version of your product or service that will evolve over time based on feedback you receive. It should contain all intended functionality of your final product or service, and eventually will be ready for production. Often, entrepreneurs build their prototypes in their garages, kitchens, or basements. You can also outsource production of your prototype to a domestic or foreign manufacturer, which we'll discuss in Chapter 18.

Rapid Prototyping

Rapid prototyping is a process used to produce a three-dimensional throwaway model of a tangible product in a short period for a low cost. The purpose of the process is to get a physical, feasibility-testable model in your hands that you can use as a learning tool to elicit feedback, pain points, and new feature ideas from potential customers. The process involves computer-aided design and specialized machinery that can build the model out of plastic, resin, or even paper. But be aware that you don't need to go to an expensive manufacturer to build a prototype—you can put one together yourself for a product or service:

- **Product Prototyping:** Produce a rudimentary three-dimensional mock-up of your tangible product out of paper, plastic, or whatever your budget allows.
- **Service Prototyping:** Prototype your service by creating a mock-up on a whiteboard or paper, or by building a mini-service. For example, if you are launching a restaurant, have menus printed and set up a table at a trade show to serve menu items to passersby, who provide instant feedback. Alternatively, set up a full-scale restaurant prototype in a warehouse to work out the visual and operational details of your business.

Prototyping is critical for testing and refining an idea before you commit large resources to an idea that may not yet fit a market.

Dragon Lore

Bring your business idea to life with a prototype as soon as possible. Validate your product or service idea in front of real customers, investors, and other stakeholders before you commit valuable time and financial resources to an unproven idea.

Having a working prototype in hand is more important for some businesses than others. That's especially true if you have an innovation that no one has ever seen before because a picture will be worth a thousand words. For example, explaining the Uno Dicycle without a prototype would be like explaining the Internet without a computer. The motorcycle-like machine is so revolutionary that the sight of just a video of it caused a feeding frenzy among the Dragons. A working prototype convinces customers and investors that your vision is more than just a pipe dream.

Uno Dicycle

Pitcher: Ben Gulak, Season 3, Episode 7
Focus: Build a Prototype

What started out as a science project in high school using wheelchair motors and gyroscopes evolved into an electric-powered, road-ready working prototype.

BACKGROUND

Nineteen-year-old Ben Gulak of Milton, Ontario, developed the Uno Dicycle after a trip to China with his parents when he was 16. He developed the electric-powered vehicle after seeing in China the enormous amount of pollution generated by scooters and motorcycles.[2] The product is designed for crowded urban centres.

PROBLEM STATEMENT

Gas-powered scooters and motorcycles generate enormous amounts of pollution.

PROPOSED SOLUTION

An eco-friendly, electric-powered, motorcycle-like dicycle.

BUSINESS CASE

- **Revenue Model:** Planning to charge a retail price of $5,000 to $5,500 per bike.
- **The Ask:** $1.25 million for 15% equity of the company.
- **Company Valuation:** $8.3 million.
- **Proof-of-Concept:** A working prototype, which was named by *Popular Science* magazine as one of the year's top-10 inventions.

DRAGONS' DEAL

After some negotiation, the Dragons offered $1.25 million for 20% of the firm.

DEAL SYNERGIES

All five Dragons went in on the deal to help Ben Gulak avoid the fatal business mistakes made by his distant cousin, a well-known story in venture capital history—the Segway.

> "It's impossible not to make an offer. The value of a concept is indeterminate and the number you threw out might be high and might be low . . . You're looking for a million and a quarter . . . If you were to do that for 30% of the firm . . . I would certainly be there."
> —Dragon to Pitcher

> "The Segway was a disaster. People need to want to be seen on it, they want to look cool."
> —Pitcher to Dragon

Pitcher Ben Gulak of Uno Dicycle showing a video of the invention that landed him on the cover of *Popular Science* for being a Top-10 Invention in 2008.

But a prototype is not just important for explaining your product or service to customers and investors. It's also critical for helping to define your product or service in the early stages of your business because it gives you something to test with real customers. Of course prototypes cost money, so your job would be much easier if you started a company like Groupon. What's been called "the fastest-growing company in history" evolved from a prototype called ThePoint.com, with just a computer, some knowledge, and serious ingenuity.

A Real-World Case Study: Groupon

"Dead-simple value that you can comprehend by looking at one page in three seconds . . ."[3]
—Andrew Mason, founder, Groupon

Many small businesses and large retailers have excess inventory and service capacity with a limited shelf life. These businesses know that if they can just get a customer in the door once with a discount, they will have earned the chance for repeat business. Groupon is a company that sets up collaborative relationships and group discounts with the vendors of these goods, services, and events, and then markets those discounts to its own database of registered users in 45 countries, including Canada, the United States, and the UK. Here's how it works: If a minimum number of people sign up for a deal of the day, then everyone who signed up gets that deal. If this "tipping point" is not met, then no one gets the deal. Groupon retains up to 50% of the revenue generated from each deal that actually "tips."

A *Forbes* magazine article calls Groupon the fastest-growing company ever,[4] with estimated revenues of $350 million in 2010, according to TechCrunch. The company launched in November 2008. Groupon could never have achieved such extraordinary growth or even have existed without a highly scalable, collaborative, go-to-market strategy.

BACKTESTING GROUPON

Looking back at the Groupon business model, we can test it to see if it meets each of the Dragons' Den Success Factors.

SUCCESS FACTOR #1: FOCUS ON A SINGULAR PAIN POINT

Small businesses have excess capacity (empty seats, unsold inventory, unused service capacity, etc.) that needs to be sold.

SUCCESS FACTOR #2: BUILD A PROTOTYPE

Groupon provides deep discounts, sometimes 50% or more, on popular restaurants, hotels, and retailers, using a collective deals model that requires a minimum number of purchasers to sign up before a deal is activated. Groupon evolved from a rudimentary prototype called ThePoint. com, which it owned.[5] The Point.com is a website where people sign on to group projects and pledge cash to make those projects happen, but don't pay a cent unless a certain number of people agree, within a set time frame, to the initial pledge. The site still exists today.

SUCCESS FACTOR #3: DEFINE THE VALUE PROPOSITION

The value proposition of Groupon stems from the outrageous deals themselves, which are provided by businesses that are given a guaranteed minimum amount of revenue before they have to honour the coupons.

SUCCESS FACTOR #4: ESTABLISH A REPEAT REVENUE MODEL

Groupon generates repeat revenue from buyers who come back to see new deals of the day that show up daily on the Groupon website and in email inboxes across North America.

SUCCESS FACTOR #5: TARGET A DISRUPTABLE MARKET

Coupon seekers are flocking to Groupon in droves because they are burnt out on meaningless discounts that businesses have traditionally offered.

SUCCESS FACTOR #6: BUILD A LEAN FEATURE SET

Groupon doesn't hold eBay auctions. It doesn't do comparison shopping. It doesn't have complex features. The website is stripped down for its *highest and best use*—deals-of-the-day group coupons that require a minimum number of purchasers to be activated.

SUCCESS FACTOR #7: COLLABORATE WITH STRATEGIC PARTNERS

On the vendor side, Groupon collaborates with business owners in postal codes across Canada and in zip codes across the United States. Each business works with Groupon to understand how to service the high volume of new business that usually comes with a Groupon deal. On the consumer side, consumers themselves collaborate on each deal because they need other purchasers to activate a deal.

SUCCESS FACTOR #8: FIND A CATALYST FOR GROWTH

Groupon triggers a *word-of-mouth windfall* every time it launches a deep-discount deal. Customers are motivated to share deals with their friends by email because each deal requires a minimum number of purchasers in order for a deal to be activated. Those friends are needed to make a deal "tip." Groupon buyers are even rewarded with $10 in "Groupon bucks" if they manage to persuade a friend to sign on and buy his or her first Groupon.

SUCCESS FACTOR #9: SCALABILITY

Web business models are inherently scalable because you can add servers and structure them from day one to handle increasing load capacity over time.

SUCCESS FACTOR #10: DEVELOP A BUSINESS MODEL

Groupon acts as a matchmaker between buyers and sellers of services and products in exchange for a share of group coupon revenues.

Self-Help Workshop: How to Conduct a Prototype Review

The best products and services evolve not through business planning but through actual use in the development phase, user feedback, and an iterative process. Their inventors start with a rudimentary version of the product or service and transform it into a shippable product or service—one that grows through a feedback loop from real product or service testers.

1. Choose a **prototyping method**.
   - ❑ Mock-up
   - ❑ Exploratory prototype
   - ❑ Evolutionary prototype
   - ❑ Other
2. Make a list of **outcomes** you want from your prototype—what do you think it will achieve? How will you measure whether it is successful? Decide your evaluation points in advance.
3. Create a product (or service) **prototype**.
4. Set up a **focus group** of six to eight people (or thousands if you have a Web app).
5. **Walk through** a demo of your product or service prototype with your focus group and ask probing questions such as:
   - What problem does this product (or service) solve for you?
   - Why would you use it?
   - What features could make it a better product (or service)?
   - What other related products or services do you wish existed?
   - What other non-related products or services do you wish existed?
6. **Summarize** your findings.
7. Use your findings to **revise and refine** your prototype.
8. **Repeat** the process regularly to improve your prototype until it is ready to go to market.

By putting together a prototype and seeing your product or service as a work-in-progress, you'll be able to refine it over time until it becomes something that is truly valuable to a large group of customers. As we'll discuss in the next chapter, defining that value in the form of a value proposition will be the key to turning your product or service into a magnet for both customers and investors.

CHAPTER 3

DEFINE THE VALUE PROPOSITION

"You have defined beautifully a small home business with enormous novelty factor. But once you get outside Milton, the appeal drops so fast you won't see it falling out of sight. It's not a business . . . As a business, I'm out."
—Dragon to Pitcher

> ### Success Factor #3: Define the Value Proposition
>
> Do something useful for your customer in a profoundly superior way. Use a novel approach to solving a problem that changes the way consumers think, act, and spend. Figure out why the world is better off with your product or service than without it.

The key to building a scalable business is to make your product or service more valuable to potential customers than what your competitors offer. People don't really care how great *you think* your product or service is if they can get other products or services that do the same thing. What matters to paying customers is *the superior outcome they get* in return for using your product or service. Take, for example, the Dyson vacuum cleaner. On the surface, it vacuums floors and carpets, as many other models do. However, what really matters to paying customers is that it doesn't lose suction like other vacuums do. The secret of the Dyson vacuum cleaner is described as "root cyclone technology," a "bagless" technology that offers superior cleaning ability because "it prevents loss of suction."

One company that understands the power of a clear value proposition is Urban Cultivator. Urban Cultivator is a producer of automated indoor mini-greenhouses and was featured on *Dragons' Den*. As you'll see in this next Dragons' Den case study, the product has clear value to professional and amateur chefs alike because herbs can't be any fresher for a chef than if you grow them yourself.

Urban Cultivator

Pitchers: Tarren Wolfe, Miles Omane, and Davin MacGregor, Season 6, Episode 14

Focus: Define the Value Proposition

> "I love this idea—it's on trend and it's an economically viable business model."
> —Dragon to Pitchers

PRODUCT DESCRIPTION

A patented mini-greenhouse for indoor use: one for commercial purposes (restaurants and hotels) and the other for domestic purposes, so people can grow their own herbs and greens.

DRAGONS' DEN BY THE NUMBERS

- **The Ask:** $400,000 for 10% of the business.
- **$6,000:** Cost of the commercial unit.
- **$2,200:** Cost of the domestic unit.
- **$200,000:** Total sales in first three months.
- **20%:** The share of the company that the Pitchers gave up.

Pitchers Tarren Wolfe, Miles Omane, and Davin MacGregor of Urban Cultivator left the Dragons' Den with a deal. They accepted one Dragon's offer and turned down two others.

THE WARM-UP: VALUE PROPOSITION DEFINED

One of history's most successful investors, Benjamin Graham, once said, "Price is what you pay. Value is what you get."[1] A value proposition is a proven superior outcome customers get from your product or service. It is disruptive if it does it in a profoundly superior way to your competition.[2] The purpose of a value proposition is to describe the superior outcome that customers can expect by using what you sell. The process of determining your value proposition involves creating a declarative statement about your product or service in one of two ways:

- **Superior Value:** Describes the unique outcome that a customer can expect from your product or service. ***Example:*** *The Dyson vacuum sucks up more dirt.*
- **Proof-of-Concept:** Describes the approach you use that is unique. ***Example:*** *The Dyson vacuum doesn't lose suction because of its bagless cyclone technology.*

Why Is Your Product or Service So Valuable?

We all make purchases because we are self-motivated to do so. If your product or service doesn't appeal to your customer's internal buying motive, you will never persuade anyone to buy from you.

There are three buying motives to appeal to:

- **Functional Value:** Describes why your product or service is useful: *"It cleans carpets better because it doesn't lose suction."*
- **Emotional Value:** Describes how your product or service makes the consumer feel: *"By using this product, I am saving energy, and that makes me feel good."*
- **Monetary Value:** Describes how your product or service makes or saves the consumer money: *"In the first year of use alone, you will realize cost savings of 5%."*

How Does Your Product or Service Work?

A useful way of determining why your product or service is valuable is to look at how a customer is currently trying to solve his or her problem without your product or service. Next, break that current problem-solving process down into micro-steps. In the software industry, the outcome of this process is called a use case. A **use case** is a sequence of steps that someone would follow to solve a real problem. Here's a rudimentary example:

1. Homeowner decides to vacuum carpet.
2. Homeowner plugs in vacuum.
3. Homeowner pushes "on" button.
4. Homeowner pushes vacuum over carpet.
5. Vacuum sucks up dirt.
6. Homeowner takes bag out of vacuum.
7. Homeowner discards vacuum bag.
8. Homeowner drives to store to buy more vacuum bags.

The purpose of a use case is to reveal annoying steps in a particular problem-solving process (such as vacuuming, moving, or cooking) that represent an opportunity to be exploited with a new or improved product or service. James Dyson did just that. Looking at number 6 and number 8 in this use case, he probably realized that there had to be a better way. The most annoying part of the vacuuming process is that much of the dirt doesn't get picked up by vacuums based on the same (old) technology. Plus, vacuum bags need to be replaced, which leads to higher costs for the consumer. During his research, James Dyson determined that vacuum bags make vacuum cleaners less powerful because they get clogged up and lead to a loss of suction. So he invented the Dyson bagless vacuum, which has *monetary value* because it saves money on bags, and has *functional value*, because it doesn't lose suction. This all leads to *emotional value*, because discriminating parents and homeowners can rest easy knowing that their carpets are as clean as they possibly can be.

In your business, once you have figured out how customers currently solve their problems, you can revise the process and build a product or service around the problem you are able to solve. Ideally, one or more steps in this sequence are truly novel. Although this is an extreme example (the Dyson took years to develop), all entrepreneurs can use some form of use case to discover their own disruptive value proposition.

Dragon Lore

If you want to succeed in the marketplace, your product or service must offer superior value over that of your competitors.

Another company that understands the concept of a value proposition is Frogbox. The inventor of Frogbox realized that not everyone likes to move using unreliable and expensive cardboard boxes. He invented a reusable and rentable plastic moving box that would appeal to the cost- and eco-conscious mover. Frogbox was one of the more popular pitches on *Dragons' Den*.

Frogbox, Inc.

Pitcher: Doug Burgoyne, Season 5, Episode 13

Focus: Define the Value Proposition

Taking a green approach, Frogbox gives customers an environmentally friendly alternative by renting reusable, plastic boxes for about the same price that most would pay to buy disposable cardboard boxes.

BACKGROUND

When Doug Burgoyne and his wife moved from Ohio to Vancouver, the cardboard packing boxes they got from the moving company soaked up moisture and lost their sturdiness while being stored in the homeowner's garage.[3] This problem inspired Doug and his business partner, Trevor McCaw, to launch an environmentally friendly alternative to the cardboard boxes used in the moving industry. They came up with eco-friendly, reusable plastic Frogbox moving boxes.

PROBLEM STATEMENT

Cardboard boxes are not a good solution for packing household items because they can get wet and mouldy, are not very sturdy, and fall apart in wet weather. They are also not environmentally friendly because they aren't reusable and often end up in landfills.

PROPOSED SOLUTION

Frogbox is a moving supply business. People who are moving go online or call Frogbox and order rental moving boxes. Uniformed delivery people show up in a branded Frogbox truck and drop off your moving boxes for as long as you need them; they pick them up when you're ready.

BUSINESS CASE

- **Revenue Model:** A franchise model where Frogbox charges franchisees a monthly royalty as a percentage of gross revenues. Franchisees rent out moving boxes, supplied by Frogbox, for a fee to people who are moving.

- **The Ask:** $200,000 in exchange for 18% ownership.
- **Company Valuation:** $1.1 million.
- **Proof-of-Concept:** $40,000 per month in revenues and growing. Operating in Vancouver, Seattle, and Toronto. The Pitchers gave the Dragons a live demonstration of the faults of competitors' paper boxes.

DRAGONS' DEAL

Doug Burgoyne, co-founder of Frogbox, agreed to part with 25% of his company in exchange for the $200,000 three Dragons offered to inject into his company, as well as their combined expertise.

DEAL SYNERGIES

From the beginning, Frogbox was established as a franchise concept. Doug Burgoyne and Trevor McCaw knew that having three key Dragons in on the deal would give them the franchising expertise, marketing expertise, and financial know-how that a franchising business needs. The strategic value was worth much more than the $200,000 injection.

> "One in six people move every year, yet there is really no good solution for moving boxes."
> —Pitcher to Dragons

Doug Burgoyne from Frogbox and his assistant demonstrate why his reusable plastic moving boxes are better than regular cardboard boxes.

Americans always seem to me to be looking for a way to make life easier. Hence we benefit from truly innovative services like Netflix. It's a service that helps us avoid late fees on movies we rent (a monetary value), because they deliver movies right to our homes (a functional value), and then let us keep them as long as we want (an emotional value).

A Real-World Case Study: Netflix

"I got the idea for Netflix after my company was acquired. I had a big late fee for *Apollo 13.*"[4]
—Reed Hastings, co-founder, Netflix

When Netflix went to market, it disrupted the way people rented movies to watch at home. The market leader at this time, Blockbuster, imposed due dates, late fees, and a rent-in-store policy. Netflix, on the other hand, mailed to you movies that you selected online, let you keep them as long as you wanted, and then gave you prepaid mailers that fit into your local mailbox. Netflix also had a massive, ever-growing inventory. Nothing could be easier unless you made movies viewable over the Web, streaming instantly—which of course, Netflix now does. The **value proposition** of Netflix is a massive movie inventory that is conveniently available.

Blockbuster had to fend off Redbox, $1-a-movie vending machines in grocery stores, Web-downloadable movies, and, of course, video-on-demand. Interestingly enough, instead of going on the offensive with a new strategy, Blockbuster repeatedly implemented a me-too strategy to fend off these competitors, offering movies through the mail, no late fees, and digital downloads. It's not surprising that Blockbuster is in deep trouble as of this writing, because its business was disrupted by multiple competitors with **disruptive value propositions**.

Netflix is the world's leading Internet subscription service for movies and TV shows, with over 23 million subscribers.[5]

BACKTESTING NETFLIX

Looking back at the Netflix business model, a historically fast-growth company, we can backtest it to see if it meets each of the Dragons' Den Success Factors:

SUCCESS FACTOR #1: FOCUS ON A SINGULAR PAIN POINT

People hate paying late fees on movies they rent from video stores and rental boxes.

SUCCESS FACTOR #2: BUILD A PROTOTYPE

Netflix evolved from a rudimentary pay-per-rent prototype to an unlimited rental system with no due dates. It started as a DVD mail-out service and is now evolving into a Web-streaming service.

SUCCESS FACTOR #3: DEFINE THE VALUE PROPOSITION

Netflix offers flat-fee unlimited rentals by mail and over the Web without due dates or late fees (or shipping and handling fees).

SUCCESS FACTOR #4: ESTABLISH A REPEAT REVENUE MODEL

Netflix generates recurring revenues from monthly subscription fees and is able to handle increasing capacity because of its high-capacity Web servers.

SUCCESS FACTOR #5: TARGET A DISRUPTABLE MARKET

Movie watchers who hate driving to the movie store to return movies and paying late fees.

SUCCESS FACTOR #6: BUILD A LEAN FEATURE SET

No popcorn. No colas. No goobers. No store locations. Just a dead-simple service offering, to mail you three DVDs at a time, for a straightforward, unlimited monthly subscription fee. Its new proposition is unlimited movies streamed to you over the Web, for a monthly subscription fee.

SUCCESS FACTOR #7: COLLABORATE WITH STRATEGIC PARTNERS

Netflix held an open competition by offering $1 million to the developer who could come up with a powerful movie recommendation algorithm.[6] Netflix also collaborates with content providers to gain access to movies and television shows that it can stream over the Web.

SUCCESS FACTOR #8: FIND A CATALYST FOR GROWTH

Netflix uses an online **affiliate program** to drive traffic to the Netflix website.

SUCCESS FACTOR #9: SCALABILITY

The Netflix low-cost operating model employs hourly and part-time workers at regional shipping hubs, to open and stuff DVD mailers using an easy-to-repeat process.

SUCCESS FACTOR #10: DEVELOP A BUSINESS MODEL

Netflix originally used a direct-to-the-consumer, home-delivery business model to cut out the costs and inefficiencies of intermediaries.

Self-Help Workshop: How to Define Your Value Proposition

One way to come up with a disruptive value proposition is to start with a yet-to-be-solved customer problem and describe the step-by-step process that consumers currently follow to solve it. One tool for doing this is the **use case**, which is a series of steps that a customer currently takes to deal with a problem you have identified. Once these steps are articulated, preferably at a microscopic level, alternative solutions to the customer's problem start to reveal themselves. You should then ask anyone and everyone, "What would you envision to be an ideal solution to this problem?"

1. Describe your **ideal customer** in general terms (you'll learn how to do a detailed target market analysis in Chapter 22).
2. Identify your product or service **category**.
3. What does your product or service do? How is the **outcome superior** to alternative solutions?
4. Describe **how your product or service works**—in micro-steps.
   Imagine your product being used or service being performed in a sequence of micro-steps. Describe each step in the fewest words possible.
5. Label each step and post it on a **storyboard.**
   Put sticky notes on a whiteboard, each containing a word that represents the step.
6. What is **novel** about your approach?
   For each step in the process, try to isolate what's novel about it, if anything. Perhaps you have a four-pronged approach, a single-stage process, or a specific input or ingredient that provides unique value to the customer.
7. What **superior outcome does the customer get** from your solution over competing brands and alternative solutions?
   Remember, there are three buying motives to appeal to:
   - **Functional Value:** Describes why your product or service is useful. *"It cleans carpets better because it doesn't lose suction."*

- **Emotional Value:** Describes how your product or service makes the customer feel. *"By using this product, I am saving energy, and that makes me feel good."*
- **Monetary Value:** Describes how your product or service makes or saves the customer money. *"In the first year of use alone, you will realize cost savings of 5%."*

8. Format your value proposition into a **single declarative sentence**.
   Fill in the blanks:
   For [*specific buyer type*], [*name your product or service*] is the only [*product or service category*] that [*What does the customer get by using your product or service?*].

9. **Revise and refine**.
   If you can't seem to put your finger on what is novel about your approach, read chapters 1 and 2 again and refine your business concept until it becomes clear. This is an immensely important aspect of building a business concept. If you are a fan of *Dragons' Den,* think about how many people have made a pitch, only to be rejected because they failed to differentiate their product or service from existing products and services.

While defining value in a way that is meaningful to a profitable group of customers is important, figuring out how much to charge for that value is equally important. In the next chapter, we'll delve deep into figuring out how much to charge for your services so you'll have enough cash flow to stay in business for the long haul.

CHAPTER 4

HOW ARE YOU GOING TO MAKE MONEY?

"Your 'baby,' as you probably called it, is gone as of today. This is not a loan. This is a business we're going into to make money."
—Dragon to Pitcher

Success Factor #4: Establish a Repeat Revenue Model

Charge a price point that will generate the highest amount of profitable revenue in the shortest amount of time. Determine a clear product roadmap that generates recurring revenues from the same customers. Make sure you have access to the staffing, financial resources, and business systems you may need to fulfill sudden increases in order volume.

A business without cash flow is not really a business at all. Without cash flow, you may not be in a position to negotiate lower wholesale costs with suppliers; you may not be in a position to pay staff to fill orders. In fact, a lack of cash flow is the worst nightmare for a budding entrepreneur: Imagine that you have to reject a high-volume order for your product or service because you simply cannot afford to pay for the staff or the suppliers you need to fill that order. Cash is the fuel that keeps your business running. If you want to build a scalable growth business that customers, investors, and other stakeholders will be attracted to, then be sure to manage your cash flow as if it were a precious fuel.

There is no simpler revenue model or business model than that of STR8TS Puzzle Game, a word game for newspapers presented to the Dragons. Because the entrepreneur only has to come up with new games on a laptop, he really has no hard costs other than to pay the staff that helps him come up with new games.

STR8TS Puzzle Game

Pitcher: Jeff Widderich, Season 5, Episode 8

Focus: How to Build a Scalable Revenue Model

"I can run this business anywhere in the world off a laptop. That's how simple this business is . . . Basically, I call the (newspapers) up and present them the puzzle. If you [license] the next hot puzzle, you're selling 5% more newspapers every day."
—Pitcher to Dragons

PRODUCT DESCRIPTION

A number puzzle game similar to sudoku that is licensed to newspapers, book publishers, and smartphone app developers.

DRAGONS' DEN BY THE NUMBERS

- **The Ask:** $50,000 for 5% royalty.
- **10%:** The royalty on revenue agreed in exchange for $150,000 in investment capital from the Dragons.
- **1.1 million:** The number of readers the puzzle game STR8TS was exposed to the day it was pitched to the Dragons.
- **$150,000:** The amount of capital offered and accepted by the owner of STR8TS in exchange for a 10% royalty.

Jeff Widderich from STR8TS Puzzle Game entering the Den with a sample of his puzzle game.

THE WARM-UP: REVENUE MODEL DEFINED

A revenue model refers to how you charge for your product or service. The purpose of a revenue model is to make sure that your business has the cash flow to meet its financial obligations as they come due and to enable your business to meet its strategic objectives. The process of establishing a revenue model involves identifying your:

- **Revenue Sources:** What do you do that generates revenue?
- **Revenue Model:** How do you charge? *Examples: Product revenue, service fees, transaction fees, licensing fees, royalties, franchising fees.*
- **Scalability:** Are you able to adapt to sudden increases in sales volume without being hindered by your current business system and financial resources?
- **Cash Flow Timing:** When do you get paid? *Examples: Upfront, milestone payments, back end using accounts receivables, a combination.* When do you have to pay your suppliers?

Revenue Sources

You can't grow your business quickly if you have to restart it every year. If last year's customers don't have a reason to pay you again this year, growth will be excruciatingly slow. Making sales to new customers is more difficult than selling to existing customers who know you and who trust you. Businesses that grow quickly generate **recurring revenues** by selling consumable products and services, product upgrades, and ongoing service agreements to every customer. They see each new customer as having a lifetime value. Once you have invented your version of the proverbial wheel, keep improving it with a new version year after year so that people have a reason to keep paying you. Look for multiple ways to charge customers, and then isolate the ones that will support the goals of each of your stakeholders—your customers, your investors, and yourself.

The percentage of customers who convert into annual repeat customers will depend on the type of product or service that you have. For example, if you sell cars or gadgets, your repeat business might take years to return—but you should try to establish an ongoing service relationship between purchases. If you run a small tea shop, however, you'll depend heavily on repeat business on a weekly or even daily basis—one of the success factors we identified in the Tim Hortons business model in Chapter 1.

Revenue Model

There are many ways to earn revenue from your product or service, and no business owner should limit himself or herself during the brainstorming phase. Your choice of model will depend on who is paying you. If the consumer or a business is paying you directly, then charge a unit price or service fee. If an intermediary such as a franchisee is paying you, then charge a transaction (franchise) fee. Here are some of the most common ways of structuring a revenue model:

- **Product Revenue:** You sell a product and receive a payment in return.
- **Service Fees:** You perform a service and receive a payment in return, sometimes based on an hourly rate.
- **Transaction Fees:** You act as an intermediary between a product producer and a consumer, and get a percentage of each product or service package sold.
- **Licensing Fees:** You let someone else produce and brand your invention, and receive a transaction fee for each unit sold.
- **Royalty Fees:** You let someone else produce and brand your copyrighted work, and receive a transaction fee for each unit sold.
- **Franchising Fees:** You receive a royalty in exchange for allowing another business owner to use your business model, systems, and branding.

Scalability

Imagine owning a small cupcake business. You sign on to advertise your business through a daily-deals website. Suddenly you receive orders for 102,000 cupcakes from 8,500 people who sign up for the deal. Because your business isn't scalable, however, you have to hire short-term staff at a higher-than-usual cost just to fill the orders. Unfortunately, you wind up taking a loss on each cupcake sold because of the increased staffing costs. This is a real-life story that happened in the UK.[1]

In this case, the owner might have been better off rejecting the orders until a more scalable business system was put in place. "Scalability" refers to having the business systems and resources in place to handle high-volume orders in very short periods without collapsing the business. If you cannot process high-volume orders without severely straining your staff or financial resources, your business is not scalable.

To make your business scalable, put the following in place:

- **Business Manuals:** Document your business processes in steps, and make them more efficient over time by removing or automating unnecessary steps.
- **Staffing Process:** Have a system in place to bring in new staff on short notice, to handle short-term spikes in order volume.
- **Supplier Process:** Look for low-cost suppliers all over the world to make sure you are taking advantage of unit volume price breaks. Establish good relationships with your suppliers so that you can depend on them when volume requirements are suddenly high.
- **Financial Backing:** Establish short-term lines of credit with the bank or a business cash reserve to make sure you can accept sudden increases in sales volume.

Cash Flow Timing

The key to keeping your business running smoothly is to manage the timing of your cash flow. A business won't survive if most of its sales are made up of accounts receivables that are paid at some random date in the future. As mentioned above, without cash flow, you can't fill orders as they come in because you aren't able to pay the staff or the suppliers whom you need to fill those orders. Nor can you expect suppliers to extend credit to a new business, or staff to work for a less-than-regular paycheque. If you want to learn about cash flow, just look at any public company's annual report and its consolidated statement of cash flows. There are three types of cash flows that you need to understand:

- **Operating Cash Flow** (when you receive payments and pay bills): "Operating cash flow" *flows* into your business when customers pay you in cash or cash equivalents. It flows out when you pay for staff, suppliers, and utility bills. The net result should be positive. If your revenue stops, operating cash flow may become negative. At that point, you could be out of business because your staff and suppliers will cut you off if you don't have the working capital to meet your financial commitments.
- **Investing Cash Flow** (when you buy assets): This type of cash flow *flows* in when you liquidate old machines and equipment to replace them with new ones. Unfortunately, it also flows out as you pay for new machines, equipment, and other long-term assets to make your product or perform your service. The net result for this type of cash flow is often negative.

- **Financing Cash Flow** (when you finance things): This type of cash flow comes from banks that lend you money and investors who inject cash into your business. Investor capital is typically easier to work with from a cash-flow standpoint, because you may not be required to make monthly payments, as would be required for a loan. Banks, on the other hand, will take your house, your car, and maybe even the doghouse if you don't pay them on time, so be sure to keep your debt to manageable levels if you can't guarantee that revenue will come in. The net result may be positive or negative.

Dragon Lore

In simple terms, cash flow is the lifeblood of your business and the timing of cash flows must be planned in advance, before you open your doors.

The core of a sound business model is a repeat revenue model. Without a repeat revenue stream that grows each year, you'll have to rebuild your business over and over again. Saif Altimimi and Shawn Swartman, the Pitchers of NoteWagon, know that students often miss classes for one reason or another, resulting in a continuous stream of repeat note-sharing among students. Because of the nature of the Web, they decided to use Wikipedia-style crowd-sourcing to make the note-sharing process more efficient. This popular technology start-up that was featured on *Dragons' Den* has a built-in repeat revenue model, because its product—class notes—are a product that will never go unneeded.

NoteWagon

Pitchers: Saif Altimimi and Shawn Swartman, Season 6, Episode 6

Focus: How to Build a Repeat Revenue Model

The business concept called NoteWagon has a built-in repeat revenue model. Students who miss class need notes, and many are willing to pay for those notes every time they miss a class.

BACKGROUND

NoteWagon was started by Saif and Shawn to capitalize on the relatively inefficient note-sharing ecosystem that already existed among students directly.

PROBLEM STATEMENT

Students who miss a class because of illness, work, or extracurricular activities need a better system for staying up-to-date with missed classes.

PROPOSED SOLUTION

Students who take succinct and articulate notes register on the NoteWagon.com website and share their notes with the community. A student who needs the notes pays cash for them. The fee they pay is shared 50–50 between NoteWagon and the student note-taker.

DRAGONS' DEN BY THE NUMBERS

- **Revenue Model:** Students buy tokens that can be exchanged for notes. NoteWagon retains 50% of all tokens exchanged, and the student sharing the notes gets the other 50%. Students can return again and again to buy the notes they need, and good students are incentivized by cash to continue to upload their course notes to the website.
- **The Ask:** $200,000 for 20% equity.
- **Company Valuation:** $1 million.
- **Proof-of-Concept:** NoteWagon was launched four months prior to the founders' appearance on the show. In the six weeks leading up to the show, the company had gained 15,000 users. The founders had previously raised an angel round of capital for the company with a $500,000 valuation. Angel investors are wealthy individuals who often invest their own money in several different start-ups at once.

DRAGONS' DEAL

$250,000 for 32.5% of the company. This deal reduced the company valuation to about $769,000 from their initial $1 million valuation.

DEAL SYNERGIES

All five Dragons joined in on the deal offer, bringing with them marketing, business, financing and growth expertise.

> "That's what I'm thinking for you. That's the problem. You need more cash."
> —Dragon to Pitchers

Saif Altimimi, Shawn Swartman, and associates pitching NoteWagon to the Dragons.

A business that will never stop generating revenue is real estate. Though the real estate market goes up and down with the business cycle, you can count on the fact that someone is always moving. And every time someone moves, a transaction fee is generated. When Dave Liniger came up with the concept for Re/Max he knew that the people behind the transactions, the agents themselves, needed support and that support would be the basis for a new kind of repeat revenue.

A Real-World Case Study: Re/Max

"Big dreams attract big people."
—Dave Liniger, Re/Max co-founder

When Dave Liniger conceived of the idea for Re/Max, most real estate brokers were focused on sharing the commission on each home sold with the real estate agent. He saw the typical commission-split concept as a highly inefficient way to run a business because the top-performing salespeople ended up supporting the underperforming sales agents in each sales office.

BACKTESTING RE/MAX

Looking back at the Re/Max business model, a historically fast-growth company, we can test it to see how it meets each of the Dragons' Den Success Factors:

SUCCESS FACTOR #1: FOCUS ON A SINGULAR PAIN POINT

Top-producing real estate agents hate the commission split because they end up "supporting the amateur, part-time and low-producing agents."[2]

SUCCESS FACTOR #2: BUILD A PROTOTYPE

Put together a prototype office before franchising it.

SUCCESS FACTOR #3: DEFINE THE VALUE PROPOSITION

In exchange for sharing office overhead and paying a management fee, Re/Max associates receive high compensation and business-building benefits and services.

SUCCESS FACTOR #4: ESTABLISH A REPEAT REVENUE MODEL

Re/Max generates repeat revenues from the agents themselves, who pay annual fees for corporate support services. Revenues do not come from the home buyers and sellers.

SUCCESS FACTOR #5: TARGET A DISRUPTABLE MARKET

Experienced, top-producing agents who hate paying commission splits.[3]

SUCCESS FACTOR #6: BUILD A LEAN FEATURE SET

Training, technology, and corporate support services.

SUCCESS FACTOR #7: COLLABORATE WITH STRATEGIC PARTNERS

Franchisees run the businesses. Re/Max provides the training and corporate support services.

SUCCESS FACTOR #8: FIND A CATALYST FOR GROWTH

Offering franchises in Canada and then in Europe. Re/Max is now in 85 countries.

SUCCESS FACTOR #9: SCALABILITY

Franchising allows for rapid expansion of the Re/Max business model because franchisees launch the Re/Max branch using their own local presence and financial resources.

SUCCESS FACTOR #10: DEVELOP A BUSINESS MODEL

Re/Max uses a business model where agents contribute to the operating expenses of the offices they work in, in exchange for high commissions and the business-building resources of the Re/Max system.

Self-Study Workshop: How to Establish a Repeat Revenue Model

The fastest way to grow revenue is to generate repeat revenue from last year's customers that you can add to new revenue from this year's customers. When completing this workshop, try to think of as many creative ways as possible that you can charge for your products or services.

1. Who **pays** you?
   - ❑ Consumer
   - ❑ Business
   - ❑ Professional
   - ❑ Middleman (licensee, franchisee, etc.)
   - ❑ Other

2. How does your product or service **generate revenue**?

3. How do you **charge** for each of the things that you do?
   - ❑ Product revenue (unit price)
   - ❑ Service fee
   - ❑ Transaction fee
   - ❑ Licensing fee
   - ❑ Royalty fee
   - ❑ Franchising fee
   - ❑ Other

4. When do you **get paid**? How do you **collect**?
   - ❑ Upfront
   - ❑ Instalment payments
   - ❑ Milestone payments
   - ❑ Back end
   - ❑ Other

5. Is your revenue model **scalable**? Can you respond to sudden increases in sales volume without spreading your staff and financial resources thin?

6. What is your **pricing model**?
   - **Price Floor:** What is the lowest price you could charge and still generate a profit?
   - **Price Ceiling:** What is the highest price you could charge and still have customers willing to pay you?
   - **Price Point:** What price point will generate the highest number of customers?

7. What is the **lifetime value of each customer**? (annual revenue × the number of years a customer will pay you, in today's dollars)

Now that you have figured out how to charge your customers, you'll need to be able to locate them easily. The framework you'll learn and implement in the next chapter will help you define your customers in a way that makes them easy to find.

CHAPTER 5

WHO IS THE IDEAL CUSTOMER FOR YOUR PRODUCT OR SERVICE?

"Let's not talk about taking over Cambodia yet, because we're in Canada."
—Dragon to Pitcher

Success Factor #5: Target a Disruptable Market

Target an addressable market segment, preferably one fraught with dissatisfaction. Make sure your customers are easy to find. Identify your customers and how to reach them, and undertake research so you can understand their buying patterns.

You don't need every "cat" to buy from you—just the ones standing on a hot tin roof. If you think about a cat on a hot tin roof, it has a singular, burning, yet-to-be-solved problem, and it will do anything for a solution. And just like that cat on a hot tin roof, the easiest market to serve is the one that has a singular pain point. Scalable-growth companies target markets that are fraught with dissatisfaction, and then build their businesses around a singular pain point that people are willing to pay them to solve. If you want scalable growth, isolate a problem and then present your offering as the best solution to the customer's problem.

Targeting a market that rallies around a cause is about as disruptable a market as you can find. There is a huge market for products that come from companies that minimize damage to the environment during the production of their products. People who believe in this eco-friendly cause are so passionate that they are willing to pay for eco-friendly clothing that is made entirely from recycled pop bottles (just to avoid having any part in damaging the environment). When Modrobes Clothing Lines & Store visited *Dragons' Den,* founder

Steven Sal Debus was so sure of his business—and the triple bottom line that he expected it to return—that he initially turned down $200,000 in capital from one of the Dragons.

Modrobes Clothing Lines & Store

Pitcher: Steven Sal Debus, Season 4, Episode 2

Focus: Target a Disruptable Market

> "It feels great to get back up and going again. It's fantastic, the store looks great. People are really, really loving everything they see in the store."
> —Pitcher to Dragons

PRODUCT DESCRIPTION

An eco-friendly clothing store and clothing line called Modrobes.

DRAGONS' DEN BY THE NUMBERS

- **The Ask:** $200,000 for 30% equity.
- **Company Valuation:** $666,666.
- **$1 million:** The amount that founder Steven Sal Debus says he has already invested in his business.
- **25%:** The percentage of his company that he gave up for $200,000 ($100k cash + $100k operating line).

Steven Sal Debus from Modrobes Clothing Line & Store explaining his plan to rebuild his Modrobes brand.

THE WARM-UP: MARKET SEGMENT DEFINED

A market segment is a homogeneous group of people who have a common set of needs. It's disruptable if the market has burning problems that are yet to be solved with the solutions currently on offer in the market. Often colloquially referred to as a "target market," it is actually more correctly defined as a subset of a target market. A target market can usually be broken down into several clusters of people with similar attributes—each called a market segment. The purpose of defining a market segment is so that:

- You can easily locate your typical customers.
- You can tailor your product or service to their specific needs.
- You can focus your marketing resources on one market.
- You can address a singular pain point with a singular value proposition.

Who Is Your Ideal Customer?

The process of defining your target market segment starts with creating a best-guess draft statement of who you are targeting. Then refine it into a declarative statement by adding:

- **Demographics:** An age, income, education, or occupational description or business type, such as *working technology professionals, schools, charities, kids, parents.*
- **Geographics:** A location description, such as *dual-income families in Toronto.*
- **Psychographics:** A personality description, such as *angry, loyal, fearful.*
- **Behaviouristics:** A behavioural description inferred from their habits, such as *their hobbies, or whether they play sports such as hockey or golf.*
- **Business Type:** A business category description, such as the office supplies industry, small private companies with 50 or fewer employees, small office/home office (SOHOs), advertising agencies.

The workshop at the end of the chapter will help you to define your target market segments.

What Is the Size of Your Market?

It's critical that you estimate the size of your market so you can determine if your business goals can be met. While the size of the market you choose to target depends on your goals, a market must be able to support your business objectives, as much as your solution serves the market itself. Furthermore, although you might be able to survive on a $5- to $10-million market, keep in mind, if you choose to seek outside investors, that most sophisticated investors look for markets with the potential to reach hundreds of millions of dollars. In fact, if you ever want to reach the most elite of all investor types—venture capital firms—you'll need to be able to show a market that is in the billions.

One market size analysis technique commonly used in the venture capital world is the TAM/SAM/SOM analysis. This analysis involves numbers you estimate using information sources you'll learn about in Chapter 20. The components of this type of market size analysis are:

- **Total Available Market (TAM):** The total industry-wide market for your product or service in a year. *Example: The number of immigrant workers who are remitting money regularly to their home countries.*
- **Serviceable Available Market (SAM):** The portion of the TAM that could conceivably buy your category of product or service. *Example: The number of immigrant workers who are remitting money regularly to the country where you have banking relationships.*
- **Serviceable Obtainable Market (SOM):** The share of the SAM you could conceivably capture. *Example: The number of immigrant workers in Canada who are remitting money regularly to the country where you have banking relationships.*
- **Compound Annual Growth Rate:** The historical growth rate of your market.

The workshop at the end of the chapter will help you gauge the size of the market you're going after.

Dragon Lore

Make sure your customers are easy to find, by clearly identifying who you plan to sell to, where they can be reached, and what their buying patterns are.

One core element of a sound business model is a clear definition of your ideal customers and where to find them. Without one, you will find it difficult to find marketing and sales outlets that specifically target them. When Easy Padala visited Dragons' Den they had done their homework. Their target market included people who remit over a billion dollars a year to their relatives in the Philippines. And with that kind of identifiable market, they didn't have a problem securing a deal from the Dragons.

Easy Padala

Pitchers: Francisco and Zeala Cortes, Season 5, Episode 3

Focus: Define the Ideal Customer for Your Product or Service

The Corteses' business model was structured on identifying a market segment they know well, and hence they knew a serious problem immigrants were facing. One of the key lessons here is that your own life experience may open the door to an idea that has a business application.

BACKGROUND

Francisco and Zeala Cortes are new immigrants to Canada. Four years ago they arrived here from the Philippines, where Francisco had worked in the banking sector.

PROBLEM STATEMENT

Many immigrants remit money to their relatives at home—in fact, the estimated value of remittances sent from Canada to the Philippines annually is $1.9 billion. The cost of each transaction is very high—as much as $30—and it can take three weeks for the money to arrive in the Philippines.

PROPOSED SOLUTION

A secure website that allows transmission of the money at a reasonable rate—$12 per transaction—and delivered within two to three days. The company has established relationships with banks in Canada and the Philippines, secured by a partner who has funds sitting in the banks guaranteeing the transactions.

BUSINESS CASE

- **Revenue Model:** Charge a fee per transaction.
- **The Ask:** $100,000 for 10% of the ownership.
- **Company Valuation:** $1 million.

DRAGONS' DEAL

Most Dragons had concerns about the control exercised by the silent partner. One partner offered $100,000 for 80% of the company but then was concerned that the Pitchers were prepared to accept that! He finally settled on $25,000 for 50% of the company and a $75,000 loan that would be paid when they could show a real purpose in what they have accomplished.

DEAL SYNERGIES

The Pitchers were keen to have the Dragons on board, saying, "It's a tough offer . . . I know we are going to grow to [be] worth millions of dollars."

Francisco and Zeala Cortes pitching Easy Padala, their remittance service, to the Dragons.

No book on starting or assessing a business concept would be complete without mentioning the fastest-growing company in history until the 1980s—Compaq Computers. The company used a second mover strategy to attack and capture part of IBM's market—the personal computer market.

A Real-World Case Study: Compaq

"From the beginning, we viewed ourselves as a large company in its formative state, not as a small company with the potential to grow."[1]
—Rod Canion, co-founder, Compaq Computer Corporation

The fastest-growing personal computer company in history was Compaq Computers (now part of HP). When computers became available for home use in the 1970s and early 1980s, this opened up a whole new market segment and a scalable-growth industry. Because so few people actually owned a personal computer at the time, the personal computer market was an underserved market and presented a huge opportunity for entrepreneurs who knew how to produce or assemble portable computers.

Hewlett-Packard, Commodore, and Tandy certainly had great starts, but Compaq beat them all. Launched in 1982, Compaq Computers became the fastest-growing computer company in the world by selling IBM-compatible personal computers to the masses. By 1987, it had sales of $1.2 billion by being in the right industry at the right time; it became, at the time, the fastest company in history to reach $1 billion in revenue.

BACKTESTING COMPAQ

Looking back at the Compaq business model, we can backtest it to see if it meets each of the Dragons' Den Success Factors:

SUCCESS FACTOR #1: FOCUS ON A SINGULAR PAIN POINT

Only IBM computers could run the software written for IBM computers, because of the BIOS that IBM controlled. The BIOS is permanent software that computers need to boot up basic hardware functionality on the computer, before Windows launches.

SUCCESS FACTOR #2: BUILD A PROTOTYPE

Compaq Computer Corporation evolved from a back-of-the-napkin idea into a $3,590 suitcase-style Compaq Portable PC that was the size of a typewriter in 1982.[2]

SUCCESS FACTOR #3: DEFINE THE VALUE PROPOSITION

Compaq built the second IBM PC-compatible computer capable of running all software that would run on an IBM personal computer. They used "clean room" techniques to legally produce the BIOS required to run all the software written for IBM computers.[3] The value to customers was that they essentially owned a computer that worked just like an IBM computer—for a lower price.

SUCCESS FACTOR #4: ESTABLISH A REPEAT REVENUE MODEL

Compaq sold ongoing support service agreements to computer buyers.

SUCCESS FACTOR #5: TARGET A DISRUPTABLE MARKET

Home computer users in 1982 had very few alternatives to the IBM personal computer, a market that was about to explode.

SUCCESS FACTOR #6: BUILD A LEAN FEATURE SET

No printer, no scanner. Just a box, a keyboard, and two floppy disk drives required for its highest and best use—running IBM-compatible software.

SUCCESS FACTOR #7: COLLABORATE WITH STRATEGIC PARTNERS

Compaq collaborated with dealers, instead of competing with them, by purposely not having a direct sales force. This collaboration engendered trust with the dealers, so the dealers would have more incentive to promote the Compaq machines over other machines.

SUCCESS FACTOR #8: FIND A CATALYST FOR GROWTH

Compaq used dealers exclusively to sell its computers to retailers, in exchange for a hefty margin on each machine sold.

SUCCESS FACTOR #9: SCALABILITY

Compaq's product was an IBM-compatible computer, so every component other than the IBM BIOS was readily available or could be produced quickly, providing Compaq with a scalable business model.

SUCCESS FACTOR #10: DEVELOP A BUSINESS MODEL

Compaq's business model was a producer model, and it used dealers to do the marketing to retailers.

Self-Study Workshop: How to Define Your Ideal Customer

The easiest way to find a customer is to clearly define who they are, where they live, how they think, and what they do.

1. Identify your **information sources** (trade associations, market research firms, industry analyses, discussed in Chapter 19).
2. Define your **market segment**.
   What homogeneous group of customers will buy your product or service?

   Example: Stay-at-home moms whose primary computer is an iPad.
   - **Demographic:** What is their age, income, education?
   - **Geographic:** Where are they located?

- **Psychographic:** What are their attitudes?
- **Behaviouristics:** What are their shared sports, job types, hobbies, purchases?
- **Business Type:** For those in B2B, what is the size of the business you are targeting?

3. What is the **total available market** (TAM) in dollars?

   What is the total industry-wide sales volume of your product or service in a year?

   Example: The number of stay-at-home moms who own computers.

4. What is the **serviceable available market** (SAM)?

   What portion of the TAM could conceivably buy your category of product or service?

   Example: The number of stay-at-home moms whose primary computer is an iPad.

5. What is your **serviceable obtainable market** (SOM)?

   What share of the SAM could you conceivably capture?

   Example: The number of stay-at-home moms whose computer is an iPad who you are able to serve.

6. What **share of the SOM** could you capture?

7. What is the **compound annual growth rate** of your market?

In this chapter you learned that defining what you are looking for, specifically the type of customer that you wish to serve, is the easiest way to find it. Now it's time to figure out what product or service features will appeal to that target customer the most. In the next chapter you'll read about ways to slim down your offering so that only the truly important features remain.

CHAPTER 6

BUILD A LEAN FEATURE SET

"The more complicated the product, the more responsibility you have to break it down to a feature set that the average guy . . . is going to understand."
— Dragon to Pitcher

> **Success Factor #6: Build a Lean Feature Set**
>
> To stand out in a sea of competition, eliminate as many unnecessary features from your prototype as you can, so that the important features have a chance to stand out. This isn't about being a one-trick pony. It is about being lean with your message and frugal with your resources so that you can survive long enough to gain market traction.

Occam's razor, a theory of simplicity widely attributed to William of Occam, states that if you take away the unnecessary steps in a theoretical method, you'll be left with the simplest solution to the problem.[1] In business, if you use Occam's razor to shave away features of your prototype that are not valuable, you'll give the important features a chance to be seen. For example, in order to help us see the iPad as something other than a laptop, Apple launched the first iPad without certain features typically found on a laptop such as USB ports, a webcam, and an off-screen keyboard. Apple included only those features that supported its *highest and best use* as a mobile multimedia platform. If you want scalable growth, pull out Occam's razor.

Few people know more about surgically removing excess features than the medical community. What doctors do best is solve our trauma problems. But when three doctors showed up in the Den, they weren't solving our medical issues. They were saving the next best thing—our all-important bananas.

Banana Guard

Pitchers: Dr. David Agulnik, Dr. Amin Sajan, and Dr. Sunil Mangal, Season 2, Episode 1

Focus: Lean Feature Set Defined

"Really what we want to prevent is needless, senseless banana trauma. [The banana carrying case] specifically prevents bruising during transport."
—Pitcher to Dragons

PRODUCT DESCRIPTION

A plastic banana-carrying case.

DRAGONS' DEN BY THE NUMBERS

- **The Ask:** $400,000 for 15%.
- **$5.99:** The price charged per Banana Guard.
- **700,000:** The number of Banana Guard units sold in three years.
- **$0:** The amount spent on advertising to sell 700,000 units of the Banana Guard.

The wildly successful Banana Guard being pitched on *Dragons' Den.*

THE WARM-UP: LEAN FEATURE SET DEFINED

A feature is a physical or functional attribute of your product or service, such as "meat-free" for a burrito restaurant, or a "10-hour battery life" for a laptop computer. A feature set is a group of these features. A feature set is lean if it is stripped down to only the must-have features that support your product or service's highest and best use. You can always add features later in a gradual, stepped fashion.

When you first launch a new product or service, you should include only the features that customers need to achieve its core purpose. Any unnecessary features make it more difficult for your most valuable features to stand out. The process of building a lean feature set involves:

- **Feature Goals:** The ways your features support the highest and best use of your product or service.
- **Feature Prioritization:** The process of paring down your wish list of features into a shortlist of features on which customers place the highest value.
- **The Product Roadmap:** The process of scheduling the release of new features and upgrades in the future when financial and/or time resources become available.

Feature Goals

A feature set is a group of features that support the highest and best use for your product or service. Features that don't support this highest and best use end up wasting valuable resources and cluttering your message, and can potentially degrade the customer's experience with your concept. The purpose of keeping your feature set down to a minimum are:

- **Brand Messaging:** Features position your product or service as the go-to solution to a customer's burning problem. If your product or service has too many features and does too many different things, you won't give the important features a chance to stand out.
- **Waste Elimination:** Features cost money to build. If you waste too much money building features that don't support your product or service's highest and best use, you'll burn through valuable cash that you could be using to improve the features that are truly valuable.

- **Go-to-Market Speed:** Features take time to build, improve, and upgrade. If you spend time building features that customers don't pay you to build, you're hurting your ability to generate revenue on the ones that they do pay you for.

Feature Prioritization

Most entrepreneurs don't have endless financial resources to add every conceivable feature to their product or service. Furthermore, if they don't get to market quickly with their new business concept, they could end up missing the market. In order to make the best use of resources, and minimize your time-to-market, it is critical to pare down your wish list of product or service features to a minimal shortlist. One feature prioritization technique, called the Kano model, was developed by Japanese professor Noriaki Kano.[2] The Kano model helps companies like Toyota figure out which features must be included and which features can be ignored when launching new products or services. The model helps you turn your wish list of features into a shortlist of must-haves, nice-to-haves, and "wow" factors.

The Product Roadmap

The product (or service) roadmap is a release schedule for your must-have, nice-to-have, and "wow" factor features. New business concepts that succeed typically release lower priority features later in a step-wise, sequential fashion as a response to customer requests. The purpose of the roadmap is to give your stakeholders (customers, investors, employees) a 5,000-foot view of where your product or service is now and how it will be upgraded in the future. It should include:

- **Current Release Features:** The shortest possible list of features (or service offerings) you can have without jeopardizing your revenue.
- **Planned Release Features:** Wish-list features not incorporated into the current offering because they weren't absolutely mandatory for commercial viability.
- **Strategic Initiatives:** Long-term projects for the next generation of your product or service.

Dragon Lore

Complicated products and services need to be broken down into a simple feature set that the average person will understand.

If you wanted the feature simplicity of a Banana Guard in the form of a waste removal tool, you would have invented the Rhinobag. The Rhinobag, which was pitched in the Den, is so simple you probably wonder why you didn't invent it yourself. But remember: the key to a successful business concept is not just coming up with a product or service. It is your ability to wrap a business model around your product or service idea, just like the team at Rhinobag proved when they visited the Den.

Rhinobag

Pitchers: Randy Uens and Mark Handley, Season 2, Episode 2

Focus: Build a Lean Feature Set

People need to get rid of household waste, and traditional metal skips (a.k.a. dumpsters) are expensive. A simple heavy-duty bag replaces the skip, and then the company charges to remove it.

BACKGROUND

Randy Uens and his partner, Mark Handley, from Belleville, Ontario, have been in the waste-removal business for a number of years and saw an opportunity to reduce costs for the consumer and at the same time make a profitable business. The waste-removal business is a multi-billion-dollar business. They were operating in Canada and wanted money to take the company international.

PROBLEM STATEMENT

The cost for consumers to rent metal dump bins is very high.

PROPOSED SOLUTION

Rhinobags are convenient, innovative heavy-duty bags that the consumer buys for $30 to $40 apiece, depending on size. The consumer can fill the bags with up to approximately 1.5 tons of waste such as concrete and shingles. When the bag is full, the consumer calls a toll-free number and pays a relatively low fee to have the waste collected.

BUSINESS CASE

- **Revenue Model:** Consumers pay to buy the bags, and then pay to have them collected when they are full.

- **The Ask:** $300,000 for 10% of the ownership.
- **Company Valuation:** $3 million.
- **Proof-of-Concept:** Projecting 25,000 bags sold, for $1 million in sales. Operating in Canada.

DRAGONS' DEAL

All five Dragons were interested in the deal and started circling the company. The Pitchers at first were adamant that the Dragons' offer was not valuing the company highly enough and asked for $1 million for 50% of the company. The Dragons persisted—all were eager to get into this market—but insisted on their lower valuation. In the end, they contributed $100,000 each to make an offer of $500,000, for 50% of the company, valuing the company at $1 million. After much consultation with his partner, Randy Uens, CEO of the company, agreed to part with half the company.

DEAL SYNERGIES

The team at Rhinobag got what most Den visitors could only dream of: interest from all five Dragons.

> "I think what's priceless to you is that there's five people, experienced in business, proven success, interested in investing in your company. And interested in the idea and engaged in it. That's priceless to you."
> —Dragon to Pitcher

Randy Uens from Rhinobag demonstrating his product in the Dragons' Den.

A Real-World Case Study: iPad

"Bernstein Research calls the iPad the fastest-selling electronic device ever."
—John Melloy, "iPad Adoption Rate Fastest Ever, Passing DVD Player," CNBC.com

"It's so much more intimate than a laptop and so much more capable than a smartphone."
—Steve Jobs, CEO, Apple

Tablet computers have been around for decades. For example, we've seen tablet computers that come with a stylus so you can write on the screen. Even Apple had its own version of the tablet in the 1990s called the Newton MessagePad and the Apple PenLite. However, tablet computers didn't really explode in sales until Apple redefined the tablet as an audiovisual device called the iPad, in 2010. It changed the tablet game by repurposing the predecessor device from being a mobile computer to being a mobile entertainment device. The iPad was so successful that by the fourth quarter of 2010, the iPad was beating the Mac in total unit volume sales.[3]

BACKTESTING IPAD

Looking back at the iPad business model, backed by a historically fast-growth company, we can test it to see how it meets each of the Dragons' Den Success Factors:

SUCCESS FACTOR #1: FOCUS ON A SINGULAR PAIN POINT

Carrying multiple audiovisual entertainment devices (books, DVD players, music, etc.) with you is cumbersome.

SUCCESS FACTOR #2: BUILD A PROTOTYPE

The iPad evolved from rudimentary prototype predecessors, including the Newton MessagePad and the Apple PenLite.[4]

SUCCESS FACTOR #3: DEFINE THE VALUE PROPOSITION

The iPad is a portable media device that combines almost every imaginable audiovisual device there is (books, email, video, music, etc.) into one simple and lightweight tool.

SUCCESS FACTOR #4: ESTABLISH A REPEAT REVENUE MODEL

The iPad generates repeat revenue from iBooks, games, and apps purchased through the app store, as well as upgrading with new versions.

SUCCESS FACTOR #5: TARGET A DISRUPTABLE MARKET

The majority of Apple iPads are purchased by current Apple product owners who thrive on innovation and are willing to pay a premium for it.[5] Apple is continually innovating, so even its own customers are given reasons to purchase new versions.

SUCCESS FACTOR #6: BUILD A LEAN FEATURE SET

The first market-ready version of the iPad didn't have a USB port or a webcam. The product was stripped down to the must-have features required for its *highest and best use*—entertainment, such as reading books and running apps. It is clearly different from a laptop, a phone, and its predecessor tablet computers.

SUCCESS FACTOR #7: COLLABORATE WITH STRATEGIC PARTNERS

Apple shares its software development kit with tens of thousands of developers who create free and fee-based apps. Every app built for the iPad by third-party developers not affiliated with Apple makes the iPad even more useful. Apple also shares its iBooks development kit with publishers that create books for the iPad.

SUCCESS FACTOR #8: FIND A CATALYST FOR GROWTH

Apple uses web apps to create demand for the iPad, which makes the iPad uniquely useful. The more web apps an iPad owner downloads, the more useful it becomes.

SUCCESS FACTOR #9: SCALABILITY

The iPad was launched with the scalability muscle of cash-rich Apple Computers.

SUCCESS FACTOR #10: DEVELOP A BUSINESS MODEL

The iPad business model is driven by a revenue-sharing model on content sales of iBooks, apps, and games. The iPad hardware itself generates repeat revenue from new versions.

Self-Study Workshop: How to Build a Lean Feature Set

The fastest way to penetrate the marketplace is to simplify your product or service down to a feature set that people will immediately understand. Features are the building blocks of your product or service that are valuable to customers. For example:

- One feature of a Frogbox moving box is that it is made of reusable plastic.
- One feature of Moxie Trades work boots is that they come in pink.
- One feature of the Banana Guard is that it is BPA-free, so it doesn't contain any harsh chemicals that could further harm your bananas.

1. Restate the **highest and best use** that your ideal customer would have for your product or service.
2. Brainstorm a wish list of every conceivable feature that your product or service would have in a perfect world. This **feature wish list** is called a "backlog" and you can add to it over time.
3. Using a **feature prioritization** technique such as the Kano model, organize your feature wish list into must-haves, nice-to-haves, and "wow" factors.
4. Pare down your list to the **shortest list of features** you can have without compromising the functionality of your product or service.
5. For each feature on your short list, state **how it supports the highest and best use** for your product or service.

   Example: The highest and best use for an iPad is mobile entertainment, so the 10-hour battery feature supports the need to have battery power for long periods.

6. For each feature on your short list, describe the **ideal customer experience** that people should have with that feature.
7. What features have **sustainable advantages** over those of your competitors'?
8. What other **assets do you own** (patents, long-term agreements, etc.)?
9. What **features will you add** in the future?

Having a lean feature set is as much about attracting customers and focusing your resources as it is about getting to market faster. In the next chapter, we'll delve into rapid market entry strategies by discussing how to find strategic partners who can help you reach your goals faster.

CHAPTER 7

WHO CAN HELP YOU REACH YOUR GOALS FASTER?

"If a large manufacturer came to you today and was willing to stay with your vision and take all of these headaches, outside of the R&D you want to provide, which everybody's going to believe you should do . . . are you okay with that? . . . For a royalty, let's say they're willing to pay you 7% of sales?"

—Dragon to Pitcher

Success Factor #7: Collaborate with Strategic Partners

Work with a virtual team of the smartest people in your domain. Partner with the leading organizations in your industry that can help you achieve your goals faster than you can achieve them on your own. Collaborate with advisors, staff, and outsourced service providers with whom you can share knowledge, successes, and achieve common goals.

The key to collaboration is that everyone has the same shared goal. A story (author unknown) has been passed on over the years to illustrate how differently people can see the same thing. It involves three bricklayers. Each is asked what he is doing. The first bricklayer says, "I'm laying bricks." The second bricklayer says, "I'm building a wall." The third bricklayer says, "I'm building a cathedral." The point of the story is that vision is in the eye of the beholder. It is important to have a shared vision in advance and also to be agile enough to change your course based on feedback from real stakeholders. You need to have a clear vision of why your product or service is valuable, or where your business is going, in order to attract the right customers, investors, and partners. If you want scalable growth, make sure all the bricklayers in your organization have the same vision.

When you run into challenges trying to generate sales yourself, you don't have to give up on your business idea. At this point, you should start considering strategic partners who have the ability to sell your product or service for you. When Jim Edison, inventor of Pop-Up Pylon, visited *Dragons' Den*, he received a whole host of advice on potential strategic partners for his business and eventually struck a deal.

Pop-Up Pylon

Pitcher: Jim Edison, Season 2, Episode 8

Collaborate with Strategic Partners

> "I'm listening to it and I think where I'm at is you're a great inventor guy. I totally get it on this cone deal. But I have to think that the best place for you to go is to the cone guy manufacturer."
> —Dragon to Pitchers

PRODUCT DESCRIPTION

A collapsible red traffic cone that collapses within its base and locks down in a flat position so several of them can be stacked.

DRAGONS' DEN BY THE NUMBERS

- **The Ask:** $150,000 for 30%.
- **Company Valuation:** $500,000.
- **50%:** The percentage of the business given up by the Pitcher.
- **39 million:** The number of traffic cones sold across North America in one year, according to the Pitcher.
- **$100,000:** The amount of personal capital Jim Edison invested in prototypes, patents, and trademarks.

Jim Edison of Pop-Up Pylon discussing the patent he has on his invention.

THE WARM-UP: COLLABORATION DEFINED

Collaboration is the process of working with other people, partners, and suppliers to achieve **common goals,** such as sales goals, production targets, or service levels. The purpose of collaboration is synergy. If done correctly, you can achieve better outcomes than you might have achieved on your own. The process of collaboration is usually triggered by a catalyst or "champion" who takes responsibility for achieving the outcome of the project. To help you start the process, we'll delve into four areas in this chapter:

- **How to Collaborate:** The foundation for a sound relationship.
- **Advisory Board:** A group of informal advisors who can help you build your team.
- **Cross-Functional Support:** Subject matter experts who you can recruit from time to time to launch strategic initiatives.
- **The 100 People You Know:** The close circle of people you probably already have on your team.

How to Collaborate

To take advantage of the power of collaboration, you need to be open minded because it involves a willingness to share resources and strategies. You can ensure a superior result by using a methodical approach. That involves:

- **Outcomes:** Develop a quantifiable list of collective outcomes for which you need partners to help.
- **Partners:** Conduct a partner search of people, suppliers, and manufacturers that you can work together with to achieve your shared goals.
- **Process:** Define clearly what you expect out of the relationship and how you plan to work together.
- **Information:** Be prepared to share information with your partners.

Advisory Board

An advisory board is a team of experienced individuals who agree to provide you with advice, contacts, or resources whenever you run into a challenge. They can introduce you to customers, investors, and suppliers. They can help to attract investors and are often investors themselves. Why would they join? Because they want to meet other people on the board, they want to be involved in a role that might lead to a paid position, or they're just looking for personal satisfaction. An informal advisory board can be the most valuable addition to your venture. It also signals to outside investors that you are not working in a vacuum because you have a sounding board of experienced people. Investors will know that your business plan is carefully thought out.

Cross-Functional Support

The founder of a company looking forward to achieving scalable growth should have a network of people who are subject matter experts (SMEs) whom he or she can bring together temporarily on short notice, for short or long periods. These SMEs are capable of doing the work the team leader defines, including designing, financing, developing, marketing, and delivering the product or performing the service. Some of these SMEs might be outsourced (such as a CFO, attorney, or marketing consultant). Others, such as product developers with technical expertise to produce and add features to your offering, might be in-house. Still others might form an informal advisory board of people who can introduce you to customers, investors, and suppliers as needed.

The 100 People or Organizations You Know

A ridiculous practice followed by some new salespeople is to make a list of the 100 people you know, call them, and try to sell them your product or service. A not-so-ridiculous practice is to make a list of the 100 people and organizations you know and categorize them by what they do and how they can help your venture. Most people will help you, especially if it doesn't cost them too much time or money. They can introduce you to suppliers, customers, and investors. They can provide feedback to grow your venture and help you address gaps. They can even provide solace when things aren't going your way. Organizations to consider partnering with include your suppliers, competitors in different geographic markets, or complementary businesses. The key to collaboration is to be as useful to others as they are to you, so when you implement this concept in the workshop at the end of this chapter, consider what you have to offer each of the people or organizations that you add to your list.

Dragon Lore

One of the most valuable ways to grow your business is to collaborate with strategic partners who can help you get things done faster than you can yourself.

Collaboration is so powerful that many businesses wouldn't exist without it. One such company, FoodScrooge, doesn't produce a tangible product. Nor do they distribute one. They simply collaborate with food manufacturers who have excess inventory and independent grocers who can distribute that food. They then find customers for that food online. When FoodScrooge visited the Den, they showed that you can build an entire business using collaborative relationships.

FoodScrooge

Pitchers: Tim Ray and Jonathan Ambeault, Season 6, Episode 10

Focus: Collaborate with Strategic Partners

The first North American company to apply the group-buying craze to bulk **food** shopping.

BACKGROUND

Tim Ray has experience in the food business. His partner Jonathan Ambeault has an IT background. They have built the first website in Canada to offer consumers the opportunity to buy food products at deep discounts—40% to 80% less than retail prices.

PROBLEM STATEMENT

Price-conscious consumers want to save on their grocery bills.

PROPOSED SOLUTION

FoodScrooge is partnering with grocery retailers that will distribute their food offers in return for 4% of gross sales. Five to seven special offers will be made each week, and customers will go to the grocery store partners to pick them up. The retailers are in it for the fee, as well as in the hope that increased foot traffic will increase their sales of other food items.

BUSINESS CASE

- **Revenue Model:** FoodScrooge sources surplus food from food manufacturers and marks it up by 25%. They then partner with independent retailers that agree to distribute the food at their locations in exchange for 4% of gross sales.
- **The Ask:** $125,000 for 15% of the ownership.
- **Company Valuation:** $833,000.
- **Proof-of-Concept:** Seven retailers in the GTA have signed up for the pilot project.

DRAGONS' DEAL

Four of the Dragons were interested in the deal, but with the company in only the second week of operations, a valuation was difficult. Three Dragons offered $125,000 for 40% of the company; another pair agreed to $125,000 for 35% of the company.

DEAL SYNERGIES

The three Dragons who went in on the deal have great marketing experience to offer the company.

> "Your biggest issue is going to be attracting consumers. You're going to have to get out there and market like crazy, and that's something that I'm good at."
> —Dragon to Pitcher

> "I am your reality, my friend; I deal in numbers."
> —Dragon to Pitcher

The FoodScrooge team presenting their Groupon-like model to the Dragons.

A Real-World Case Study: Domino's Pizza

"Delivering pizzas fast is not a matter of driving fast; it's a matter of getting the pizzas in the oven fast."
— Tom Monaghan, "The Pioneering Pizza-Delivery Chain I Started Almost Didn't Make It Out of the Oven" (with Julie Sloane), *Fortune Small Business*

If you want to expand a retail business model like Domino's Pizza to many geographic locations quickly, you need capital and a local presence in each one of those markets. So you have two options: (1) come up with the capital yourself and manage each of the local stores yourself (the Starbucks model) or (2) collaborate with local entrepreneurs, called franchisees, who bring their capital and local teams into the business (the Domino's Pizza model).

Domino's achieved scalable growth by collaborating with local entrepreneurs, called franchisees, and by delivering a lean product—a pizza with pepperoni and a soft drink. It disrupted the entire pizza-delivery industry by promising that your pizza would arrive 30 minutes from when your order was placed—or it was free. Was the world better off because it now had a new place to buy pizza? No. There were many pizza restaurants before Domino's arrived on the scene. Domino's Pizza achieved scalable growth because it created a disruptive value proposition that no one else could meet—it solved the uncertainty of not knowing when your pizza would arrive with its "30 minutes or it's free" promise.

BACKTESTING DOMINO'S PIZZA

Looking back at the Domino's Pizza business model, we can test it to see how it meets each of the Dragons' Den Success Factors:

SUCCESS FACTOR #1: FOCUS ON A SINGULAR PAIN POINT

When Domino's Pizza started in the 1960s, pizza-delivery companies were notorious for delivering orders in unpredictable amounts of time.

SUCCESS FACTOR #2: BUILD A PROTOTYPE

Domino's Pizza evolved from DomiNick's,[1] a rudimentary version of the first Domino's Pizza store prototype.[2]

SUCCESS FACTOR #3: DEFINE THE VALUE PROPOSITION

Domino's Pizza achieved scalable growth early on by delivering a quality pizza to its customers in a predictable amount of time. The company uses an assembly-line pizza-making process that streamlines the cooking process, which helps make delivery time predictable. For years, Domino's Pizza offered its "30 minutes or it's free" delivery promise, and its revenue exploded.

SUCCESS FACTOR #4: ESTABLISH A REPEAT REVENUE MODEL

Repeat pizza orders from current customers.

SUCCESS FACTOR #5: TARGET A DISRUPTABLE MARKET

Domino's operates in a $35-billion market.[3] By delivering to a timetable, it disrupted its competitors who couldn't or didn't match the promise.

SUCCESS FACTOR #6: BUILD A LEAN FEATURE SET

Domino's offered a simple menu of pizza only before it achieved incremental growth by also offering soft drinks. The company maintained this stripped-down menu to meet its highest and best purpose—hot pizza delivered in a predictable amount of time. It maintained its basic menu until 1992, when it finally added bread sticks—its first non-pizza menu item.[4]

SUCCESS FACTOR #7: COLLABORATE WITH STRATEGIC PARTNERS

Domino's Pizza grew rapidly by collaborating with franchisees across the country. Today, the company has more than 9,000 stores worldwide.[5]

SUCCESS FACTOR #8: FIND A CATALYST FOR GROWTH

The catalyst for growth for Domino's Pizza has been *franchising.* Essentially, the company is able to piggyback on the efforts of local entrepreneurs who want to build a pizza business fast by using the proven Domino's Pizza banner and business model.

SUCCESS FACTOR #9: SCALABILITY

Tom Monaghan built the company around a highly scalable assembly-line process called the "makeline" and a franchise business model that could penetrate new markets quickly.

SUCCESS FACTOR #10: DEVELOP A BUSINESS MODEL

Domino's Pizza used a franchise business model and highly streamlined process to penetrate new markets quickly.

Self-Study Workshop: How to Build Your Team of Advisors

Entrepreneurs are in business to get things done, not necessarily do them themselves. Collaborating can cut your time-to-market in half, give you access to people with personal ties to key decisions makers, and provide valuable strategic advice.

1. Make a list of the **100 people you know or organizations you could partner with** (suppliers, vendors, complementary businesses, etc.) to produce and sell your product or service.

     This list can be longer, but start with 100.

2. What **subject matter experts** are required to run your business?

3. What **deep market experience** is required to win customers in your market?

4. What **cross-functional support** do you require to support your day-to-day operating efforts?

5. Considering your needs from the previous steps, **categorize** your list of 100 people by what each person brings to the table.

6. Develop a **gaps list**—a list of skills or connections (customers, suppliers, investors) that you need access to.

7. **Contact** people on your list.

     Tell them about your business concept and ask if they would be able to assist you on a paid or non-paid basis in the future. In addition, ask them if they know anyone who can fill in any of the gaps on your gaps list.

8. Prepare the groundwork for your team-building efforts by getting **commitments** from critical hires and advisors.

The importance of strategic partners cannot be overstated because they have the ability to help you reach new markets faster. In the next chapter, we'll further develop this concept by discussing how to use events that can trigger growth.

CHAPTER 8

HOW CAN YOU TRIGGER A SUDDEN INCREASE IN SALES?

"You should be going to let someone else distribute them for you. It's better to make 10% on a large number than try to push that yourself."
—Dragon to Pitcher

Success Factor #8: Find a Catalyst for Growth

Cross-market your product or service through other businesses, people, and partners. Consider shared revenues, referral fees, or just a straight exchange (subject to industry laws and regulations).

Sometimes a business needs more than just a great business model to trigger a breakthrough in sales. Eventually, you need to *flip the switch* using a trigger such as an event, partner, or other catalyst. Scalable-growth companies seek out these partners in the form of piggyback marketing and co-branding relationships that can double or triple their revenues in an instant. On a sales chart, this breakthrough is called an "inflection point," because your revenue goes up with little or no added cost to you. If you want scalable growth, seek out a catalyst that triggers a huge increase in sales overnight.

One company that visited *Dragons' Den* found a catalyst in YouTube. After taking a video of her daughter signing, using her My Smart Hands solution, Laura Berg posted the video on YouTube. Then the unexpected happened. Her video had more than 2.5 million views, enough to bring huge attention to her company.

My Smart Hands

Pitcher: Laura Berg, Season 5, Episode 12

Focus: A Catalyst Defined

"I posted a video [on YouTube] of my daughter showing parents what babies are capable of, and to date that video has had over 2.5 million views."
—Pitcher to Dragons

PRODUCT DESCRIPTION

Sign language and play classes for hearing babies and toddlers.

DRAGONS' DEN BY THE NUMBERS

- **The Ask:** $100,000 for 40% of the business.
- **50%:** The percentage of the business given up by the Pitcher.
- **2.5 million:** The number of views that Laura Berg's sign language video on YouTube had by the time she presented on the show.
- **$50,000:** The revenue the Pitcher had earned in the year prior to making it onto the *Dragons' Den* set.

Laura Berg presenting her website for teaching babies American Sign Language.

THE WARM-UP: CATALYST DEFINED

A catalyst is a person, action, or event that triggers a rapid increase in sales you otherwise wouldn't have achieved on your own. The purpose of a catalyst is to help you build market traction faster than you could on your own. Because every business category is different, your catalyst will be unique.

Go-to-Market Strategy

A go-to-market strategy refers to the steps you need to take to reach an addressable (i.e., clearly identifiable) market. Your strategy should clearly identify your:

- **Product Category:** Are you laying bricks or building a cathedral? (See the discussion on differing visions in the opening paragraph of Chapter 7.)
- **Target Customer:** Are you selling to resellers or directly to the consumer?
- **Channels:** Are you selling directly or through intermediaries that constitute distribution channels?

Catalysts

Every business needs a catalyst, and once you find that catalyst, you may experience a rapid increase in sales revenue. A catalyst is anything that helps you achieve a strategic objective faster than you could achieve it on your own. Some of the most powerful catalysts are:

- **Complementary Products:** Your product or service complements another product or service (e.g., salt and pepper; rum and cola).
- **Franchising:** Your business model is successful and can be replicated easily in other markets (e.g., Domino's Pizza, Chapter 7).
- **Affiliate Marketing:** Other websites drive traffic to your website, and you pay them for that traffic (e.g., Netflix, Chapter 3).
- **Dealer Promotions:** You don't have a standalone sales force that competes with your distributors (e.g., Compaq, Chapter 5).
- **Viral Marketing:** Your product or service has a "wow" factor that people are willing to talk about over and over (e.g., Groupon, Chapter 2).

- **Piggyback Marketing:** You're able to strike a fee deal with a business that can represent your product or service to its customers (e.g., getting a deal with QVC, which is like a TV version of a retail outlet; it gives you access to an extremely high volume of viewers that QVC has already established).
- **User-Generated Content:** You create a community or website around content that is produced by the visitors to that site. Then you sell things to that community. Examples of user-generated concept sites are Wikipedia and Facebook—the content on the sites is generated by the visitors themselves.
- **Strategic Investors:** You are able to take on a financial investor who also has extensive contacts with suppliers, vendors, or manufacturers in your industry (e.g., when Microsoft invested in Apple in the 1990s it brought expertise that Apple needed to make Microsoft Office products work on Mac computers).

A Low-Cost Catalyst

Out of all the catalysts that are available to most start-ups, none is stronger than piggyback marketing. Piggyback marketing is a go-to-market strategy that uses channels already in place to sell your product or service. The key to the strategy is to find products or services that are already being sold to your ideal customers and then strike a marketing agreement with their product managers. This may involve shared revenues, referral fees, or just a straight exchange, depending on what is legal in your industry. It's one of the fastest ways to go to market because you're putting your product or service in front of customers whom someone else has spent money to attract. For example, you partner with a toolbox manufacturer and sign a revenue-sharing agreement with it to include your multi-purpose tool as a part of its toolbox offering. On the Web, you advertise your product on Google or Facebook and piggyback on the millions of users of these sites.

Dragon Lore

It's better to make a small percentage of a large number than a large percentage of a small number.

Another company that visited the Den also found a catalyst in an unexpected place. After changing their name from HapiFoods Group to Holy Crap Cereal, the company received an inordinate amount of attention from a word-of-mouth brush fire that was triggered by the new name. Plus, as a side effect of being on the *Dragons' Den* show itself, their sales reportedly blew through their initial $600,000 target and reached $5 million in sales within a year of being on the *Den*.[1]

Holy Crap Cereal

Pitchers: Brian and Corin Mullins, Season 5, Episode 7

Focus: How to Trigger an Increase In Sales

What started out as a "survival" cereal exploded in sales after a simple name change to Holy Crap Cereal. At the time of the pitch, the product sold through farmer's markets, but the all-natural product now sells online and through some grocery stores, including IGA and Sobeys.

BACKGROUND

Husband-and-wife team Brian and Corin Mullins founded their company as the HapiFoods Group. About three weeks after the product launch, the name was changed to Holy Crap Cereal in response to the number of calls and letters they had received where people said, "Holy crap, this is amazing."

PROBLEM STATEMENT

People need natural ways to lower their blood sugar, blood pressure, and cholesterol.

PROPOSED SOLUTION

Originally developed as a survival food, Holy Crap is an all-natural mixed cereal of organic hulled hemp hearts, buckwheat, and chia, and includes cranberries, raisins, and apples for sweetness. It is gluten-free, wheat-free, lactose-free, and vegan, and promotes digestion.

BUSINESS CASE

- **Revenue Model:** Produces and sells cereal directly and through retailers.
- **The Ask:** $120,000 for 20% equity.

- **Company Valuation:** $600,000.
- **Proof-of-Concept:** In the company's first few months of sales, changing the name helped increase revenue by 400%. They reached $65,000 in revenue in approximately 50 days of sales at farmer's markets. Sold online and in grocery stores.

DRAGONS' DEAL

$120,000 for 20% equity.

DEAL SYNERGIES

One Dragon came in on the deal with a distribution company, manufacturing contacts, and financing.

> "I've got a distribution company. I've got guys who can make this stuff. Whatever you need me to do, I'm ready to do a deal."
> —Dragon to Pitchers

Husband-and-wife team Brian and Corin Mullins pitching their Holy Crap cereal.

There is nothing more catalytic than mixing alcohol with a soft drink. It's a recipe that cannot only change the nature of the two individual components, but it can also change the revenue of the brands behind them.

A Real-World Case Study: Bacardí Rum

At 150 years old, Bacardí rum is older than Ford, Hershey's Chocolate, and even Coca-Cola. The company began in a tin-roof distillery in Santiago de Cuba on February 4, 1862, and has grown into the world's favourite and most-awarded rum. Its logo was inspired by a colony of fruit bats in the rafters of the original distillery. Founder Don Facundo Bacardí Massó pioneered key rum-making standards that have made his Bacardí rum the go-to-ingredient for the daiquiri, the mojito, and, of course, the Cuba libre (i.e., rum, cola, and lime).

BACKTESTING BACARDÍ

Looking back at the early years of the Bacardí business model, we can backtest it to see if it meets each of the Dragons' Den Success Factors:

SUCCESS FACTOR #1: FOCUS ON A SINGULAR PAIN POINT

Before Bacardí rum, the rum of the time—known as fire water or *aguardiente*—was crude and unpalatable to the emerging Cuban middle class. Consumers with discriminating taste were more likely to drink whisky or Cognac than the harsh-tasting rum that was available to them before the smooth-tasting Bacardí rum came about.

SUCCESS FACTOR #2: BUILD A PROTOTYPE

The first samples of Bacardí rum were offered directly to consumers at the distillery. Local consumers and sailors in port showed up with their own refillable barrels, since glass bottles were not widely available at the time.

SUCCESS FACTOR #3: DEFINE THE VALUE PROPOSITION

Bacardí rum was the world's first light-bodied spirit because it was (and still is) a smooth, mixable alternative to other, harsh-tasting, rums.

SUCCESS FACTOR #4: ESTABLISH A REPEAT REVENUE MODEL

In the 1800s, sailors, sugar planters, and other locals lined up at the tin-roof distillery daily, barrels in tow, to fill them with rum. They would return once they were empty.

SUCCESS FACTOR #5: TARGET A DISRUPTABLE MARKET

An emerging middle class that had previously turned to imported spirits like Cognac and whisky now had a smooth-tasting, premium, light rum alternative that they could purchase domestically.

SUCCESS FACTOR #6: BUILD A LEAN FEATURE SET

In the early years, Bacardí rum was sold directly from the distillery, unbottled, to local consumers, sailors, and sugar planters who brought their own containers.

SUCCESS FACTOR #7: COLLABORATE WITH STRATEGIC PARTNERS

The business was a joint venture with founder Don Facundo's younger brother to buy the first distillery in Santiago de Cuba—150 years ago, on February 4, 1862.

SUCCESS FACTOR #8: FIND A CATALYST FOR GROWTH

The catalyst for growth for Bacardí rum was the cocktail culture of the early 20th century. Not only was Bacardí rum used as the main ingredient in a mixed drink made famous in Daiquiri, Cuba, but returning U.S. soldiers from the Spanish-American War requested that it be mixed with their Coca-Cola.

SUCCESS FACTOR #9: SCALABILITY

The existing distillery in Cuba was purchased by founder Don Facundo Bacardí Massó and adapted to accommodate his quality standard.

SUCCESS FACTOR #10: DEVELOP A BUSINESS MODEL

In its early days, the company had a direct sales model, with free samples used to create demand. Local consumers and sailors arriving at the nearby port visited the distillery to refill their own barrels with Bacardí rum before departing on their next voyage.[2]

Self-Study Workshop: How to Find a Catalyst for Growth

When hard work doesn't pay off fast enough, an external trigger or catalyst can help you achieve your business goals faster.

1. **What** are you selling?
2. To **whom** are you selling?
3. What is your sales and marketing **approach**?
4. What events (holidays, deadlines, purchases, etc.) **trigger** the purchase of your product or service?

5. What other products and services **complement** your product or service?

6. What **organizations or associations** regularly communicate to your target customers?

7. List potential partners or outside businesses that can help you cross-market your product or service.

8. What **agreement** can you strike with these strategic partners to cross-market each other's services?

9. Do you know intermediaries who can **connect** you with these businesses and partners?

10. What's your **go-to-market strategy** (in one sentence)?

After reading and implementing the concepts in this chapter, you will no doubt have discovered a multitude of ways to trigger a rapid increase in sales. As you'll read in the next chapter, handling the pressure of that sudden increase in sales will require that you have a scalable business system.

CHAPTER 9

IS YOUR BUSINESS IDEA SCALABLE?

"Is your vision with the money to create a think tank where you'll take a product to a certain stage and then license it to others and then build the next cool thing, or is your idea to actually become the Henry Ford of the motorcycle world?"
    —Dragon to Pitcher

Success Factor #9: Build a Scalable Business System

Establish a repeatable operating process. Work with suppliers that will work with you on short notice. Standardize your product or service as much as possible. Find a repeat customer model.

Think about your old personal computer that slowed to a crawl as you added more software and data. It eventually collapsed under the pressure of newer, ever more demanding software programs, larger amounts of data, and increased interaction with you. Sooner or later, you had to wipe the system clean and reinstall the operating system. Or you saved yourself time and headaches and scrapped it altogether. If you chose to buy a new one, the new system started out really fast, but over time the same problem happened again. In other words, the new personal computer system wasn't scalable either. In business, scalability refers to the ability of a business and its systems to handle increased customer activity without slowing to a crawl because of a lack of staffing or financial resources.

One of the most *scalable* business models ever presented on *Dragons' Den* was NoteWagon. The key to NoteWagon, as you'll see, is that it is a completely automated and highly scalable website. Because people who use the website generate the content that is sold, or traded, the business can handle large volumes of customers with little stress on system resources.

NoteWagon

Pitchers: Saif Altimimi and Shawn Swartman, Season 6, Episode 6

Focus: How to Build a Scalable Business Model

"I could never take great notes [in university]. I always found myself borrowing my friends', making a copy and then referencing it later . . . Students register for free on our website [NoteWagon] and then share their notes with the community. The [note-sharing] student then exchanges cash for course notes."
    —Pitcher to Dragons

PRODUCT DESCRIPTION

An online note-sharing service for university students. The service targets influential opinion leaders on school campuses to get users to sign up.

DRAGONS' DEN BY THE NUMBERS

- **The Ask:** $200,000 for 20% of the business.
- **Company Valuation:** $1 million.
- **15,000:** The number of users that NoteWagon had when the founders met the Dragons.
- **$250,000:** The amount of investor capital offered by five Dragons.
- **5:** The number of Dragons who agreed to the deal.

Saif Altimimi and Shawn Swartman being grilled by the Dragons.

THE WARM-UP: SCALABILITY DEFINED

Scalability is the ability to handle sudden increases in customer volume without being constrained by staff or financial resource limitations. The purpose of scalability is to have a business system that doesn't crash under the pressure of increasing customer volume. The process of incorporating scalability into your business system starts with:

- **A Repeatable Process:** A process that is streamlined and operating manual-driven so others can repeat the process.
- **Flexible Suppliers:** Suppliers that will work with you on short notice at low or high volumes, ensuring you have access to a continuous supply of raw materials as needed, without having to overly commit financial resources in advance.
- **Standardized Output:** A standardized product or service delivery process, instead of a customized product or service process.
- **Repeat Customers:** A business model that provides for a never-ending stream of customers for your product or service. If you sell a one-and-done product or service that never needs to be repurchased, it becomes harder to scale your business.

Repeatable Process

If you think about a cookbook, it is nothing more than an operating manual that can be followed by anyone. It has pages in it, complete with lists of ingredients, step-by-step directions, and suggested cooking times to achieve a standardized product. If you skip one of the steps, your cheese soufflé might not turn out so well. Just like a cookbook, an operating process is designed to provide a step-by-step, repeatable process that can be performed by anyone. One model to draw valuable lessons from is the franchise business model. A franchise is nothing more than a business model that someone has chosen to let others use in exchange for a fee. Franchisors protect their brands by developing highly efficient and repeatable business processes. They start by documenting their step-by-step processes early on, until they have a repeatable process and predictable product or service output that anyone can follow. Then they package that process and license it out for an ongoing royalty.

Flexible Suppliers

If you were going to buy a car, you would never go to one lot, ask the dealer how much, and then pay the price he asked. You'd shop around, do your homework in advance, and know exactly how much the car was worth before you made a commitment. When sourcing suppliers for your business, you should ensure you follow the same negotiating process as you would if you were buying a car. However, unlike the car-buying process, working with suppliers is more of a collaborative process, where they provide you with the customized raw materials for your business. Keep in mind that they need you as much as you need them, so make sure you are never in a position of weakness. Feeling like you have a gun to your head when you need more raw materials on short notice can cause you to make bad business decisions. Make sure that procuring suppliers is an ongoing part of your overall business process.

Standardized Output

A standardized product or service is more about having a predictable level of quality than it is about having a cookie-cutter product or service. For example, a hair salon franchise concept can have a standardized process, while at the same time offering a customized look and feel to the final output. The operation can be standardized in terms of types of clientele served, time spent, and geographic preferences. Being scalable means you can repeat a process over and over, with a predictable outcome that doesn't have to be one-size-fits-all.

Repeat Customers

If cash flow is the lifeblood of all businesses, repeat customers are the heart of your business. Customers who come back to you—because they have consumed or are finished with what you originally sold them—will allow you to achieve predictable growth. Restarting your business annually will not. However, if you happen to sell a tangible product that is not consumable, you can consider adding an ongoing service agreement to the original purchase to generate repeat cash flow going forward.

Dragon Lore

Systematize your business so anyone can repeat the process and achieve the same predictable product or service output.

Another highly scalable business model that appeared on *Dragons' Den* is CardSwap. The company uses a Web-based application to help gift card owners sell their unwanted cards. Because the trading system operates online, there is little or no disruption to the core business system if volumes suddenly increase. The only part of the business that might become stressed is the gift card shipping operation, since cards have to be sent in by sellers and then sent back out to buyers. But the shipping process itself can also be highly automated.

CardSwap

Pitcher: Frances Ho, Season 6, Episode 2

Focus: How to Scale Your Product or Service

Websites, if set up correctly, are the poster child for scalable business systems. Web application technology can be structured to handle high-volume traffic loads at very low incremental cost.

BACKGROUND

After trying unsuccessfully to get rid of unused gift cards on Craigslist, Frances Ho conceived of the idea for a card-swapping website where people could turn their gift cards into cash.

PROBLEM STATEMENT

Some 40% of gift cards go unredeemed.

PROPOSED SOLUTION

CardSwap is a website where you can sell your unwanted gift cards for cash. The site pays the site visitor up to 90% of the value of the gift card.

BUSINESS CASE

- **Revenue Model:** CardSwap buys and resells gift cards and keeps the profit.
- **The Ask:** $500,000 for 33% equity.
- **Company Valuation:** $1.52 million.
- **Proof-of-Concept:** Over $1 million in revenue over the last 12 months on the sales of gift cards; $80,000 in profit over the last 12 months. Over 100,000 users on the site.

DRAGONS' DEAL

$500,000 for 50% of the company.

DEAL SYNERGIES

Two Dragons came in on the deal, bringing restaurant industry contacts and online business model expertise to the table.

> "I think it's worth a million dollars."
> —Dragon to Pitcher

Frances Ho of CardSwap explaining her value proposition to the Dragons.

A Real-World Case Study: Mint.Com

> "Observe the world around you. Everything you do—and especially everything you hate to do—solves a real problem and the world is yours."[1]
> —Aaron Patzer, founder, Mint.com

The hardest part of cutting your monthly spending budget is in determining where your money goes. Aaron Patzer became so thoroughly annoyed with this problem and the available solutions he experimented with that he resolved to come up with his own Web application to solve the problem. His painkiller solution, Mint.com, became the fastest growing personal finance website in history. It simplifies the task of categorizing your bank transactions and searches through them to find ways to save you money. The "wow" factor of Mint.com is that it figures out ways in which you can save $50 or more per month[1] by looking at your bank account transactions—all in minutes and completely free. Its business concept is to help you find ways to lower your monthly bills, in exchange for a referral fee paid by the vendors who can save you money on those bills. Its revenue model is referral fees from the financial institution vendors.

Within two years of launch, Mint.com made such a splash in the personal-finance industry that Intuit Inc. bought the company for a reported figure of $170 million. Today, Mint.com tracks billions of transactions for millions of users.

BACKTESTING MINT.COM

Looking back at the Mint.com business model, we can backtest it to see if it meets each of the Dragons' Den Success Factors:

SUCCESS FACTOR #1: FOCUS ON A SINGULAR PAIN POINT

People don't follow budgets because they don't have the time to track and categorize dozens of purchases from multiple bank and credit card institutions.

SUCCESS FACTOR #2: BUILD A PROTOTYPE

Mint.com evolved from a rudimentary private beta into the most popular personal-finance Web app through an iterative process that incorporates valuable suggestions, bug reports, and requests from thousands of beta tester emails.

SUCCESS FACTOR #3: DEFINE THE VALUE PROPOSITION

Mint.com automatically builds, tracks, and analyzes your family budget from your transactions so you can stay on track financially—for free. Mint.com uses account aggregation technology that pulls and sorts all your financial transactions from multiple bank and credit card institutions into a neat little budget, all in one place. The service is kept free because Mint.com is paid by vendors if they find a credit card (or other vendor) that you switch to that would save you money.

SUCCESS FACTOR #4: ESTABLISH A REPEAT REVENUE MODEL

Mint.com generates repeat revenue from the vendors who pay them a referral fee every time a Mint.com user switches to them.

SUCCESS FACTOR #5: TARGET A DISRUPTABLE MARKET

Young professionals between the ages of 22 and 35 bank online and are constantly looking for "bigger, better, stronger."

SUCCESS FACTOR #6: BUILD A LEAN FEATURE SET

Mint.com doesn't balance portfolios, doesn't estimate taxes. The service is stripped down to the must-have features required for its *highest and best use*—categorizing monthly expense transactions so you can see how much you are spending per month by category.

SUCCESS FACTOR #7: COLLABORATE WITH STRATEGIC PARTNERS

Mint.com initially collaborated with Yodlee, a provider of data aggregation software, because it needed a way to help customers see all their financial data in one place.[2] Through a licensing agreement, Mint.com was able to go to market faster than it could have had it built the technology itself.[3] Mint.com was later bought by Intuit and no longer required Yodlee as a partner.

SUCCESS FACTOR #8: FIND A CATALYST FOR GROWTH

Mint.com *syndicated their blog content* to other blogs that had ready-made audiences, in exchange for return links.[4]

SUCCESS FACTOR #9: SCALABILITY

Just like other famous Web applications, Mint.com is inherently scalable because of the server technology that houses the software online.

SUCCESS FACTOR #10: DEVELOP A BUSINESS MODEL

Mint.com figured out that if you offer a great Web business model free to users, you can attract a huge volume of followers quickly. Mint.com makes money on referral fees when its users sign up for bank, credit card, and brokerage accounts on the site.

Self-Study Workshop: How to Build a Scalable Business

Scalability is all about building flexibility into your operating process. Making your business more efficient involves having suppliers, systems, and resources in place to react to short-term spikes in business activity.

1. Set up a **note-taking system** on your computer or in a notebook to track the steps.
2. Break down your **method of producing your product or performing your service** into 7 to 10 steps, as if you were telling someone else how to do it.

3. Revise and refine your notes over time into a **cookbook of sorts**, complete with the supplies required, the inputs involved, and the detailed micro-steps involved for each stage.

4. List **at least three suppliers** for every raw material used in the production of your product or delivery of your service.

5. Describe your process for acquiring **new staff** on short notice:
   - ❑ Temp agencies
   - ❑ Staffing firms
   - ❑ Headhunters
   - ❑ Other

6. What part of your product or service offering is **standardized?**

7. What part of your product or service offering is **consumable**?
   - ❑ Product or service itself
   - ❑ Service agreements
   - ❑ Planned obsolescence (will need to be replaced in the future)
   - ❑ Other

Making sure that your business doesn't collapse under the pressure of a sudden increase in revenue has been the theme of this chapter. In the next chapter we'll discuss how to put the previous nine success factors together into a sustainable money-making system.

CHAPTER 10

DO YOU HAVE A SUSTAINABLE MONEY-MAKING SYSTEM?

"The business model essentially is: students will buy into token packages of virtual currency and exchange these tokens for notes. During that exchange of tokens we retain 50% of it, and the [note-selling] students then get allocated the other 50% as payment."
—Pitchers to Dragons

> ### Success Factor #10: Develop a Sustainable Business Model
>
> Use trial and error to find the most profitable market for your product or service. Build a long-term, sustainable money-making system around your product/market focus.

Product-centric entrepreneurs are at risk of succumbing to something my wife and her medical practitioner colleagues refer to as the "Wile E. Coyote Effect": the moment in your product-centric business when your sales are running along smoothly, then suddenly pause and plunge just like Wile E. Coyote after he runs off a cliff in pursuit of the Road Runner. Innovators who don't build sustainable business models around their products or services are at risk of being copied, undercut, or succumbing to sudden market shifts (think Yahoo! when Google entered the market). Once you have found the most profitable market for your product or service, build a business around it by establishing a sustainable money-making system.

Two businesses, literally founded on out-of-the-box thinking, demonstrate how you can have two different business models for seemingly identical underlying products: plastic boxes. Frogbox and Bottle Bin both figured out before visiting the Den that it's not the product—the plastic box—that determines your success. It's the business model you build around that product that leads to success.

Frogbox vs. Bottle Bin

Frogbox Business Model vs. Bottle Bin Business Model

Season 5, Episode 13	Season 6, Episode 4
Product: A reusable plastic box	**Product:** A reusable plastic box
Revenue Model: Rent the box for a fee.	**Revenue Model:** Sell the box for a fee.
Business Model: Use a **franchise business model** to rent reusable green plastic boxes through franchisees in major cities to consumers who use them to move their personal belongings from one home to another. Charge a 7% royalty fee to franchisees.	**Business Model:** Use a **producer business model** to wholesale bottle boxes to beer stores, which mark them up and retail them to their customers. Charge a per-unit wholesale price to beer stores.

You can do a lot with a bucket, as Frogbox and Bottle Bin showed in their separate visits to *Dragons' Den*.

THE WARM-UP: BUSINESS MODEL DEFINED

A business model is a *sustainable money-making system* that describes your product or service sold, the customer served, and your repeat revenue model. While you may have figured out how to get people to pay you (and you are to be congratulated for that!), this does not mean you have a sustainable business model on your hands. The purpose of a business model is to define how you are going to repeat your success again and again in the future. The process of finding a business model involves clarifying the following components:

- **Product (or Service) Sold:** A tangible item (or intangible service) that people are willing to pay you for. ***Example:*** *Reusable plastic containers for storing, organizing, and transporting empty beer, wine, and liquor bottles.*
- **Customers Served:** To whom is it valuable? ***Example:*** *Customers who frequent the beer store or liquor store.*
- **Repeat Revenue Model:** A method of charging that sustains your business, such as renting, selling for a per unit price, or licensing your invention to a manufacturer in exchange for a royalty fee. ***Example:*** *We charge $10 retail and $8 wholesale per box.*

Is Your Product a Business?

Imagine coming up with a carrying case that protects bananas from bruising. You find a manufacturer that can produce it for you at low cost. Then you persuade retailers in Canada to stock your product. Because your innovation keeps bananas from bruising during transport, banana-loving consumers start coming out of the woodwork and buy them in the United States, the UK, and indeed, all over the world. In three short years, your sales balloon to 700,000 units, and you and your two partners find yourselves with a money-making product on your hands. This, of course, happened to three enterprising doctors who appeared on *Dragons' Den* with their product, the Banana Guard. Do they have a product or a business? Well, it depends. It will be a business if they build a system for generating repeat customers in the future and create a sustainable competitive advantage that keeps competitors at bay.

A Product-Centric Approach

Finding a market for a product or service involves a trial-and-error approach. You have to seek out customers who not only will want your offering but who also are willing to pay you a price that is profitable for you. Once you find a product/market fit, you'll need to develop a business model that helps you sustain and grow your revenue over the long term. For example, once you have come up with a concept for a quick-service restaurant that people will flock to, your business model might be to *franchise the concept* in exchange for a royalty of

X% of franchisees' monthly revenues. Or once you have invented a hockey board game that your research and testing indicates will be a big hit, your business model might be to *license* it for a royalty to a game manufacturer that has an ecosystem in place, including distribution channels to bring your innovation to market faster than you possibly could. And once you come up with your own build-a-bar chocolate store for kids, your business model might be to establish a *retail store* where you can hold workshops, bar-building birthday parties, corporate team-building events, and chocolatier courses.

Business Model Types

Once you establish a market for your product or service, you need to build a business model around it. There are many ways to categorize business models, but for simplicity's sake, here are two general categories:

- **Owner/Operator Models:** If you are interested in growing your business organically and maintaining control of your baby, you might choose to operate your business model yourself in one or more markets. Your growth will come from setting up shop in one geographic market at a time.
- **Licensing Models:** If you have perfected a business model and are willing to let others use it for a fee, franchising or licensing your business model or product to others might be a good option for you. This direction is best for people who are interested in expanding quickly but are not necessarily interested in running the day-to-day operations in each market themselves.

Owner/Operator Models

- **Producer Business Model:** You produce your own product or perform your own service. Your revenue is based on the fee you charge directly to consumers, to wholesalers, or to intermediaries. Your gross profit is your selling price minus your cost of goods sold.
- **Merchant Business Model:** You resell the products or services of others. Your revenue is based on marking up prices that you pay for your inventory. Your gross profit is your selling price minus your wholesale price.
- **Agency Business Model:** You act as an intermediary between buyers and sellers, but you produce nothing and carry no inventory. Your job is to handle the paperwork of the

transaction, without necessarily being a part of the fulfillment. In exchange, you receive a transaction fee or commission on each deal made.

Licensing Models

- **Franchising Business Model:** You license your business model to franchisees. Your revenue is an upfront franchise fee and an ongoing royalty fee, for example, 7% of franchisee revenues.
- **Licensing Business Model:** You license your product to a manufacturer that has an established distribution system in place. Your revenue is an ongoing licensing fee, for example, 7% to 15% of wholesale revenue.

Dragon Lore

A single SKU product is not a business unless you build a long-term, sustainable, money-making system around it.

To further illustrate the power of a business model in action, we can delve deeper into the Bottle Bin business model. Remember, Frogbox (discussed earlier) also had a plastic bucket at the centre of its business model, but Bottle Bin found a completely different use, market, and revenue model for what is essentially the same thing: a plastic bucket.

Bottle Bin

Pitchers: Chris, Trevor, and Kathleen Williams, Season 6, Episode 4
Focus: Develop a Business Model

An inspired idea can occur at any time and in the unlikeliest places. Bottle Bin was conceived to solve a general household problem. Andy Williams opted for the owner/operator approach to control the business, and grew the business plan from there.

BACKGROUND

While sitting in his kitchen, Andy Williams, the company president, came up with the idea to find a way to organize and store empty beer and wine bottles, and make it more convenient to return empties to the store. He then brought his children Chris, Trevor and Kathleen on board and sent them to pitch the business concept on *Dragons' Den.*[1]

PROBLEM STATEMENT

Canadians return more than 8 billion deposit-bearing glass bottles for refund every year. Empties are inconvenient and difficult to store, and the glass often breaks when dropped on the way to the store.

PROPOSED SOLUTION

A reusable container with a dual-handle carrying system for homeowners to store returnable empty bottles. The container holds 18 standard wine bottles, 24 beer bottles, or 48 beer bottles when stacked on top of each other.

DRAGONS' DEN BY THE NUMBERS

- **Revenue Model:** Charges $10 retail through liquor stores and other retailers and retains a $2 profit per bin.
- **The Ask:** $150,000 for 20% of the business.
- **Company Valuation:** $750,000.
- **Proof-of-Concept:** $375,000 in sales in four months for 50,000 units. Just finished delivering to 400 beer stores across the country, with pilot programs in British Columbia, Alberta, Saskatchewan, and Newfoundland. A province-wide rollout in Ontario at the beer store; available at P.E.I. liquor stores.

DRAGON'S DEAL

$150,000 for 20% of the business.

DEAL SYNERGIES

The Pitcher secured a deal offer from one key Dragon, who can give them potential access to the returnable bottles of one of the leading pizza restaurant franchises in Canada and the United States.

"I really like the idea. I think it's smart. It's one of those things that retailers are going to go, yes, is there some way for me to get my brand in people's homes to bring them back to the store? This is a really smart idea."
—Dragon to Pitchers

The team from Bottle Bin pitching their proven concept to the Dragons.

Businesses that start with a foundation for success often get away from those very success factors—then have to rediscover them later in the development of the business. Research In Motion—maker of the BlackBerry—became successful at the outset because of its security-rich communication features. After fighting a losing battle against the iPhone—a battle that was like a high-end restaurant trying to compete with McDonald's on price—RIM recently announced that they are returning to their roots, and that's probably a good idea. It seems quite logical that they need to highlight their strength as *the only* business mobile phone that is secure enough with data to use in a serious business. There is a reason why the President of the United States uses a BlackBerry, and success like that is a hint as to what RIM's future branding should be based on. With courier services, if you absolutely positively have to get it there overnight, then use FedEx. And if you absolutely positively need your mobile communication to be secure, why not use a BlackBerry? Here's a look back at the early days of the Blackberry.

A Real-World Case Study: Research In Motion

"The key is to prepare for growth. Otherwise, you won't grow. Or you will fail when you grow."

—Mike Lazaridis, founder, Research In Motion, quoted in "How the BlackBerry Duo Plans to Stay In Motion"

In 1996, Research In Motion (RIM), based in Waterloo, Ontario, established the first two-way messaging pager, called the BlackBerry.[2] Soon after, government, technology-sector, and financial-sector employees became so dependent on the security-rich communication features of the BlackBerry that some people started nicknaming it the CrackBerry. While RIM finds itself in a highly competitive environment today, and its co-founders have apparently relinquished day-to-day control, its early life as a high-growth company through the BlackBerry is a solid example for review.

BACKTESTING RIM

Looking back at the Research in Motion business model, we can backtest it to see if it met each of the Dragons' Den Success Factors when it first launched:

SUCCESS FACTOR #1: FOCUS ON A SINGULAR PAIN POINT

Government and corporate workers and executives needed secure, mobile, two-way communication to improve communication when they were out of the office.

SUCCESS FACTOR #2: BUILD A PROTOTYPE

What started out as the first wireless technology developer in North America[3] created a two-way pager with a monochrome display that later evolved into the first smartphone to allow wireless email.

SUCCESS FACTOR #3: DEFINE THE VALUE PROPOSITION

The early BlackBerry allowed people to securely communicate with others regardless of where they were.

SUCCESS FACTOR #4: ESTABLISH A REPEAT REVENUE MODEL

A monthly subscription fee was charged for an always-connected wireless service.

SUCCESS FACTOR #5: TARGET A DISRUPTABLE MARKET

Government and corporate employees require the high levels of communication security that the BlackBerry is known for.

SUCCESS FACTOR #6: BUILD A LEAN FEATURE SET

The first BlackBerry was a simple-to-use monochrome two-way pager that allowed people to communicate with each other while on the go.

SUCCESS FACTOR #7: COLLABORATE WITH STRATEGIC PARTNERS

Partnered early on with telecommunications companies, including what used to be called Rogers Cantel and BellSouth Wireless Data, as well as hardware companies like Compaq, to reduce its time-to-market.

SUCCESS FACTOR #8: FIND A CATALYST FOR GROWTH

RIM added email service to the device, which triggered widespread use. It gave the product away to opinion leaders in Congress and corporate America to speed up adoption.

SUCCESS FACTOR #9: SCALABILITY

Research In Motion produces scalable hardware and achieves connectivity scalability through partnerships with telecoms.

SUCCESS FACTOR #10: DEVELOP A BUSINESS MODEL

The BlackBerry generates revenue for Research In Motion primarily through the sale of the device itself, user-license fees, and per-account fees on data connectivity services.

Self-Study Workshop: How to Develop a Business Model

A revenue-generating product or service is not a business in itself. A business is a sustainable money-making system that is built around one or more products or services. The Holy Grail of business is a game-changing business model that combines two or more traditional business models into something that changes the way a large number of profitable customers think, act, and spend.

1. Is your business a **product or a service** business model?
    - ❑ Product Business Model: Produce and sell a product.
    - ❑ Service Business Model: Perform a service.

2. Is your business a **merchant or agency** business model?
   - ❏ Merchant Business Model: Sell your own products and services.
   - ❏ Agency Business Model: Sell someone else's products and services.

3. Is your business a **producer or licensor** business model?
   - ❏ Producer Model: Produce your own product or perform your own service.
   - ❏ Licensor Model: License the intellectual property of your product to others for a licensing fee.

4. Is your business a **franchising/licensing business model or an independent owner/operator** business model?
   - ❏ Independent Owner/Operator Model: Operate your own business model.
   - ❏ Franchising/Licensing Model: License your business model to others who pay you a royalty fee.

5. Is your business model a **traditional or game-changer** model?
   - ❏ Traditional Model: Pick a pure business model.
   - ❏ Game-Changer Model: Combine two or more traditional business models to disrupt your industry.

6. **Revenue Model:** How do you charge and who pays you?

7. **Business Model Statement:** Describe your sustainable money-making system in two or three sentences.
   - ❏ Product Sold/Service Performed
   - ❏ Customers Served
   - ❏ Repeat Revenue Model

8. Why is it a **sustainable,** long-term business model?

Now that you have read and implemented the first 10 chapters of this book, you should have a more refined business concept that is ready to be tested. In Part II of this book, we'll discuss how to make sure that both you and your business are ready for the pressure of the market by taking you through the feasibility study process.

PART II

THE FEASIBILITY STUDY

Complete three assessments to determine how prepared you are to start your business: a self-assessment, a business assessment, and a feasibility study.

CHAPTER 11

WHAT DO YOU BRING TO THE TABLE?

"I don't care about your feelings. I care about your money. I want to make you stinking rich."
　　—Dragon to Pitcher

Assessment #1: Self-Assessment

Take an inventory of the financial, emotional, and physical sacrifices that you are willing to make to bring your business concept to the market. Launch your business concept with your eyes wide open, so that you are not shocked when the highest highs and lowest lows start to creep into your entrepreneurial psyche during the launch phase.

We have all seen the proverbial fish out of water, flapping back and forth. Pulled from the water where it happily thrives, it suffocates in its new environment. Many new entrepreneurs suffer the same initial shock when they leave a salaried or hourly position to enter the entrepreneurial world. The things you used to take for granted are no longer there: your computer breaks down, and you realize that you no longer have tech support to call; your printer stops working mysteriously, and the cash that you are lacking to fix it means you have to go into your meeting empty-handed; you're out of paper 30 minutes before you have to make that big proposal, and now you have to email it instead. The good news is that diverse backgrounds are precisely the reason so many entrepreneurs with sound business models succeed. Former corporate-world professionals understand immediately how to maintain a disciplined daily work schedule. Stay-at-home moms know how to multi-task and wear multiple hats. Hourly workers know how to get a job done within a limited amount of time and won't complain about working overtime. If you want to eliminate any fear whatsoever, embrace your past experiences—don't run from them.

One person who did just that was George Schmidt from Mag Roll-Up. After driving a truck for many years, he found one little annoyance that turned into a business windfall for him. Every time he had to wind up the straps used to tie down the loads on his truck, he wondered, like most entrepreneurs, how it could be done faster and easier.

Mag Roll-Up

Pitchers: George Schmidt and Laurie Johnson, Season 5, Episode 15

Focus: What Experience Do You Bring to the Table?

"Right now I'm a truck driver . . . For many years I was driving [a] truck, and the straps to hold down the load [were] hard on the arms and shoulders and back, so I invented something that goes fast and easy."
—Pitcher to Dragons

PRODUCT DESCRIPTION

George Schmidt brought an entire career's experience to his product: an adaptor that fits on electric drills that allows truck drivers to wind up the straps that hold down the loads on flatbed trucks.

DRAGONS' DEN BY THE NUMBERS

- **The Ask:** $50,000 for 100% of the business.
- **$25:** The retail price of each attachment.
- **20:** The number of straps on a flatbed truck.
- **9 million:** The number of flatbed trucks in North America.
- **$20,000:** The amount a trucker can save over the course of a year by speeding up the delivery process using the Mag Roll-Up.
- **10%:** The net royalty offered as part of the deal.
- **$50,000:** The amount offered by one Dragon for 80% of the business.

George Schmidt demonstrating his simple attachment for rolling up straps on a flatbed truck, the Mag Roll-Up.

THE WARM-UP: SELF-ASSESSMENT DEFINED

A self-assessment measures how fit you are to take on the business concept that you are proposing. The entrepreneurial world is not a meritocracy where hard work automatically pays off. It takes the right opportunity, good management, and a lot of luck. Entrepreneurs who succeed know as much about seeing an idea through to the end as when to quit. Overcommitting to a business idea that isn't going anywhere can be detrimental to your financial and emotional well-being. One way of staying on track is to conduct a self-assessment. The purpose of a self-assessment is to make sure you know exactly what you are getting yourself into personally when you decide to launch a new business concept.

Step 1: Personal Motivation—What inspired you to launch your business concept, and what will keep you inspired?

Inspiration: What inspired you to launch your business concept?
Many businesses are inspired by a need that entrepreneurs have in their business or personal worlds. When entrepreneurs fill those voids for themselves, they decide that others may want the same solution. They then go out and build a prototype product or service and begin the process of launching the business concept. When the obstacles and challenges

of entrepreneurship unfold from there, it is important to stay connected to what originally inspired the launch of the business. But it is equally important to know what to do if your business isn't showing signs of earning back your investment and providing positive cash flow.

Role Modelling: What real-world business success would you like to be similar to?
One way to stay on track from day one is to use another successful business as a big-picture role model for what it is you're trying to do. That's not to say that you should follow a me-too strategy by replicating a competitor's strategy. However, you can look at other industries to find companies that have used an approach that might work for your business. For example:

- We want to do for financial advice what H&R Block did for tax preparation.
- I want to be the Martha Stewart of the personal chef industry.
- We want to do for soup what Mr. Sub did for sandwiches.
- We want to do for chicken what Boston Pizza did for pizza.

Outcomes: What do you want out of your business?
Outcomes are what you want both financially and emotionally in return for launching your business concept in the first place. It is critical that you set clear personal outcomes for your business so that pride doesn't keep you committed to a business that isn't going anywhere. For example:

- **Short-Term Goals (One Year):** What would have to happen in the next 12 months for you to feel successful? ***Example:*** *Generate enough income from my business to pay for my basic living expenses and not go into personal debt.*
- **Medium-Term Goals (Two to Three Years):** What would have to happen in the next two to three years for you to feel successful? ***Example:*** *Hire a business manager so that I can stay focused on developing the best business systems, and have more time with my family.*
- **Long-Term Goals (Five+ Years):** What would have to happen in the next five-plus years for you to feel successful? ***Example:*** *Sell my business for two to three times annual sales within five years.*

Step 2: Personal Inventory—What experience and expertise do you bring to the table?

Prior experience in your industry can give you access to contacts, resources, and efficiencies that your competitors may lack. At the same time, being a domain expert in your industry can be extraordinarily helpful when launching a new product or service because you won't have a learning curve to overcome. Your efforts can be focused more on action than on finding your way. And if, instead, you're a generalist or jack of all trades, you will find your diverse skills suddenly come to life when you go to launch a new business concept. Skills fall in one of two categories:

- **Soft Skills:** Non-technical skills, such as how to sell, how to develop rapport, or how to work a room.
- **Hard Skills:** Technical skills, such as how to produce PowerPoint presentations, how to make your product, or how to perform a specific service.

Step 3: Personal Resources—What amount of time and money are you able to commit?

Time Resources

A business has a strange way of taking over your psyche. That's because you are now the boss and you're responsible for everything that goes on. But even if you are highly dedicated to your business idea and want to sacrifice everything to make it succeed, you won't be giving your business everything it needs if your personal world falls apart around you. Be sure to structure your day to include family time, work time, and personal time so you can counterbalance the psychological demands of growing a business. Also, have a clear vision of the type of business you are seeking to develop. Here are some guidelines (not hard-and-fast rules) to consider:

- **Hobby Business (10 hours/week):** A part-time business designed to supplement income from another line of work.
- **Lifestyle Business (40+ hours/week):** A full-time business designed to provide an annual salary that supports your family's lifestyle.
- **Growth Business (60 to 80 hours/week):** A full-time business designed to provide an annual salary plus a future liquidity event that can make you a very rich entrepreneur.

Financial Resources

Launching a new business concept is not an all-or-nothing process. Although it is certainly your prerogative to leverage your home, cash out your retirement plan, and max out your credit cards, treat such actions with extreme caution. For every person who wins by betting the farm, there are countless others who have destroyed their lives. The wisest course of action might be to launch your business concept while you are still working. One way of controlling the financial risk you take is to structure your personal finances into wealth "buckets," like those shown below. A wealth bucket is a dollar amount of money that you set aside for a specific funding goal. Then set limits on how much of each of those buckets you are able to sacrifice without putting your family at risk. These wealth buckets include:

- **Living Expenses:** Cut all discretionary expenses out of your budget while you are not drawing a salary.
- **Emergency Fund:** Set aside 6 to 12 months' worth of living expenses before you commit full time to your business, if possible. Consider exiting the business once you burn through your emergency funds. Be cautious about taking on an external debt load, be it from family members or arm's-length investors.
- **Major Assets:** Put off major expenses—such as the purchase of a car or house, or taking a vacation—until your business is generating free cash flow to pay you a salary. As a general guideline, don't tap into the equity of your major assets to fund your business.
- **Education Funds:** Don't raid your children's college education fund while you are starting your business.
- **Retirement Funds:** Set aside 15% of any salary you do draw from your business. As a general guideline, don't tap into your retirement accounts to fund your business.
- **Net Worth:** Try not to risk more than 5% to 15% of your total net worth on your business. Use outside capital sources or exit the business once you reach the upper end of this threshold.

These too are guidelines, not hard-and-fast rules. There are many people who have risked it all and succeeded, but they are few and far between. These guidelines are here for the rest of us and can help keep you financially solvent. Seek advice from an accountant who has experience with entrepreneurs.

Step 4: Personality Type—What personality traits do you bring to the table?

Entrepreneurs don't have the luxury of typecasting themselves based on past behaviour. The most successful entrepreneurs adapt to their new surroundings by overcoming past work styles, problem-solving approaches, and levels of risk tolerance. The key to adapting to new market opportunities as they present themselves is to know yourself in advance, so you can get out of your own way.

Work Style

Your job as an entrepreneur is to get things done, not necessarily to do things yourself. It is important to understand your own personal work style so that you understand your own built-in limitations.

- **Delegators:** Delegators get things done through other people. They save valuable time by getting others to do their work. The downside of being a delegator is that you can burn through *financial resources* very quickly if you pay others to do everything.
- **Do-It-Yourselfers:** Do-it-yourselfers like the personal challenge of doing everything themselves. They conserve cash by doing everything in-house. The downside of being a do-it-yourselfer is that valuable *time resources* are often wasted on low-value projects.
- **Collaborators:** Collaborators work well with others and put the outcome of their work above themselves. They conserve both time and financial resources by leveraging strategic relationships with others to achieve an overriding goal. The downside of being a collaborator is that you have to check your ego at the door because you end up having to share the accolades that go with a successful outcome.

Problem-Solving Approach

Entrepreneurs run into brick walls all the time. However, the most successful ones deal with problems head-on so that they can move on to bigger and better things. How you deal with problems as they arise can determine whether your business survives or fails. There are two approaches:

- **Problem Solver:** Entrepreneurs who take this approach to problems deal with thorny situations head-on. If you are a problem solver, make sure you don't get sidetracked putting out fires all day. Systemize your business processes to reduce the number of problems that occur.

- **Problem Avoider:** Entrepreneurs who take this approach to problems avoid thorny situations like the plague and sometimes just ignore them. Not recommended. If you are a problem avoider, make sure you have someone on your support team on speed dial to call if you run into an unexpected challenge.

Risk Tolerance

When you sign a hypothetical contract to become an entrepreneur, you are agreeing to seek profit at the risk of loss. Risk is a big part of the game. Take too much risk and you might end up penniless. Take too little risk and you might not capitalize on the one and only opportunity you have to make your business concept fly. Part of dealing with risk is understanding your personal tolerance for it:

- **Risk Taker:** Entrepreneurs who take this approach to risk often see opportunity everywhere. They are prone to betting the farm on ideas that may have no basis in reality.
- **Risk Manager:** Entrepreneurs who take this approach to risk weigh the costs and benefits of each decision to be made. The downside of being a risk manager is that you can start to see risk in everything. You might miss a valuable opportunity because you can't make a decision quickly enough.

Step 5: Barriers—What will you do when you hit a brick wall?

Most business problems are never as bad as they seem. One way to deal with business problems is called "root cause analysis." Root cause analysis is at the heart of many Lean Six Sigma efforts at highly efficient organizations such as Dell, Toyota, and Intel. Essentially, you start with a problem and dig deeper to get to the cause behind it by asking questions about the problem. Then you make the required changes based on your conclusions about the initial problem.

5 Whys

One deceptively simple problem-solving concept used at the Toyota Corporation is the 5 Whys.[1] It is such a simple concept that you can apply it to just about any problem in order to discover a solution to that problem. Here are two self-explanatory examples:

PROBLEM: MY BUSINESS IS STARVING FOR CASH

- Why? Because our customers don't pay upfront.
- Why? Because we don't ask them to.
- Why? Because we offer flexible payment terms.
- Why? Because we think customers won't pay us upfront.
- Why? Because one of our first customers asked us if he could have payment terms and we haven't changed the policy since.

Solution: From these five responses you might conclude that very few customers actually request payment terms and that you should stop offering them. By not offering them, you may be able to resolve your cash flow issue almost immediately.

PROBLEM: I DON'T SPEND ENOUGH TIME WITH MY FAMILY

- Why? Because I wear many hats in my business.
- Why? Because I don't have enough staff.
- Why? Because I can't train people to do my job.
- Why? Because I don't have a how-to manual for roles in my business.
- Why? Because I haven't taken the time to make one.

Solution: From these five responses you might conclude that you are taking on too many roles in your business. It might be time to create an operating manual for each area of your business so you can hire staff to do some of things you shouldn't be doing yourself.

Support Circle

Bringing a sound business concept to market requires an unwavering commitment to your vision. A support circle you can turn to any time you have a challenge or need feedback can be one of the most critical resources you have. There are three types of support any entrepreneur with a new business idea can set up for low or no cost:

- **Family and Friends:** Family and friends can be the best and worst type of support for your business. Supportive family members can bring you out of a tailspin when one obstacle after another presents itself. At the same time, they can also be the ones who tell you to trudge forward on an idea that really has no hope of succeeding in the marketplace.

- **Advisory Board:** A formal or informal advisory board can help you ride out the highs and lows of your business. A seemingly insurmountable obstacle can usually be overcome after a quick chat with someone on your advisory board who has done this before.
- **Business Coach:** A business coach can make you accountable at weekly or monthly checkpoints to the short-, medium- and long-term outcomes you've set in advance.

Step 6: Personal Boundaries—Knowing when to say when

Business is about money, not personal ego. Putting your entire life at risk for an idea that has no long-term merit is bad business and could prevent you from finding one that does have merit. For every entrepreneur who bet his or her home, retirement, and family life for an idea and won big, there are many others whose lives were ruined by a business idea that got out of control. This is not to say that you shouldn't take the risk or that you can keep any of this from happening. Just be sure to set your personal limits so you know when to bring outsiders in or when to exit the business. Consider your:

- **Financial Limits:** What is the greatest amount of personal capital that you are able to invest without putting your family at risk? Maybe $10,000 is what you can afford, and after that, you need to look for outside investors.
- **Time Limits:** What amount of time are you able to invest daily and over the long term without destroying your family life? You might decide that you will give yourself three years, at which point you will consider exiting the business or bringing in outsiders if your goals are not being met.
- **Emotional Limits:** What amount of energy are you able to invest without destroying your health? This is also tied to your risk profile—take on more risk than your system can handle and you may take on too much stress.

Dragon Lore

Anytime someone tells you that you have a ridiculous idea, remember the Banana Guard, which sold 700,000 units before its inventors appeared on *Dragons' Den*. Test and prove your idea, and don't let the sceptics derail you if your business plan has a solid foundation.

Learning how to capitalize on personal skill sets is what differentiates a successful entrepreneur from one who struggles. When Katherine DaSilva launched eStudent.ca she just started putting her entire skills history on paper in the form of a teaching materials website.

eStudent.ca

Pitcher: Katherine DaSilva, Season 3, Episode 2

Focus: Self-Assessment

Katherine DaSilva brought many key skills to the table when she conceived the idea for an online Web application for students learning English, French, and Spanish grammar. She was not only a teacher looking for classroom resources to help teach her students, she also brought the ability to write more than 20,000 pages of teaching material (per resource) by hand typing on a computer. Without this writing skill, she would have burned through inordinate amounts of personal financial resources paying others to write, in an attempt to bring her business concept to life.

> "When I present the software at the end of the presentation, I'm greeted with a standing ovation from the audience of teachers and students, who say, 'This is unbelievable. Where have you been all our lives? And more importantly, who the hell are you?'"
> —Pitcher to Dragons

BACKGROUND

Pitcher Katherine DaSilva, founder of eStudent.ca, grew frustrated with grammar resources available to her as a teacher and to her students in the classroom. That's when she was inspired to produce eStudent.ca, a software-based grammar resource for teachers and students.

PROBLEM STATEMENT

When teachers create tests, exercises, and assignments, they often have to pore through several books on a single subject just to find what they are looking for.[2]

PROPOSED SOLUTION

eStudent.ca is a single-source, 20,000-page-per-language grammar resource for teachers to create tests at the click of a mouse. It comes complete with verb conjugators, practice exercises, and test generators.

BUSINESS CASE

- **Revenue Model:** $1,750 site license per school.
- **The Ask:** $250,000 in exchange for 30% of the company.
- **Company Valuation:** $833,333.
- **Proof-of-Concept:** $500,000 in sales to date. Invited to present the software at various educational conferences.

DRAGONS' DEAL

$250,000 for 50% of her company.

DEAL SYNERGIES

The Dragon who went in on the deal brings deep marketing experience to the table, along with an investment of $250,000 for 50% of the company.

Katherine DaSilva and her husband in the Dark contemplating the offers she has received for her learning solution, eStudent.ca.

Self-Study Workshop: Conduct a Self-Assessment

Take a personal inventory of your resources and the sacrifices you are willing to make to bring your business concept to the marketplace. This self-assessment is more about understanding your limits than it is about setting them. When you understand your limits, you'll be in a better position to objectively weigh the costs against the benefits of important business decisions.

Step 1: Original Inspiration—What inspired you to launch your business concept, and what will keep you inspired?

- ❑ Original Inspiration: *Example: I couldn't find the resources I needed to teach my students effectively.*

❏ Role Model: *Example: Atomic Tea wants to be the Starbucks of tea.*

❏ Outcomes: *Example: My exit strategy is to sell my business in five years.*

Step 2: Personal Inventory—What experience and expertise do you bring to the table?

2.1 **Expertise:** What relevant skills do you bring to the table?

❏ **Hard Skills:** What relevant hard (technical) skills do you bring to the table?

Examples: Product design, computer programming, knitting, gourmet cooking.

❏ **Soft Skills:** What relevant soft (non-technical) skills do you bring to the table?

Examples: People skills, sales, negotiating.

2.2 **Experience:** What experience do you have in this type of business? Are you a domain expert in this industry or a jack of all trades with transferable skills that work in any industry?

❏ **Domain Expert:** Build a support team around you to handle those tasks you are not good at.

❏ **Jack of All Trades:** Cleary define your highest and best use so you don't waste time on tasks that would be better done by someone else.

Step 3: Personal Inventory—What is your commitment to this business?

3.1 **Time Commitment:** What amount of time daily are you ready, willing, and able to commit to launching your business concept?

❏ Full time (maybe eight hours or more per day)

❏ Part time (maybe four hours or less per day)

❏ Hobby time (maybe four hours per week)

3.2 **Emotional Commitment:** Why do you want to be in this business? Are you physically prepared for the stresses that come with bringing a business concept to market? Is your family prepared for the amount of time and energy your business is going to take?

3.3 **Financial Commitment:** What are you willing to sacrifice financially to bring your business concept to market?

❏ Up to $10,000

❏ Up to $100,000

❏ Up to $1,000,000

❏ Other

Do you have an alternative source of income or a reserve amount of cash set aside for living expenses, to support yourself financially during the first 6 to 24 months of launching your business concept?

❑ Yes

❑ No

Do you have assets to fall back on if this business doesn't work?

❑ Yes

❑ No

Step 4: Personality Type—What personality traits do you bring to the table?

4.1 **Work Style:** How do you complete tasks and projects?

❑ Delegator

❑ Do-it-yourselfer

❑ Collaborator

4.2 **Problem-Solving Approach:** How do you react to sudden challenges and obstacles?

❑ Problem solver

❑ Problem avoider

4.3 **Risk Tolerance:** How do you handle risk?

❑ Risk taker

❑ Risk manager

Step 5: Barriers—What will you do when you hit a brick wall?

5.1 **Support:** Everyone needs someone to "talk them off the ledge" once in a while. Who will act as your emotional support when you are faced with seemingly insurmountable challenges?

❑ Friend (name one)

❑ Family member (name one)

❑ Business coach (name one)

❑ Advisory board (name one)

Step 6: Personal Boundaries—Knowing when to say when.

6.1 **Time Limit:** What amount of time do you give yourself to make your business work?

❑ One year (e.g., then I go back to work)

- ❑ Three years (e.g., then I partner with someone else)
- ❑ Five years (e.g., then I liquidate the business)

6.2 **Financial Limit:** What amount of capital will you personally limit yourself to committing to?

Starting and running a business can take you through higher highs and lower lows than you've ever experienced in your life. Hopefully this chapter has made you more aware of your strengths and weakness so that you can manage them better. It's now time to summarize why you feel that your business will succeed using the one-page business case format that you'll follow in the next chapter.

CHAPTER 12

WHY WILL YOUR BUSINESS SUCCEED?

"If this thing works, and you've proved that it works with a couple of newspapers, let's get on with it."
—Dragon to Pitcher

> ### Assessment #2: The One-Page Business Case
>
> Complete a hypothetical summary of why your business concept is justified. This summary should describe your overall vision and financial justification for your business concept. It is not intended to be a multi-day research project. Just two to three hours of brainstorming should suffice.

A new business idea is like a science fair project. You start out with a hypothesis describing what will happen if you pursue your business concept. You map out your idea in your head or on paper, and then you set up an environment where you can conduct a series of tests to prove that your hypothesis is true. These tests start with a simple prototype product or service and a hypothesis that it can solve a real problem. You then move to a pilot test stage, where you look for proof not only that your concept works but also that people will actually pay you for it. And finally, you conduct a full-scale feasibility study to make sure your business concept has market, technical, and financial feasibility on a larger scale. If your feasibility study passes with flying colours, you build a business plan around it, and you commit larger amounts of your own capital or investors' capital to the project. By this point, your business has been well thought out. The starting point for your business equivalent of a science project is called a **one-page business case**.

When the children of Bottle Bin founder Andy Williams ended up on *Dragons' Den*, what made their pitch successful was their pilot program. One critical way to show every stakeholder in your business that you have a winning concept is to actually generate sales in a very short period of time. As you'll see from the Bottle Bin pitch below, their $375,000 pilot test proved instrumental to their success in business but also in securing a deal from the Dragons.

Bottle Bin

Pitchers: Chris, Trevor, and Kathleen Williams, Season 6, Episode 4

Focus: Business Case Defined

"We have a pilot program in B.C., Alberta, and Saskatchewan. We have a full province-wide rollout here in Ontario at the beer store. We know from our current stats that we're selling about, with just a sign, five bins per store per week . . . First parts came off the line four months ago. So, in those four months, we had $375,000 in sales. We sold 50,000 units."
    —Pitcher Chris Williams of Bottle Bin

PRODUCT DESCRIPTION

The world's first reusable container for returnable glass bottles.

DRAGONS' DEN BY THE NUMBERS

- **The Ask:** $150,000 for 20% of the business.
- **4:** The number of months the Bottle Bin founders had been in business before going on the show.
- **$375,000:** The revenue to date over those four months.
- **50,000:** The number of units of Bottle Bins sold by the Pitchers.

Pitcher Trevor Williams explaining the lean feature set of the Bottle Bin, a reusable beer and wine bottle-carrying container available at beer stores.

THE WARM-UP: BUSINESS CASE DEFINED

A business case is the business equivalent of a hypothesis. It is a one-page summary of the reasons why you expect that your product, service, or business concept is financially justified. The purpose of a one-page business case is to help you weed out a not-so-clever business idea before it gets out of hand—financially or time-wise. The process of writing a business case typically involves two to three hours of brainstorming on the following:

- **Background:** What was the inspiration behind this business?
- **Problem Statement:** What problem does your business solve?
- **Current Alternatives:** How does the customer currently solve the problem?
- **Proposed Product or Service:** How does your product or service work?
- **Business Case:** What is the financial justification for your business?

BUSINESS CASE: WHY DO YOU FEEL THAT YOU HAVE A WINNING BUSINESS IDEA?

A business can turn your entire world upside down. Once you become gripped by it and the financial potential it has for your life, you start to develop tunnel vision. Pretty soon your family, friends, and colleagues become less of a priority, and your business starts to take on a life of its own. It is imperative that you map out the reasons why your business is financially justified before you take the leap.

One-Page Summary

This process starts with a quick, back-of-the-napkin-type summary of your business idea—your business case. A **business case** is a one-page description of why your business is justified. You could certainly produce a 20-page document, but for your purposes here, you need a one-page summary, because at this stage the business idea is only a hypothesis. A business case shouldn't be confused with a feasibility study or pilot test, which are real-world tests of your business idea. Rather, a business case is the outcome of two to three hours of brainstorming your business idea over a glass of wine, a coffee, or a tea cooler from Atomic Tea, (a previous visitor to *Dragons' Den*).

Stakeholders

There will be many stakeholders who will depend on you to make a sound business decision, so it's important to summarize your business idea succinctly. A business should not be started unless it supports the needs of various stakeholders involved in your business. People with something at stake include customers, who will be parting with their hard-earned money to pay you for a product or service that they hope will solve their problem. They include investors, who invest in your business idea in exchange for a reasonable return on investment (ROI). They include company founders (you, and your partners if you have any), who will need the business to meet their own financial requirements, including their salary needs and future profit potential.

Guidelines

A business case is not a full-blown research project. If it takes you more than two or three hours to summarize your hypothesis, then you might have to rethink your idea. Here are some simple guidelines:

- Keep your answers to the questions posed above (in "The Warm-Up: Business Case Defined" section) to one sentence.
- Keep the entire business case to one page.
- Keep your business case to general assumptions. Do not include detailed research.
- Treat the business case like a scientific hypothesis, not a full-blown research project.

> **Dragon Lore**
>
> If you want to shorten your go-to-market cycle, emulate business role models that have already achieved in their industry what you are trying to achieve in yours.

Proving your business concept to a group of investors can certainly become easier if you have an emotional attachment to your business. When Jack Dell'Accio showed up on *Dragons' Den,* he also backed his personal passion for the business with $1.3 million in real revenue, the irrefutable stamp of good quality on a successful business case.

Essentia Memory Foam Mattresses

Pitcher: Jack Dell'Accio, Season 3, Episode 8

Focus: The Business Case for Your Business

All businesses need revenue, and having $10,000 worth of revenue would be enough to excite any investor. But founder Jack Dell'Accio came with much more than that—$1.3 million in revenue, plus the ability to discuss the scientific background behind his product. Without this revenue, it would have been highly unlikely that the Dragons would have given his retail concept, one that they normally steer clear of, a second look.

> "If you do want to be involved in the greater picture, I am willing to walk down that road with you."
> —Jack Dell'Accio, founder of Essentia

BACKGROUND

When a family member was diagnosed with cancer, Jack Dell'Accio was inspired to produce the world's only natural memory foam mattress. Physicians had made him aware of the toxins in everyday items like couches, carpets, TVs, plastics, and even mattresses.[1]

PROBLEM STATEMENT

The leading brand of memory foam mattress is made of synthetic, chemical-based memory foam.

PROPOSED SOLUTION

Essentia Memory Foam Mattress is the world's only natural memory foam mattress that's not made with synthetic chemicals. It's a water-based latex version of the synthetic chemical-based memory foam mattress that is currently on the market. Latex foam is healthier because it doesn't contain the harsh chemicals or glues that are used in the urethane production that is involved in many competitors' products.

BUSINESS CASE

- **Revenue Model:** Sells memory foam products direct to consumer through retail outlets.
- **The Ask:** $350,000 for 30%.
- **Company Valuation:** $1.17 million.
- **Proof-of-Concept:** $1.3 million in revenue in the opening year of sales. A hotel has already tested the brand in its properties.

DRAGON'S DEAL

$350,000 for 50% of Essentia's Canadian business.

DEAL SYNERGIES

The deal came with cash, plus the financing expertise of a Dragon with deep venture capital expertise.

Jack Dell'Accio of Essentia Memory Foam Mattress pitching to the Dragons.

Self-Study Workshop: The One-Page Business Case

Pretend you are a lawyer in a courtroom with limited time to convince a jury of friends, family, customers, and suppliers that there are real financial and non-financial needs for the product or service you plan to launch. Summarize the overriding reasons why you think that you have a winning business concept.

1. **Background**

   Describe the original inspiration for your business concept.

   Example: I started noticing an increase in the number of newspaper stories about potential links between electronics devices in the home and cancer. While electronics manufacturers continue to present "proof" that there is no link, the fact that cigarette manufacturers said the same thing—that they didn't see a link between smoking and cancer either— scared me to death. So I decided to build a prototype solution called, with deliberate irony, the Kill Switch.

2. **Problem statement**

   Define the problem your product or service solves or how your product or service improves upon a current alternative in the marketplace.
   - What problem does it solve?
   - What current product or service does it improve upon?

   Example: All of the electronic devices in our homes are exposing us to an enormous amount of radiation while we sleep. This radiation is being linked to a noticeable increase in cancer over the last 50 years.

3. **Proposed product or service**

   In two to three sentences, discuss what your product or service is and how it works. Think in terms of its functional use, its cost-cutting ability, and its ability to increase revenue (if it's a product or service that other businesses will buy from you).

   Example: The Kill Switch is a button you put on your wall that powers down all of your electronics wirelessly. It comes with a set of attachments that you put in each of the wall sockets that you use to power your computers, iPods, cell phones, and television sets. It also comes with a software app so that your computers and cell phones can be shut down first, before the power is cut. It can even be programmed to shut itself off at night, and power down and power up your electronics on a timed schedule.

4. **Business case** (financial justification)

The heart of the business case is the financial justification for your product, service, or business.

- Reason 1 (Revenue Model).
Example: Electrical product manufacturers pay us a royalty fee for the use of our trademark and business systems.

- Reason 2 (Revenue Target/Revenue to Date/Users to Date).
Example: $450,000 in the last 12 months.

- Reason 3 (Profit Potential).
Example: 30% profit margin.

- Reason 4 (Projected ROI).
Example: Ten times initial investment within five years.

- Reason 5 (Start-up funds required).
Example: $300,000.

- Reason 6 (Proof-of-Concept).
Example: Prototypes tested, awards received, customers to date, revenue to date.

5. **Conclusion**

Summarize in one sentence the overriding justification for your product or service.

What is the financial justification for your business concept? What is the non-financial justification for your business concept? What personal mission are you on?

Example: We just signed a licensing deal with a global electronics company to manufacture and distribute 50,000 units for a fee.

A one-page business case is one more step in the process of formalizing your rationale for your business, so that you don't overcommit to a weak business idea. Now that you have completed a hypothetical summary of why your business is justified, it's time to take another step in the feasibility study process by testing it using the real world feasibility study process in the next chapter. This is where you dip your foot in the market to gauge its temperature—before you dive in head-first.

CHAPTER 13

IS YOUR IDEA TECHNICALLY AND FINANCIALLY FEASIBLE?

"It's almost as if we were a junior mining company looking for copper and we went and discovered a gold vein, but we need someone like [a Dragon] to help dig it up for us."
—Pitcher to Dragons

> **Assessment #3: Feasibility Study**
>
> Complete an analysis of the commercial viability of your business concept. This analysis should be completed before you write your business plan, and may deem your business plan unnecessary if the outcome is that your business won't work.

Every business needs a kill switch, something to shut it off before it gets out of hand if it's simply not going to work. In business, that kill switch is the feasibility study. A properly conducted feasibility study should test for market, technical, and financial feasibility *before* you write your business plan. You can't move forward with your business idea just because it *appears* to solve a problem or because your spouse loves it. The feasibility study is the litmus test for determining if your business is a go or a no-go. If you want scalable growth in revenue, put your concept through a feasibility study before you go any further.

Commercial viability, also known as feasibility, starts with the creativity of the entrepreneur. And one area where creativity is being applied is the world's oldest profession, which is not what you might think it is—it's water filtration. Without clean water we simply can't survive. But finding a way for *individuals* to pay for that water, instead of governments, is a more recent phenomenon. When the founders of Q Water visited *Dragons' Den*, they showed how the core of commercial viability is branding and that being able to brand a simple commodity like water can lead to a financial windfall.

Q Water

Pitchers: Paula Tekela and Stephen Beaumont, Season 5, Episode 9

Focus: Business Case Defined

"We install a filtration system in the restaurants. It eliminates bottled water 100%. It eliminates the transporting of bottles, the recycling of bottles, the inventorying of bottles. The profit margins for the restaurants are huge and the water tastes great."
    —Pitcher to Dragons

PRODUCT DESCRIPTION

Premium water filtration systems for the hospitality industry, complete with towers, decanters, and jugs.

DRAGONS' DEN BY THE NUMBERS

- **The Ask:** $250,000 for 33% of the business.
- **30:** The number of Q Water filtration systems sold as of the day it was pitched on the show.
- **$180,000:** The revenue to date of Q Water.
- **$3:** The approximate amount charged by the restaurant per glass of Q Water sold.
- **$200:** The planned monthly charge to each restaurant that wants to rent the system.

A pure branding play—Q Water rebranding tap water in restaurants.

THE WARM-UP: FEASIBILITY STUDY DEFINED

Until now, you've been in the pre-feasibility stage figuring out what needs to be incorporated in your product or service launch to be successful. Now it's time for a full-scale **go/no-go assessment** of your business idea. The purpose of a feasibility study is to weed out the make-or-break issues that could help or hinder your business concept. The process of conducting a feasibility study involves:

- **Market Feasibility Testing:** Is the market large enough to support your business goals?
- **Technical Feasibility Testing:** Does your product or service work as promised, and can it be produced at the volume scale that is required to support your business goals?
- **Financial Feasibility Testing:** Are your potential revenue and profit enough to support your business goals?

THE FEASIBILITY STUDY

A feasibility study is a written summary of the key aspects of your business model that provide support for your business model. As a general guideline, try to keep it to two pages, though some studies are as short as one page, or as long as or longer than full-scale business plans. Writing a feasibility study involves the process of thinking through a business idea and documenting it on paper. Its purpose is to determine the market, technical, and financial feasibility of your business. It is not a business plan. *It is a precursor to a business plan.* It serves as a pre-business planning checkpoint to help you make a final go/no-go decision on your business model. If you decide to move forward with your business, the research yielded by the process is included in the business plan, a planning document that helps delineate what actions need to be taken in order to capitalize on your market opportunity.

The Market Feasibility of Your Concept

Market assessment techniques are discussed in detail in Chapter 19. In the meantime, let's simply say that the key to estimating the demand for your product or service is to make your estimates realistic. Crazy market share predictions are meaningless if you can't trace them back to actual steps you will take to make them happen. For now, we can review the core components of market-size analysis. If you read Chapter 5, you may already have these numbers in place from previous research, so you can just plug them in for this chapter's Self-Study Workshop. Just to recap, here are the definitions:

- **Total Available Market (TAM):** The total industry-wide market for your product or service in a year.
- **Serviceable Available Market (SAM):** The portion of the TAM that could conceivably buy your category of product or service.
- **Serviceable Obtainable Market (SOM):** The share of the SAM you could conceivably capture.
- **Compound Annual Growth Rate:** The historical growth rate of your market.

The Technical Feasibility of Your Concept

Technical feasibility is a screening framework that helps you assess whether your product or service can be delivered in a timely manner. The purpose of the process is to demonstrate that you will be capable of producing a fully functional, market-ready product or service, in real-world conditions, when customers are waiting. When you list the components of your product or the tangible components of your service, consider trade-offs that are possible if some of them prove to be cost-prohibitive.

What Technical Resources Are Required?

A business needs an endless flow of resources to build its products or deliver its services. Breaking down your offering into its component parts will not only help you assess your capabilities but also enable you to put a cost on each component later. When testing whether your product or service can be delivered as promised, consider these resource needs:

- **Know-How:** The methodology required to produce your product or service.
- **Labour:** The level of skill required.
- **Raw Materials:** The types of inputs required.
- **Equipment:** The type of equipment and technology required.
- **Other Inputs:** Any other miscellaneous resources required.

What Are the Technical Constraints?

When you produce a product or perform a service in a testing environment, time is not an issue because a customer is not waiting. However, once you go to market, time becomes a major issue. A customer won't care how good your product or service is if you can't deliver it when it's needed. When considering your technical feasibility, keep the following in mind:

- **Time Constraints:** Will you be able to deliver your products and services when your customers want them?
- **Location Constraints:** Will your environment enable you to deliver your offering in an efficient manner?

The Financial Feasibility of Your Concept

Financial feasibility is a screening framework for your business concept that helps you assess whether you can turn a profit on each product or service unit sold, and if you can operate your overall business at a profit. The purpose of conducting a financial feasibility study is to make sure that your expected revenues will exceed your expected costs (including your required return on your business). Of course, at this point you might want to call the accountant in the family to help you put together your estimates, but here are the basics.

Revenue Estimate

Revenue estimates should be realistic, not pie in the sky. A financial feasibility study is not a sales pitch you are using to convince others that your business will be successful. These numbers are here to give you a realistic set of expectations of the success potential of your business idea.

Revenue Formula

The background behind the components of this formula will vary depending on what you sell. Your definition of what a unit is might be an hour of time, one product, or a service contract. But the core formula itself should stay the same:

$$\text{Revenue Estimate} = \text{Estimated Units Sold} \times \text{Price of Each Unit}$$

Costs to Run Your Business

Two of the main categories of costs that you need to watch for in your business, assuming you don't have any debt-financing costs, are:

- **Cost of Goods Sold:** Estimated units sold × cost per unit of product or service sold (cost of resale goods, costs of raw materials for products produced, labour performed).
- **Selling, General, and Administrative Expenses:** Estimated costs to market and sell your product or service plus the costs required to run your business (rent, utilities, office salaries, office supplies, insurance, licenses, etc.).

Profitability of Your Business

The two areas of your business that determine profitability are your costs of goods sold and your costs of overall operation. The two measures that you must take are gross profits (revenues from sales, less cost of goods sold) and operating profits (which net out your expenses like rent, administration, and marketing). If your gross profits are in the black but your operating expenses are too high and trigger a loss, then ultimately your business will need to be shut down. Throwing money at it to keep it afloat is like throwing money to the wind.

Gross Profit Formula (Product Profit)

This is the profit of your business before selling, general, and administrative expenses are reflected:

$$\text{Gross Profit} = \text{Revenue} - \text{Cost of Goods Sold}$$

Operating Profit Formula

This is the pre-tax and pre-interest profit of your business:

$$\text{Operating Profit} = \text{Gross Profit} - \text{Selling, General, and Administrative Expenses}$$

Dragon Lore

Sometimes the best feasibility study is to just get your product or service out into the hands of real, paying customers.

To conduct a feasibility study, you don't have to spend a fortune. But you do need to test your concept on three fronts. First, determine whether there is a market for what you intend to sell. Next, figure out a way to build it so that you can see if it works. And finally, determine if you'll be able to sell it at a profit. The founder of My Smart Hands got her first indication that she might have a hit on her hands (so to speak) when she posted a demonstration on YouTube for free.

My Smart Hands

Pitcher: Laura Berg, Season 5, Episode 12

Focus: Feasibility Study

Pitcher Laura Berg simplified the concept of a market feasibility study when she posted her concept on YouTube. By the time she got in front of the Dragons, she'd had 2.5 million views, a clear sign that her concept of teaching sign language to preverbal babies had a large potential market.

BACKGROUND

Laura started her company as a way to stay at home with her daughter. She combined her passion for teaching with her knowledge of sign language.

PROBLEM STATEMENT

Hearing impaired and preverbal babies need a way to communicate.

PROPOSED SOLUTION

Classes, videos, flashcards and books that teach parents how to use American Sign Language to communicate with their preverbal babies and hearing-impaired children. Consists of a licensed eight-week class.

BUSINESS CASE

- **Revenue Model:** Charges a licensing fee of $140 to instructors and an annual renewal fee plus a fee for manuals that instructors are required to pay. Operates almost like a franchise where instructors are licensed to use the My Smart Hands course material.
- **The Ask:** $100,000 for 40% of the business.
- **Company Valuation:** $250,000.
- **Proof-of-Concept:** Will do at least $100,000 this year. Posted a video on YouTube and had more than 2.5 million views. Has more than 100 instructors in 12 countries.

DRAGONS' DEAL

$100,000 for 50% of the business.

DEAL SYNERGIES

The marketing expertise and educational publishing expertise of two key Dragons.

> "I will introduce you to the largest educational publishers in the world . . . we will start a bidding war. And you will become very rich."
> —Dragon to Pitcher

Laura Berg and her daughter sign "I'm in" to the Dragons.

Self-Study Workshop: Conduct a Feasibility Study

In order to prove your concept, you need to conduct a feasibility study to make sure that your business concept is worth pursuing.

1. **Team and advisors**
   - Describe the background of the members of your team who have domain expertise in your product or service category and deep market experience in winning customers in your target market segment.
   - Describe the access you have to the functional expertise that will be needed to round out your team.

2. **Business model**
   - Describe how you plan to make money.

3. **Market feasibility**
   - Describe the size of your market opportunity.
   - Describe the market you plan to target.
   - Describe your competitive advantage.

4. **Technical feasibility**
   - Describe the status of your product or service prototype.
   - Describe the resources that you have in place to scale your business idea (i.e., produce volume).
   - Describe the results of any product or service pilot testing that you have completed.

5. **Financial feasibility**
   - Quantify your start-up capital requirements.
   - Quantify your projected revenues in years one, two, and three.
   - Quantify your cost of goods sold.
   - Quantify your annual operating expenses.
   - Quantify your annual profit.
   - Quantify your projected break-even point in years or months.
   - Quantify and qualify the source of capital to which you have access to fund your start-up.

6. **Conclusion**

   Can you succeed with your business idea? This must be a brutally honest assessment.

Parts I and II of this book have been about refining and testing your business concept to figure out what your product or service offering needs to include to be successful. In Part III of this book, you'll refine your concept even further by delving deep into the story behind your product or service, and how you plan to commercialize it.

PART III

THE PRODUCT ROADMAP

Define your product or service in four key areas: your brand story, brand definition, product definition, and product development.

CHAPTER 14

MANAGING YOUR PRODUCT ROADMAP

"I think it's an idea that's just late. Eleven years ago [the entrepreneur] set out on a mission and four years ago he should have stopped."
   —Dragon to Pitcher

Product Roadmap

Screen your business concept using the 10 Dragons' Den Success Factors. Determine where your concept fits in the product lifecycle. Keep your product or service in the growth stage of the lifecycle for as long as possible by defending your points of differentiation.

Steve Jobs was considered the Wayne Gretzky of product managers. He was also a great motivator and used company-wide mantras to effectively push his teams beyond their limits. One core theme of all his slogans was that people don't always know what they want until somebody gives it to them. Just think of the following examples. Most people were fine using a Rand McNally paper map until GPSs in cars blew the driving experience out of the water. The Brother typewriter was working just fine for most until the word processor went mainstream. AOL's dial-up Internet access was quite life-changing until Wi-Fi access came about. All of these companies—AOL, Rand McNally, and Brother—were eventually disrupted by a new product or service innovation that changed the way the underlying need was met.

But your business doesn't have to be high-tech to require a product roadmap. Some products are not necessarily at risk of being innovated out of existence, because people will most likely covet them for as long as the product is available. One such product is smoked salmon. The business process behind this type of product still needs to be mapped out and sometimes the process takes outside investor capital. When the founders of Yukon Smoked Salmon visited *Dragons' Den*, they had little or no business plan but left with sound business advice and a small amount of capital.

Yukon Smoked Salmon

Pitchers: Lewis and Samson Hartland, Season 5, Episode 9

> "I'll give you the $20,000 in $5,000 increments as you finish the business plan first and develop a process and program for getting this turned into a business."
> —Dragon to Pitcher

PRODUCT DESCRIPTION

A premium smoked salmon, smoked personally by the Hartlands using their special marinades; Lewis has been smoking salmon for 30 years, and in the past four years has started selling it.

THE ASK

$20,000 for 15% equity in the company.

THE DEAL

$20,000 for 20% equity as a convertible loan to be released in $5,000 increments.

THE OUTCOME

After being on *Dragons' Den* . . .

- As a start-up company, the Hartlands appreciated the business advice they received from their Dragon.
- Signed a deal with a smoked salmon facility in France.
- Had hundreds of orders within hours of their appearance on the show.

Father-and-son team Lewis and Samson Hartland pitching their Yukon Smoked Salmon to the Dragons.

THE WARM-UP: PRODUCT ROADMAP DEFINED

All businesses start with an idea. But if you don't take action daily to refine that idea into a sound business concept, the market will soon pass you by. In the next four chapters you'll learn how to define your product or service in four ways:

- **Storytelling:** Describe your product or service in terms of your original inspiration and how it works.
- **Brand Definition:** Describe your product or service in terms of what you want it to be known for.
- **Product Definition:** Describe the product that customers would be willing to pay you for.
- **Product Development:** Describe your product or service in terms of how it is made.

Treat this chapter as a quick checkpoint before you work on your product description: it includes a refresher on concept assessment and explains what to do in each stage of the product lifecycle.

Concept Assessment Recap: Do You Have a Slow-Growth or Fast-Growth Business Idea?

Entrepreneurs become attached to their business ideas. The thrill of the chase, social pressure, and fear of failure can sometimes make an entrepreneur feel like there is no turning back. But the truth is, the sooner you kill a bad idea, the sooner you'll find a better one. So it's important to screen your business concept before you commit heavy financial, emotional, and time resources to a business idea that won't make you money in the long term. Now that you are ready to commercialize your concept, retest your business concept against the 10 Dragons' Den Success Factors. If you don't meet all 10, that doesn't mean you can't have a successful business. But if you are able to meet them all, then you are improving your likelihood of success.

The 10 Success Factors

1. **Focus on a Singular Pain Point:** Does your product or service solve a burning problem?
2. **Build a Prototype:** Do you have a working prototype?
3. **Define the Value Proposition:** Is your business concept uniquely valuable to customers?
4. **Establish a Repeat Revenue Model:** Do you have a repeat revenue model?
5. **Target a Disruptable Market:** Are you targeting a large, definable untapped market?
6. **Build a Lean Feature Set:** Is your initial product or service based on a streamlined set of features?
7. **Collaborate with Strategic Partners:** Do you have potential partners who can help you achieve your goals?
8. **Find a Catalyst for Growth:** Do you know what events will trigger your biggest increase in sales?
9. **Scalability:** Do you have systems in place to handle a sudden increase in order volume?
10. **Develop a Business Model:** Do you have a sustainable money-making system?

The Product Lifecycle: Where Does Your Product or Service Fit in the Product Lifecycle?

The product lifecycle is a strategy metaphor that can help you predict the level of competition you can expect, the strategy you should follow, and the sales growth you might be in for once you go to market. The purpose of product lifecycle analysis is to help you assess the feasibility of your business concept before you invest heavily in it. The process of analyzing the product lifecycle involves a "gut check" review of where your idea fits in the lifecycle and an understanding of what to do about it. The four core stages of the product lifecycle are:

- **Introductory Stage:** Market demand for your type of product is *low*. No one has ever seen anything like it, and you have no proof that consumers will buy it. You are competing in an "incubator" environment.
- **Growth Stage:** Market demand for your type of product is *growing rapidly*. Although similar offerings exist, your product has several unique features that haven't been copied yet. You are competing in a "land grab" environment.
- **Maturity Stage:** Market demand for your type of product is *levelling off*. There is nothing unique about your offering. The market is saturated with competition. The only way to distinguish your offering is through costly branding campaigns. You are competing in shark-infested waters.
- **Decline Stage:** Market demand for your type of product is *shrinking*. People no longer want your type of product unless you offer deep discounts. Competitors are exiting the market. Your product or service category is becoming a dinosaur.

Extending Your Stay in the Lifecycle

Managing the product lifecycle means knowing what to do in each stage of the lifecycle. If you discover that your product or service is in the maturity or decline stage, set up an incubator or business creation unit to come up with the "next big thing."

The Product Cycle

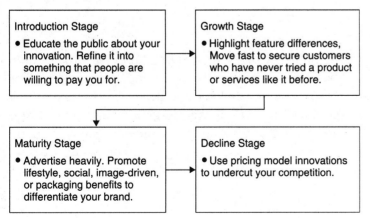

*These are sample actions, not hard-and-fast rules.

Dragon Lore

The business world is a kill-or-be-killed world. Evolve your products and services over time, or another more innovative business may enter the market and displace your business. Understand where your product or service fits in the product lifecycle to keep from being out-innovated.

When it comes to the product lifecycle, especially in the technology industry, you have to be on your toes at all times. Because most software or web application solutions can be written with a computer and a smart technical mind, the world is on equal footing when it comes to the capital required to build some programs. But the founders behind ScribbleLive know that it's not just a unique product that gives you a sustainable competitive advantage, it's also your history. The fact that co-founder Michael De Monte has been in the new media business since 1983 certainly helped to make their pitch stand out.

Product Snapshot: ScribbleLive

Pitchers: Michael De Monte and Jonathan Keebler, Season 4, Episode 6

Live publishing platform that will help big media companies attract millions more users to their websites.

HOW IT WORKS

ScribbleLive is a live publishing platform, similar to blogging software, that permits multiple users to comment on one event, and post text, photos, or video to one place. ScribbleLive will direct traffic to any Web event that people are talking about. Media companies will pay a monthly subscription to put ScribbleLive on their websites, increasing traffic and therefore advertising revenue. During the G20, for example, one newspaper had six reporters in different locations commenting on the event—giving multiple perspectives on that one event. And media companies like Rogers, Hearst Publishing, and The Score were already customers.

THE ASK

$250,000 for 20% equity.

THE DEAL

$250,000 for 30% equity.

KEY FEATURES

- The technology permits multiple users to collaborate on discussing an event.
- Users can post text and add photos and video.

CORE BENEFITS

- Media companies add ScribbleLive to drive traffic to their websites.
- More traffic equals more advertising revenue.

TESTIMONIAL

"I didn't really get how useful Twitter was for mass reporting until ScribbleLive appeared."

—Janine Gibson, *The Guardian,* reporting at the G20

Michael De Monte and Jonathan Keebler from Toronto present ScribbleLive, their online publishing platform, to the Dragons.

Self-Study Workshop: Product Roadmap

1. Describe the **market demand** for your type of product or service.
   - ❑ Low
   - ❑ Growing rapidly
   - ❑ Levelling off
   - ❑ Declining

2. How **innovative** is your idea?
   - ❑ It's a brand-new innovation that no one has ever seen before.
   - ❑ It's an innovative product or service that a small number of companies are selling.
   - ❑ It's a copycat product or service that we plan to advertise aggressively.
   - ❑ It's a product or service type that is outdated.

3. What is the **level of competition** in your industry?
   - ❑ No competition: *0 players*
   - ❑ Light competition: *2 to 3 players*
   - ❑ Heavy competition: *5 to 10 players or more*
   - ❑ Competitors exiting the industry in droves

4. What is the **trend of total industry-wide sales** volume for your product or service category?
   - ❑ Slowly increasing
   - ❑ Rapidly increasing
   - ❑ Stable and levelling off
   - ❑ Declining rapidly

5. What is your **competitive strategy**?
   - ❑ Educate people about my invention
   - ❑ Feature-driven differentiation
   - ❑ Brand-driven differentiation
   - ❑ Deep discounts

6. Where does your product or service fit in the **product lifecycle**?
   - ❏ Introductory stage
   - ❏ Growth stage
   - ❏ Maturity stage
   - ❏ Decline stage

7. When do you plan to release your product or launch your service to the market?
   - ❏ Within 30 days
   - ❏ 1 to 3 months
   - ❏ 3 to 6 months
   - ❏ 6 to 12 months
   - ❏ Other

Understanding where your product or service fits in the product lifecycle will help you know if you have a true innovation. But even if you have a copycat solution, what truly distinguishes a brand in the marketplace is the story behind it. In the next chapter we'll discuss how to bring your story to life by creating a brand experience.

CHAPTER 15

WHAT IS THE STORY BEHIND YOUR CONCEPT?

"My best friend was severely wounded in Afghanistan. So I promised him that I would share his mission . . . I figured out one way—orange blossom. I buy the oil from their orange blossom crops—the legal crops—to empower the economy, and I convert it into a product that's North American–ready. It's perfume—Afghanistan orange blossom— and perfume has one of the highest profit margins . . . The farmer makes money, the supplier makes money, the retailer makes money, and I make money."
     —Pitcher to Dragons

> **Product Description Method #1: Storytelling**
>
> Give people the backstory behind your new concept. Help people understand what you are selling by giving them usage scenarios. Reinforce this story through every interaction you have with your market.

There is nothing more awkward than trying to explain a business idea to a customer, a banker, or an investor who simply cannot understand what you are talking about. When this happens, it's usually best to stop talking about technical features and *start telling your story*. For example, the idea for the billion-dollar Chipotle restaurant chain came about when founder Steve Ells, who frequented authentic tacquerias in the Mission District of San Francisco, became fascinated with the process they used to serve giant tortillas stuffed with ingredients and then wrapped in foil. He was further inspired by how few people were needed to serve a long line of customers in a small retail space. This inspiration led to the creation of the first of many Chipotle stores that make up the billion-dollar-plus Chipotle restaurant chain.[1] To understand how unique the Chipotle experience is, just visit one of its fast-casual restaurants. You will most certainly notice the giant burritos, how streamlined the process is, and how quickly the lines move. When you hear the story of the founder's inspiration, the brand becomes more interesting. By telling the story of how your product or service came about, you will give your stakeholders—your customers, suppliers, investors, and bankers—an opportunity to become interested in your brand in a way that doesn't feel like a sales pitch.

Your story doesn't have to be deep or complicated. It just has to be told because it creates a personal connection between you and the product you are selling. For example, the founders of Dig It Handwear visited the Den and told their story of how their own manicures were damaged while gardening. So they set out to build the first glove that is designed specifically for women who *do* mind getting their hands dirty in the garden, but who also love to garden.

Dig It Handwear

Pitchers: Wendy Johannson and Claudia Harvey, Season 4, Episode 8

> "When we started in the Den, we had one SKU, Dig It Handwear, and now we have four SKUs . . . It's been an exciting two years, and the value of our company has doubled."
> —Pitcher to Dragons

PRODUCT DESCRIPTION

Gardening gloves with cushion tips to protect a woman's manicured nails.

THE ASK

50,000 for 10% equity.

THE DEAL

$50,000 for 10% equity.

THE OUTCOME

Within two years of being on *Dragons' Den*, Dig It Handwear . . .

- Landed a spot on The Shopping Channel.
- Increased distribution from 32 retailers to 350, including Home Depot.
- Increased product line from one SKU to four SKUs, including Eye Dig It sunglasses.

Pitchers Wendy Johannson and Claudia Harvey from Dig It Handwear, whose broken fingernails inspired a business that led to shelf space at a major retailer.

THE WARM-UP: STORYTELLING DEFINED

At the core of every business is a story, and that story is what makes your business interesting to people. The process of storytelling starts with the timeline of events that led to your idea. It includes your vision of how your goods or services will be used in practice. And it comes to life with the series of interactions that your customer will have with your product or service. The process of writing your story involves putting together your:

- **Brand Story:** Everything about your product's or service's history that makes it interesting.
- **Brand Experience:** The set of interactions with customers that you will use to tell your brand story.

Brand Story: What's So Interesting about Your Product or Service Idea?

People don't talk about products or services unless they are interesting. And sometimes the products or services themselves are really not interesting at all. But when you tell the story behind the product or service, you give the customer a deeper reason to become attached to it. Bill Bowerman of Nike used his wife's waffle maker to mould urethane into a prototype sole that would give runners more traction. Partner Phil Knight then sold these soles out of the back of his car at track meets. The product is now one of the leading lifestyle brands on the market.[2] Howard Schultz of Starbucks travelled to Italy and fell in love with the coffee-house experience that Italians were enjoying daily. He returned to the United States, tested the concept in Seattle, purchased the Starbucks brand with investors, and built it into the empire that it is today.[3] Chris Haney and Scott Abbott of Trivial Pursuit were looking to invent a challenging alternative to Scrabble, so they built a prototype, found a manufacturer, and grew it into the highest-selling trivia-based board game in history. Each one of these stories forms the basis for the brands that they have become today.

A brand story is the timeline of events that inspired your business concept and made it what it is today. The purpose of sharing your brand story is to make your product or service more interesting to current and potential customers. A brand story can change over time, but your marketing efforts should attempt to keep your brand centred on a singular story-line. One market space where brand storytelling has no equal is the world of professional sports. People develop personal relationships with the players on the field or ice, and the teams they belong to, by listening to interviews, commentary, and the backstory of the teams they root for. They dress in team colours, get emotionally attached to their favourite players, and even get in arguments with others over whose team is better. By the time the game actually airs, fans are so fired up about their team that the game almost seems like an anticlimax to the story itself.

To tell your brand story, start by looking at your original inspiration for your business and then inject the essence of that story into the brand experience that you provide to your customers. The three core elements of a brand story are:

- **Backstory:** How your product or service came about.
- **Theme:** What is truly interesting about your business idea.
- **Vision:** The powerful singular direction in which your business is going.

Brand Experience: How Will Customers Remember Your Product or Service?

Every time you make contact with a customer, you leave a footprint. And if those footprints don't look and feel the same, your business won't be memorable. To establish a consistent theme across all interactions with the customer, start with a high-level **operational concept** for your product or service and then brand each interaction or **touchpoint** with a consistent look and feel.

Operational Concept

An operational concept is a bird's-eye view of how and where your product will be used (or how and where your service will be performed). Each step of the process must reflect a consistent theme. The three core elements of your operational concept are:

- **Trigger Events:** The likely problem or event that would give rise to a phone call or a visit from a customer to your place of business to purchase from you.
- **Step-by-Step Operation:** The general process that someone will follow to experience your product or service.
- **Environment:** The place where your product or service will be experienced by your customers.

Touchpoints

Every physical, visual, and auditory interaction that you have with a customer needs to be mapped out in advance and branded with a consistent look and feel. Each interaction is called a touchpoint, and when you put a set of touchpoints together with a consistent theme, you have a brand experience. For example, if you are selling a high-end product, you can't send out discount coupons or use cheap packaging. Your price, packaging, and even advertising have to reflect the premium brand you are trying to establish. If you are running a gift basket business, you need to make sure that your ordering and delivery process is streamlined, since gifts should arrive on time.

Although touchpoints are unique to each business type, there are a common set of touchpoints found in all business types:

- Brand name, logo, and advertising choices
- Initial contact with customers

- Packaging
- Operational process
- Payment process
- Delivery process
- Environment (where your product is used or service performed)
- After-sales support (warranties, guarantees, support line offered)

Dragon Lore

A brand experience is much more than a narrative that you print in a newspaper or repeat in front of the Dragons. It's a consistent look and feel at every point of contact between your business and your customer.

When it comes to brand experience in the apparel industry, Moxie Trades founder Marissa McTasney is an expert. She built a construction-wear product line, a brand, and a company for women, around a poor buying experience in a men's construction-wear retail outlet. And then she showed up on *Dragons' Den* with an entire group of female customers who are committed to her brand.

Product Snapshot: Moxie Trades

Pitcher: Marissa McTasney, Season 3, Episode 4

Work wear and gear for female contractors, carpenters, and factory workers.

HOW IT WORKS

Before Moxie Trades, women had to buy their safety gear from men's stores, whose boots, belts, and other work wear weren't made for female bodies or appealed to women's fashion sense. Moxie Trades products are specifically designed for women.

THE ASK

$600,000 for 49%.

THE DEAL

Marissa McTasney of Moxie Trades asked for $600,000 for 49%. The Dragons offered $600,000 for 75%. She rejected the deal. However, soon afterward, one of the dragons had second thoughts, with an offer—$600,000 for 50%, which she accepted.

KEY FEATURES

- Aimed at a specific market segment of women working in construction and other trades.
- Sized for women; shaped for women.
- Sold at retailers across the country.

CORE BENEFITS

- You can wear pink if you want to!
- Improved fit, since the products are customized for women.
- Products address women's needs.
- The Moxie brand is supported by Marissa's advocacy for women working in the trades.

TESTIMONIAL

"My guess is that as a female in a very male-dominated industry, there is a sense of pride in being a female and you want to differentiate yourself but still be considered equal, so I think these are almost badges of honour."
—Dragon to Pitcher

Pitcher Marissa McTasney of Moxie Trades leaving the Dragon's Den after rejecting the deal offered by the Dragons.

Self-Study Workshop: Your Brand Story and Brand Experience

Tell the brand story, also known as a backstory, of your product or service. Then design a series of customer interactions that reflect that story.

Brand Story

1. How did your **business idea** come about?
2. What is **truly interesting** about your product or service?
3. What would you describe as being the **singular direction** that your brand is going into the future?

Brand Experience

1. What events **trigger the purchase** of your product or service?
2. In **what way** do you see your product being used or service being enjoyed?
3. In **what type of environment** will your product be used or service be enjoyed?
4. List every way in which a customer will **come in contact** with your business.
    - ❑ Brand name, logo, and advertising choices
    - ❑ Initial contact with customers
    - ❑ Packaging
    - ❑ Operational process
    - ❑ Payment process
    - ❑ Delivery process
    - ❑ Environment (where your product is used or service performed)
    - ❑ After-sales support (warranties, guarantees, support line offered)
    - ❑ Others
5. Describe the **core theme** that will be infused into every interaction with your customers.

Often what distinguishes a business is the entrepreneur's personal connection to the product or service he is offering. It gives the customer an emotional reason to buy in the form of a story that the customer can relate to. And that unique story becomes hard for someone else to copy. In the next chapter we'll discuss how to further refine your brand's story, by figuring what features and benefits should be highlighted in your brand's design.

CHAPTER 16

WHAT DO YOU WANT YOUR BUSINESS TO BE KNOWN FOR?

"I think you're actually on to something in terms of the fact that you've gone to a higher-end product line for dogs for owners that care deeply about what they feed their dogs . . . so I think that's a smart idea."
—Dragon to Pitcher

> **Product Description Method #2: Brand Definition**
>
> Identify the mission behind the products and services that you sell. Build distinguishing features, attributes, and benefits that reflect that mission. Design the visual identity of your product or service with a look and feel that communicates that mission.

Many entrepreneurs use a top-down approach to branding. They start with a company name, a nice logo, and a powerful set of colours. They call this their brand and then move on to more important things like advertising their new logo to customers. Unfortunately, the amount of money wasted marketing new products and services this way each year could probably run a small country. The idea that a brand is simply a recognizable logo is a myth that has been perpetuated by the old cattle-branding methods used by ranchers looking to protect their cattle from thieves. Branding is a business-wide identity for your business that must be infused into every feature, attribute, benefit, and process of your business. It's an in-depth process that aligns every point of contact you have with a customer with a singular theme. Your logo then reinforces that identity and makes your product or service as recognizable as a branded cow.

There is no business where the power of branding is more exemplified than the cosmetics and skincare industry. The distinction between products can be so fine that you have to use something other than your product to make people realize just how good it is. When Pierre Pelletier of Olivier skin care products visited *Dragons' Den*, he managed to not only captivate the audience with his brand, but even seemed to captivate the heart of one of the Dragons when he applied his lotion to her hands.

Olivier Skin Care Products

Pitchers: Pierre Pelletier and Clarence LeBlanc, Season 6, Episode 12

> "Since the time we talked, we have now perfected our skin care consultant program. It is actually an incredible program which is the most compensated package you can find on the market."
> —Pitcher to Dragons

PRODUCT DESCRIPTION

A skin care consultant program where, for a fee, you become a sales rep for Olivier skin care products and you get paid a percentage commission from the first dollar earned.

THE ASK

$200,000 for 20% equity.

THE DEAL

Advertising endorsement deal by two Dragons for a 5% ongoing royalty plus 20% equity. No cash exchanged in the deal.

THE OUTCOME

After being on *Dragons' Den* the first time, Olivier . . .

- Perfected its skin care consultant direct sales program.
- Has 71 sales reps, each selling an average $500 per month per rep.

Pierre Pelletier and Clarence LeBlanc from Olivier are back, pitching their skin care consultants program to the Dragons.

THE WARM-UP: BRANDING DEFINED

A brand is a distinctive mark that permanently identifies your business. It's much more than a logo. If built correctly, it works like a set of footprints that leads customers back to your business again and again. For a brand to have value, each footprint must look and feel the same, and reflect something that people place a value on. Now, you might wonder why branding is being talked about in the product description section of a business book, rather than in the marketing section. It's because a brand is not something you hot-stamp onto marketing materials after your concept has been developed. A brand is a business-wide theme that needs to be built into the business concept's DNA during concept development.

The branding process involves three core elements:

- **Core Purpose:** The ongoing mission behind the products or services that you sell. *Example: We sell auto-off light switches, but our core purpose is electrical safety.*
- **Point of Differentiation:** The unique features, attributes, and benefits of your offering, including the ones you purposely exclude. *Example: Our products are the only fireproof widgets on the market.*
- **Visual Identity:** The look and feel of your product or service, including its name, logo, colours, and overall design.

Core Purpose: What Do You Want to Be Known For?

Businesses survive by creating value for their customers. If that value-creation process does not have a consistent theme, your business and its message will wander aimlessly toward random opportunities. One year your website might help students share their notes at college, the next year it might help entrepreneurs share their business plans. Pretty soon your customers will forget what it is you are known for. The key to building a powerful brand is to become known for doing one thing really well. That one thing is your core purpose and it is reinforced using a name, logo, set of colours, and a consistent look and feel. A core purpose is not a slogan. Instead, it is the mission behind your business. If strategized correctly, it could become the source of a complete line of products and services. Here are some examples:

- **Symantec:** "Securing and managing your information-driven world."
- **New York Times:** "Enhance society by creating, collecting, and distributing high-quality news, information, and entertainment."
- **Cadbury:** "We create brands people love."
- **Verizon:** "We bring the benefits of communications to everybody."
- **Twitter:** "Connects you to the latest information about what you find interesting."

If your core purpose becomes valuable enough, your customers will start treating your brand as their own. For example, the purpose of Cadbury is to produce chocolate that people love, so when it announced that it was ending its famous Wispa chocolate bar, Wispa lovers everywhere in the UK were outraged. After an outpouring of consumer feedback, Cadbury brought the Wispa back to life and put it back on the shelves. The purpose of Netflix is to make it easier to rent movies, so when it announced that subscribers would have to use two different websites to access movies online—Qwikster.com for DVD-by-mail and to netflix.com for streaming video—it lost hundreds of thousands of subscribers in a few short months. So Netflix responded to their customers by killing the idea and reverting back to the single-website concept. And, of course, we all know what happened to Coca-Cola's revenue when it introduced New Coke. Today, Coke is more popular than ever.

Keep in mind that two businesses can have a different core purpose even though they sell the exact same product or service type. For example, if two companies sell customized chocolate bars, Company A might create value by packaging its chocolate bars for parents who give them away at birthday parties, whereas Company B might create value for business owners by packaging its chocolate bars as promotional products for small business owners to give away. Each company's unique core purpose will lead to a completely different business strategy.

Point of Differentiation: Why Is the World Better Off with Your Concept Than Without It?

Unique Features

A feature is a distinguishing physical or descriptive attribute of your product or service. To keep your product or service streamlined, make sure that each feature that you invest in supports the core purpose of your product. There are two types of features:

- **Functional Features:** Components that perform a function that the customer places a value on.
- **Non-Functional Features:** Attributes of your product or service, such as performance, convenience, and speed.

Unique Benefits

A benefit is the reason a feature is important. For example, one feature of the car you buy might be light-coloured seats. One benefit of that feature is that your seats won't be boiling hot when you sit on them on a sunny day because light colours deflect sunlight. There are two core categories of benefits:

- **Rational Benefits:** Measurable value the customer derives from each feature. *Example:* *"I save $3,000 a year by using the product."*
- **Emotional Benefits:** Intangible value the customer derives from each feature. *Example:* *"The product gives me peace of mind."*

Excluding Features and Benefits

Some of the best brands on the market exclude features on purpose. The features that are excluded are considered off-brand because they don't support the overall message that the business is trying to communicate. For example, Tim Hortons coffee shops don't sell milkshakes because milkshakes don't reflect the brand. Groupon doesn't hold eBay-style auctions for goods it sells because auctions wouldn't reflect the brand. And iPads don't come with external keyboards because external keyboards don't reflect the highly mobile nature of the iPad brand.

Identity: What Is the Look and Feel of Your Product or Service?

In order for your business to be remembered, it needs a name, logo, and colours that reflect the underlying core purpose of your business. For example, Panasonic's Toughbook laptops have an industrial look and feel, and logo to match, because their brand promises a rugged, durable, any-environment product. Frogbox rental moving boxes have an environmentally friendly look and feel to them because their brand promises an eco-friendly experience. Chipotle restaurants have a premium cafeteria look and feel to them, to reflect the fast-casual nature of the Chipotle brand. The two core elements of an identity are:

- **Corporate Identity:** Create a logo and slogan that reflects your brand. You can visit logo-making websites such as 99designs.com to crowd-source paid logos, or free logo websites such as www.logomaker.com.
- **Industrial Design:** Because of the varied nature of the business concepts that are being assessed, this book is not the proper forum to discuss industrial design in depth. That said, your product or service components should reflect the quality level that you are providing. For example, Victorinox Swiss Army knife products use only the highest-quality rust-resistant steel. The look and feel of all its products, including its fragrances and travel gear, remind us of the classic red Swiss Army knife we all grew up with.

Rebranding: What Do You Do If Your Brand No Longer Resonates with Your Customers?

Sometimes a brand gets off track. As more and more customers interact with a business, the business owner or brand manager starts to feel pressure to respond to requests for new features, new products, and new services to keep customers happy. The more features that are added, the more incomprehensible the brand becomes as the features that truly matter get hidden behind the features that really don't. Soon the same customers who made all those "new feature" requests start to flock elsewhere. When this happens, the business needs to reset the course by:

- Redefining its core purpose.
- Redefining its point of difference.
- Redesigning the "look and feel" identity.
- Stripping away anything that doesn't reflect that new core purpose.

In some rebranding cases, the underlying business concept itself might need to be radically overhauled or repurposed. A mom-and-pop coffee and tea shop that is losing customers to Tim Hortons might consider scrapping the coffee altogether just to compete. It could rebrand itself by adding finger sandwiches and change the look and feel of the environment to appeal more to the tea enthusiast than to the coffee lover. A mom-and-pop fitness studio that is losing customers to Bally Total Fitness might consider rebranding itself as an after-school fitness zone for kids. It could realign all of the features, attributes, and benefits of the studio around the needs of kids. And a burger restaurant that is losing business to Harvey's might consider switching to meatless hamburgers that look and feel exactly like real hamburgers, complete with whole-grain and gluten-free buns.

Dragon Lore

Try to associate your business with a lifestyle or functional mission.

When building your brand, keep in mind that a brand is much more than a catchy slogan and a nice-looking logo. Some brand names might not sound catchy, but it's the story behind them that triggers a following of loyal customers. Canadian Recycled Plastic Products, a name that would send shivers through Madison Avenue because of its lack of memorability, has a business so wildly popular that they can't keep up with demand. Lucky for them, their customers and the Dragons are more interested in the recycled materials that are used to produce their products, than their less than memorable brand name.

Product Snapshot: Canadian Recycled Plastic Products

Pitchers: Trudie Wiseman and Jamie Bailey, Season 5, Episode 3

Outdoor furniture made from recycled plastic.

HOW IT WORKS

The company manufactures outdoor furniture crafted from recycled plastics. The company's values reflect the owners' strong core values and belief in turning out practical, reliable products that help save the environment. And Trudie and Jamie have an unusual problem: they can't keep up with demand and are turning down sales!

THE ASK

$1,000,000 for 30%.

THE DEAL

$1,000,000 for 50%.

KEY FEATURES

- A green product.
- Made from recycled plastic.
- Furniture comes in various colours.
- UV-resistant.

CORE BENEFITS

- Environmentally friendly.
- No painting or staining required.
- Zero maintenance.
- Retail price is the same as comparable wooden products.

TESTIMONIAL

"Green products are just flying."
—Pitcher to Dragon

Chairs made by Canadian Recycled Plastic Products are delivered to the Dragons.

Self-Study Workshop: Branding

A brand is an identity that your company or your product is known for. If it is not known for something, then you don't have a brand. Use this self-study workshop to develop the core elements of your company's brand.

1. Name your **three favourite brands** and write down what each is known for, then visit their websites or pick up their products and see if your answers are reflected in their visual identity.

2. **Core Purpose:** What is the mission behind your product or service?

3. **Core User:** What customer type would place the highest value on this core purpose?
   - ❑ Consumer
   - ❑ Professional user
   - ❑ Business owner
   - ❑ Salesperson
   - ❑ Other

4. **Unique Features:** What are the three most valuable components of your product or service?

5. **Unique Benefits:** For each feature listed above, state why the feature is important.

6. **Exclusions:** Branding is as much about excluding features as it is about including them. A brand becomes diluted when it includes anything that does not support its core purpose. What are some of your product's or service's features that you really don't need?

7. **Look and Feel:** How does the look and feel of your product or service reflect your underlying core purpose?
   - **Touchpoints:** List all the ways in which your customers come in contact with your product or service.

   Examples: Customer service, packaging, usage.

   - **Aesthetics:**
     - *Logo*
     - *Name*
     - *Colour scheme*
     - *Design*

8. **Brand Statement:** Write a declarative statement of what you want your product or service to be known for.

   Brand Statement = Core Purpose + Core User

Think of your brand definition as a theme for your product or service that will make it attractive and recognizable for your customers. It will also help guide your business. Now, to define the features and benefits that will go into your product or service, turn to the next chapter on Product Definition.

CHAPTER 17

WHAT PRODUCT WILL CUSTOMERS BE WILLING TO PAY YOU FOR?

"There's a reason that it's called women's intuition and not men's intuition, and I don't actually care what you think about it. I think this is exactly the kind of idea that I want."
—Dragon to Dragon

Product Description Method #3: Product Definition

Determine if you have the right product or service. Validate your idea. Then focus on building the product correctly.

Markets are highly efficient ecosystems in which customer needs evolve over time. Entrepreneurs and established companies are always at risk of being out-innovated, out-advertised, or even copied by an overzealous competitor. Think about what happened to tanning salons, print encyclopedias, typewriters, and even buggy whips. All were innovations at one time but were later displaced by changing needs, wants, and preferences. Print encyclopedias were out-innovated by Encarta and Wikipedia. Tanning salons were out-innovated by spraying salons. And, of course, typewriters were wiped out by computers. Even movie theatres are being out-innovated by video on demand. Fortunately, entrepreneurs who thrive in a survival-of-the-fittest environment and continue to innovate are often rewarded beyond their wildest dreams. By developing a clear definition of your product or service, you will have a better understanding of whether it has the revenue potential that you are expecting.

However, defining your product in a way that cuts through the clutter of heavy competition in the marketplace might take as much creativity in packaging as it does in product design and definition. When makeover entrepreneur Andi Marcus of Mistura visited *Dragons' Den*, she showed how a simple packaging decision means the difference between business success and toiling for years trying to draw attention to your business. Packaging six of her products into a 6-in-1 solution helped to distinguish her line of makeup in one of the most competitive market landscapes you can find.

Mistura

Pitcher: Andi Marcus, Season 4, Episode 1

> "There's a lot more than meets the eye to a deal like this. It's actually very, very educational, and it's worthwhile because it sets you on the path for future success."
> —Pitcher to Dragons

PRODUCT DESCRIPTION

A six-in-one makeup solution that acts as a foundation, a concealer, a blush, a lipstick, a bronzer and an eyeshadow, and that adapts to the skin tone of each woman who uses it.

THE ASK

$200,000 for 10% equity.

THE DEAL

$200,000 for 25%.

THE OUTCOME

Within four months of being on *Dragons' Den*, Pitcher Andi Marcus planned to use the cash infusion to . . .

- Hire marketing consultants and staff.
- Put solid inventory in place.
- Open up a call centre.
- Expand the product line.

Andi was later named as one of Ottawa's Top 40 under 40.

Pitcher Andi Marcus with her all-in-one beauty product.

THE WARM-UP: PRODUCT DEFINITION DEFINED

A great product that no one is willing to pay you for is not a product at all. Spending years perfecting the design of your new concept, only to find out later that nobody wants it, could turn into a financial disaster. In the early days of your business, first determine if you are selling the right product or service. Garner feedback from potential users, suppliers, and any other stakeholders to determine the features, attributes, and benefits that truly matter. Then—and only then—spend resources converting your prototype into a market-ready commercial product or service. The process of defining your product or service includes:

- **Product Description:** What features, attributes, and benefits do people want?
- **Product Environment:** Where will your product be consumed or service performed?
- **Product Stakeholders:** Who has an interest in your success and who do you report to?
- **Product Reaction:** What type of feedback are you getting from prospective customers?
- **Product Line Extensions:** What other similar product ideas can you commercialize in the future?
- **Product Protections:** How have you protected your idea?

Product Description: Describe the Features, Attributes, and Benefits of Your Product

There is nothing more boring than listening to an entrepreneur list product specifications ad infinitum. Most people want to tell time, not build the watch. However, for those who want to know every last detail about what you sell, there are myriad ways of describing your product or service:

- **Features:** Components of your product or service that are uniquely valuable in your product or service category, such as free delivery, a 10-hour battery, or a frying pan handle that doesn't get hot.
- **Attributes:** Intangible characteristics of your product or service, such as reliability, convenience, and performance.
- **Benefits:** Why each feature is important.
- **Point of Differentiation:** What makes your product or service different from competitive products and services currently on the market.
- **Operational Concept:** How your product or service works, including how many times it is used.
- **Proprietary Features:** A feature that you own, which can't be copied without the person or company doing so infringing on your legal rights. (See "Protecting Your Idea" below.)
- **Documentation:** The supporting documentation that comes with your product or service.
- **After-Sales Support:** The ongoing operational support that is required to support the customer.

Product Environment: Where Will It Be Used or Consumed?

The location at which your product is used or service performed can lead to critical decisions regarding design, payment methods, packaging, durability needs, and ongoing service agreements. For example, the designers of the Panasonic Toughbook clearly understood the power of environmental context when they came up with their line of highly durable laptop computers. Military personnel, construction workers, and anyone who works in a rough environment expose their laptops to dirt, liquids, and even the occasional drop. Today, Panasonic owns the rugged laptop space, and it's all because their designers knew before anyone else the power of context. When considering your product or service's environment, look at:

- **Users:** The person who uses your product or benefits from your service. ***Example:*** *Our moving boxes are lifted by people with various levels of strength.*
- **Environment:** The place where your product will be used or service performed. ***Example:*** *Our moving boxes often sit outside in the rain, on living room floors, and in the backs of moving trucks.*
- **External Entities:** Products or services that will interact with yours in that environment. ***Example:*** *Our moving boxes are stacked on moving dollies and hand trucks that are dragged up and down stairs.*

Product Stakeholders: Who Needs This Thing to Work?

The person who uses your product or receives your service is not the only person whose needs have to be met. In many cases, as with many items that are purchased by the head of a household, the actual consumers of the item are not the ones who pay for it. One person may shop for it; another person may put the money up to buy it; a third person may consume it. Still another person may need it to generate a certain amount of profit in order for the business to stay open. Appealing to every person in the chain is a balancing act and everyone's interests have to be aligned. These people are called "stakeholders" because they all have an interest in your success. And if you don't meet the needs of every stakeholder, your "simple product that Canadians need" might turn into a complete financial disaster. Stakeholders include the following:

- **Decision maker:** The person who is in charge of whether the purchase happens or not. ***Example:*** *The grandparents who want to bring the family together for an annual get-together with the grandchildren.*
- **Shopper:** The person who researches the features, attributes, and benefits of your offering. The decision maker may delegate the decision to the shopper. ***Example:*** *The mom who wants to make sure that everyone's needs are met.*
- **User:** The person who consumes the product or receives the service. ***Example:*** *The extended family that goes on a trip to a bed and breakfast.*
- **Designer:** The person who builds your product or develops your service.

- **Investor:** The person who invested in your business who needs to know that your business can generate a liquidity event that pays him or her a cash return in the future.
- **Bank:** The bank needs to know that your business can generate a positive cash flow high enough to cover any loans.
- **Supplier:** The supplier needs to know that any volume discounts that it provides will be met with actual sales in the future.
- **Regulator:** The regulators need your product or service to comply with all applicable laws in the markets in which you operate.

Product Reaction: What Level of Interest Is There for Your Idea?

The initial reaction you receive from prospective customers or focus groups can be another rich source of ideas. While you certainly shouldn't give anyone control of your goals, be sure to take heed of any negative patterns in the way people respond to your business idea. In the early stages of your business, regularly track and review feedback from:

- Prospective customers
- Suppliers
- Existing competitors
- Press reviews and industry analysts (if you are lucky enough to get in front of them)

Product Line Extensions: What Other Related Products or Services Could You Launch?

A product or service is not a business unless you can build a sustainable revenue model around it. One way to keep revenues coming in is to keep upgrading the original product. Another way is to create variations of your initial offering that appeal to new market segments. These new products or services are called line extensions, and they can keep your business from becoming a one-trick pony. It's generally a good idea to make sure that all line extensions reflect the core purpose of your brand. For example, it's probably not a good idea for a makeup company to start selling chocolate, because chocolate doesn't reflect the company's core purpose. But it could start selling chocolate-flavoured lipstick for teenagers. And a moving box rental service should probably stay out of the rental car business, unless the company decides to change its core purpose. But it could start renting out larger containers to commercial businesses that are moving from one location to another. The processing of making sure that line extensions fit your brand is called "staying on brand."

Protecting Your Idea: How Will You Protect Your Idea?

The right time to tell the world about your business idea depends on the nature of your product or service. Share your idea too soon and the people around you might kill your enthusiasm, or worse, steal your idea. Share your idea too late and you might find that you are committing to a concept that is no longer (or never was) relevant to anyone. Keep in mind that the ultimate protection for your business is a loyal customer. So if you have a good idea, get it out into the market in a timely manner. But there are protections available to you. Because people interchange the terminology like it's going out of style, here is a simple chart to give you some background. Of course, this is not legal advice, so always speak to an intellectual property lawyer first if you think you have an idea that is protectable.

What Can Be Protected?	Protection	Term of Protection*
Authored works such as drawings, software programs, books, articles, or music.	Copyright	Life of the author plus 50 years.
Inventions such as equipment or processes.	Patents	Up to 20 years.
Symbols, names, and logos that you use to identify your product or service.	Trademarks	Potentially indefinitely.
Trade secrets: formulas or processes that you keep a secret.	Non-disclosure agreements (a.k.a. confidentiality agreements)	For as long as you or your employees don't leak it to the public.
Contracts with your employees to keep them from leaving your business, setting up shop in the same business, and stealing your customers.	Non-compete agreements	Depends on the locality.

*In Canada.

Another example of how product definition and packaging decisions can mean the difference between success or failure was clearly demonstrated when honey entrepreneurs John and Justin Rowe, from Honibe, visited *Dragons' Den*. By making honey portable using a dehydration technology, and guarding their process secrets, they have been able to penetrate an otherwise mature and hyper-competitive honey market.

Product Snapshot: Honibe

Pitchers: John and Justin Rowe, Season 5, Episode 12

The world's first pure, non-sticky honey that you can hold.

HOW IT WORKS

The Pitchers use proprietary technology to dehydrate honey into drop form.

THE ASK

$1,000,000 for 20%.

THE DEAL

$600,000 for 35% plus a $400,000 line of credit.

KEY FEATURES

- Proprietary technology dehydrates honey into drop form.
- A portable dry honey product that is being extended to lozenges and candy drops.

CORE BENEFITS

- The honey comes in drop and sprinkle form, for easy transport.
- Can be used in restaurants and coffee shops as a sugar alternative.

TESTIMONIAL

> "I love honey. It's very good. It's such a good idea."
>   —Dragon to Pitcher

Honibe products, a pure hard-candy form of honey, being pitched on *Dragons' Den*.

Dragon Lore

In the early days of your business, put more emphasis on making sure that you have chosen the right product to market than on building your product correctly. Building a product correctly is certainly important, but you don't want to spend years building a dream product or service that nobody is willing to pay you for.

Self-Study Workshop: Product Definition

A product definition is the technical description of your product or service. Use this self-study workshop to hone your definition of what customers will get in exchange for the price they are paying. This type of information can be used in brochures and the product section of your website.

1. What are you **selling**?
2. How does it **work**?
3. How is it **different** from competitors' products or services that are currently being offered on the market?

4. What **features, attributes, and benefits** of your product, service, or business will customers be most willing to pay you for?

5. Does your product, technology, or service offer something **unique** to the market?

6. **Where will it be consumed** or performed, and how does that impact your design?

7. Who are the **stakeholders** in your business, and what are their overriding goals?
   - ❑ The decision maker
   - ❑ The shopper
   - ❑ The user
   - ❑ The investor(s)
   - ❑ The bank(s)
   - ❑ The supplier(s)
   - ❑ The regulator(s)

8. What are your plans for **line extensions,** improvements to your current offerings, or planned obsolescence of your current offerings?

9. Do you have **legal protection** in place for any of your features?

A product definition forces you to commit to a short-term path and set of features for your product. In the next chapter you'll determine whether to buy or build your product, or license your service model from others, and how to research suppliers.

Chapter 18

Should I Buy or Build My Product?

"There is a path here for a very quick upside for you. You don't want to be in the shoe manufacturing business. [You] want to license this to a large shoe manufacturer."
    —Dragon to Pitcher

Product Description Method #4: Product Development

Business ideas are free. If you're like most entrepreneurs, you probably see them everywhere. Unfortunately, an idea is not a concept until you have turned it into a prototype. And a concept is not commercially viable until you have tested it and figured how to produce it and sell it at a profit. The decision whether to *buy* or *build* your product is based on many factors, including cost, your ability to find suppliers, and time-to-market. This is where the rubber meets the road in your business, so take this part of the development process very seriously.

The best thing about starting a clothing line is that a prototype can be put together at low cost in your kitchen or basement. But once you commercialize your product, and your order volume starts to increase, you'll have to find ways to produce that higher volume at a lower cost. And since the Dragons are all about cutting costs to increase profit, sooner or later the discussion of producing your clothing line offshore will come up, as the pitchers of Dressed n' Case and Squito Wear found out when they showed up on *Dragons' Den*.

Dressed n' Case vs. Squito Wear

Dressed n' Case Business Model vs. Squito Wear Business Model

Season 6, Episode 10	Season 6, Episode 15
Problem: Finding an offshore manufacturer to cut costs and increase margins.	**Problem:** Finding an offshore manufacturer to cut costs and increase margins.
Dressed 'n-case is a bag that converts into a swimwear cover-up that Kimberley Rosadiuk has had manufactured in Canada. She has people emailing and calling her, wanting to rep the product, but can't get her inventory up because her manufacturing costs are too high.	Edith Sinclair has been sewing Squito Wear, a suit to keep the bugs off, in her basement and can't keep up with demand.
Kimberley's Dragons' Deal **The Ask:** $175,000 for 25% equity. **The Deal:** $175,000 for 55% of the company and help her get offshore manufacturing in Asia.	**Edith's Dragons' Deal** **The Ask:** $75,000 for 20% of the business. **The Deal:** $75,000 to take over manufacture, marketing, and distribution of the product, paying a royalty of 6% to 8% on every product sold.
Kimberley Rosadiuk demonstrates her Dressed n' Case cover-up that's a dress and a bag all in one to the Dragons.	Pitcher Edith Sinclair demonstrates Squito Wear to the Dragons.

WARM-UP: PRODUCT DEVELOPMENT DEFINED

Product development is the process of converting a feasible business concept into a market-ready offering. The purpose of product development is to make sure that your product or service is both profitable for your business and valuable for your customers. There are four key elements to consider:

- **Industrial Design:** What are the components of your product or service? How will it be designed and by whom?
- **Cost Estimation:** How much will it cost to produce your product or perform each unit of your service?
- **Sourcing Suppliers and Vendors:** Where will you find suppliers, vendors, and manufacturers who meet your market, technical, and financial needs?
- **Supplier Evaluation:** How will you make your final decision on which supplier to go with?

Industrial Design

After you have screened your business idea and concept using the Dragons' Den Success Factors in this book, it's time to actually cost out your product or service. Start by deconstructing your product or service into its component parts. Keep track of your list on a spec sheet or a bill of materials. Then make a buy or build decision for each component based on market, technical, and financial feasibility considerations. Most people see this part of the process as being a product-only exercise. However, services do have tangible components and those tangible components need to be valued, as well as the variable labour required to perform each unit of service. Although the topic of industrial design is beyond the scope of this book, here are two key factors to consider:

1. Design Criteria

- **Usability:** How easy is it to use your product or service?
- **Attributes:** Quality, size, weight, aesthetic needs, performance, and other requirements.
- **Materials:** Ingredients that you need to produce from scratch.
- **Components:** Parts that you will buy off the shelf to build your product or perform your service.

2. Trade-Off Criteria

Most entrepreneurs have resource constraints when starting out. As a result, sometimes trade-offs must be made early on just to get your business off the ground. Three areas to address during the design process are:

- **Cost vs. Quality:** Will my chosen components and materials meet my margin goals? Can the chosen components be used to build a product or service that will perform as expected? Will the chosen components meet the quality and performance requirements of the market I'm targeting? Can I trade off quality to get costs down to a profitable level?
- **Buy vs. Build:** Should I build the product myself, or have someone else manufacture it for me? This decision is based on cost and time-to-market. If a manufacturer can build your product better, cheaper, and faster than you can yourself, you might consider licensing your idea to it.
- **Build vs. License:** Should I build the product myself or license the concept to another manufacturer? Licensing agreements can give you access to a larger audience than you might be able to reach yourself. But building it yourself puts less pressure on you to reach high-volume targets.

Cost Estimation

Business is about making money. If you have a great product or service that can't be produced at a profit (sales minus cost to buy or build), then you won't have a business. A starting point for your estimate is market research into costs and mark-up guidelines for your industry. Also keep in mind that quotes you receive from suppliers should include price breaks for volume orders. So be sure to complete a detailed sales volume estimate during your market assessment efforts later. Although detailed cost estimation for your specific situation might be highly complex, you can certainly begin the process by understanding some simple formulas.

Per-Unit Cost

Unit costs tell you how much profit you can generate per unit sold. That per unit profit can then be used to pay for overhead such as selling, and general and administrative expenses. There are two product costs to consider when buying or building a product or structuring a service: **fixed costs** and **variable costs**. These costs don't consider operating costs (location, etc.), which are considered later when you put together your business plan:

- **Fixed Costs:** Set-up charges, including what it costs to design the specs of your product or service.
- **Variable Costs:** A component cost per unit produced. Includes labour and raw materials or ingredients per unit of product or service unit performed.
- **Contribution Margin:** The amount per unit sold that "contributes" to your fixed costs. Contribution Margin = Price Per Unit – Variable Cost Per Unit
- **Break-Even:** The total number of units of your product or service that have to be sold to break even on your fixed costs. These are not hard-and-fast rules. You can calculate a break-even in many different ways, including the break-even that covers your design and set-up costs, a break-even to cover your business start-up costs, or the monthly break-even on your entire business to cover your monthly operating costs.

Gross Profit Calculation
- **Revenue** = Price × Product or Service Unit Sales Volume
- **Cost of Goods Sold** = Per Unit Fixed Costs (total set-up and design) + Variable Costs (total per unit costs)
- **Gross Profit** = Revenue – Total Cost of Goods Sold
- **Break-Even** = Total Fixed Costs / Per Unit Gross Profit

Sourcing Suppliers and Vendors

You are responsible for the quality of your suppliers' work. Their work becomes a part of your product or service: if anything goes wrong with their inputs, you'll be held responsible. It's important to screen suppliers and vendors thoroughly, so make use of the supplier evaluation checklist in this chapter. Although it's important to be wary of suppliers that don't initially impress you, there is no need to exclude a vendor just because an aggressive sales rep puts you off or a rude secretary was having a bad day. Be sure to dig deeper than just making a phone call. Also, your choice of *where* your suppliers and vendors are located (offshore or domestic) depends on your business's overall branding and your ability to visit suppliers in person.

For most start-ups, referrals might be the most cost-effective way to source and pre-screen vendors. Some referral sources for vendors are:

- **Trade Associations:** Call the trade association for your industry and ask for a list of trade shows, conferences, and trade magazines. Its job is to protect and promote the interests of your industry, so it should be more than happy to help.
- **Trade Shows:** Attend trade shows and speak to attendees. This is one of the ways that the creators of Trivial Pursuit figured out how to launch their bestselling game.
- **Trade Magazines:** Suppliers and vendors advertise in trade magazines.
- **Trade Conferences:** Trade conferences are the choke points for your industry, where the key players in your industry congregate on an annual basis.
- **Direct Calls to Manufacturers:** Call vendors and suppliers that you learn about at the trade shows, conferences, and through online searches.

To supplement your face-to-face or phone conversations with industry participants, you can also search online using:

- **Industry Canada:** Resource information by industry, industry statistics, and trade data can be found at www.ic.gc.ca.
- **Google Searches:** A good starting point is a Google search for "supplier for _____."
- **ThomasNet:** An industrial search engine with which you can source product and product suppliers in Canada and the United States.
- **Alibaba.com:** An online exchange where you can source and communicate online with manufacturers and vendors from around the globe.
- **Freelance Exchanges:** Online expertise exchanges such as Guru.com, eLance.com, and Desk.com, where freelancers can be sourced for various projects.

Supplier Evaluation Checklist
The procurement process in business is similar to any other shopping experience. It's a process of screening vendors and suppliers in a timely manner, using various quantitative and qualitative factors. You can start by listing your suppliers and rating your initial interactions with them using a sliding scale. Then, after you have narrowed your list down to a shortlist of

vendors that meet your needs, you can do more in-depth research by visiting them in person or by talking to their references.

Rate each supplier you have sourced on a scale of 1 to 7 for each of the following items:

- Product/component quality fit
- Cost fit
- Payment terms
- Location fit
- Turnaround time and timeliness
- Experience
- Collaboration: Will vendor work with you to achieve your goal?
- Working conditions
- Years in business
- Customer case studies/references provided
- Site visitation allowed
- Employee attitude
- Quality process
- Other

Dragon Lore

An idea is not a business until you find someone who can produce your product or perform your service in a way that meets your market, technical, and financial needs.

Your method of production not only plays a key role in your cost structure, but it can also become a big part of what makes your business attractive to its market. When Barb Stegemann of The 7 Virtures visted *Dragons' Den*, her story about why she chose suppliers in Afghanistan drew instant attention from the Dragons.

The 7 Virtues

Pitcher: Barb Stegemann, Season 5, Episode 15

The 7 Virtues produces a line of fragrances made with essential oils sourced from international suppliers in Afghanistan and Haiti, who use the revenue to rebuild their communities.

HOW IT WORKS

The company buys the oil from Afghan orange-blossom farmers and converts it into market-ready perfume products. The farmer makes money, the supplier makes money, and the company makes money.

THE ASK

$75,000 for 15% equity.

DRAGONS' OFFER

$75,000 for 15% equity.

KEY FEATURES

- The initial fragrances are made of high-quality oils from Afghanistan. An addition to the product line uses oils from Haiti.
- A scent that North Americans want.
- Uses orange blossoms grown by Afghan farmers.

CORE BENEFITS

- Gives Afghan farmers a new legal cash crop that is an alternative to selling illegal poppy seed.
- Pays $8,000 for one litre of orange blossom oil, which impacts 400 people in a community.
- It smells good.

TESTIMONIAL

"I should be your partner, and I think this is smart. I like it because it's not charity. And it is helping the economy. And they do need to figure out how to make a living and they do need to be able to survive. So I love what you are doing."
—Dragon to Pitcher

Barb Stegemann setting up to pitch her perfume company The 7 Virtues to the Dragons.

Self-Study Workshop: Product Development

Find suppliers that can make your product or service for a cost that meets your margin goals. As always, if you are not a numbers person, seek advice from someone who is, such as the accountant in the family or through a referral from a friend.

1. What are the **tangible components** of your product or service?
2. Who will **draw the specs** of your product or map out your service?
3. What is the **fixed cost** to design your product or service?
4. What is the **variable cost** per unit to buy or build each tangible component of your product or service?
5. What is the **variable cost of labour** to produce each unit or perform each deliverable of your service?
6. What is the **contribution margin** per unit of your product or service?
7. How many units of your product or service do you need to sell to **break even**? In other words, how many units of your product have to be sold or service units performed to cover your fixed costs, your fixed start-up costs, and your total annual fixed costs?

8. How will you **produce** your product?
   - ❏ Buy
   - ❏ Build
   - ❏ Other
9. Who are your **top three suppliers or vendors** for each component of your product or service?

In parts I, II and III of this book, you have refined your business concept, tested it for feasibility, and committed to a clear product or service definition. In Part IV you'll delve deep into the mechanics of the market in which you'll be operating so you'll be able to develop a clear go-to-market strategy in Part V.

Part IV

Defining Your Market

Research the market environment in which you will operate, including the business cycle, the industry, the competitive landscape, and your target market.

CHAPTER 19

THE BUSINESS CYCLE

"People are doing this like crazy right now. You're getting coins. You're getting all kinds of stuff coming back. Every jewellery shop in the country is selling gold . . . trying to buy gold."

—Dragon to Pitcher

> **Market Assessment #1: The Business Cycle**
>
> Track the business cycle. Understand what the economy means to your business concept. Start a business in spite of the business cycle, not because of it.

Imagine this scenario. Financial panic hits the largest economy in the world. Banks are closing. Overpriced real estate prices are collapsing. And rumours are starting to spread that a once-great country could be headed for bankruptcy. People are losing jobs left and right, and the rest of the world is wondering if the country will continue to maintain its dominance. In this real-life scenario, the name of the president in power wasn't Bush, it was Van Buren. And it wasn't 2008, it was 1837, the year Tiffany & Co. and Procter & Gamble were founded. Two enterprising entrepreneurs, Charles Lewis Tiffany and John B. Young,[1] found a market for their skills in one of the worst financial periods in U.S. history to date: the Panic of 1837.[2] Two other entrepreneurs, William Procter & James Gamble, found a market for their candle-making and soap-making skills in the same year.[3] Today their companies, Tiffany & Co. and Procter & Gamble, are powerhouses in their respective industries, and all because of four entrepreneurs who were determined to succeed in spite of the business cycle. They all knew that businesses are started when the *entrepreneur* is ready—not necessarily when the economy is.

One industry that never loses its lustre is the food industry. But industry participants do respond to business cycle fluctuations by changing the industry's pricing strategies and by modifying its offerings to lower-cost options. Entrepreneurs Tim Ray and Jonathan Ambeault understand food, and apparently the business cycle, because their discount food buying website is perfect for a time when the economy is uncertain and wallets are lean. FoodScrooge, as the name implies, offers high-value food to the price-conscious consumer. They were able to translate the group-buying craze into an investor frenzy when they visited *Dragons' Den.*

FoodScrooge

Pitchers: Tim Ray and Jonathan Ambeault, Season 6, Episode 10

"If we can get consumers into these local grocery store retailers, they're going to buy additional items while they're in that store."
—Pitcher to Dragon

PRODUCT DESCRIPTION

The first North American company to apply the group-buying craze to bulk food shopping, a non-discretionary item in a contracting economy.

THE ASK

$125,000 for 15% of the business.

THE DEAL

$125,000 for 35% of the business.

THE OUTCOME

After being on *Dragons' Den* . . .

- Six months after launching the business, the Pitchers were bought out by WagJag, a division of Torstar, which operates like Groupon, with daily offers, including for groceries and travel. "The fastest exit strategy in history," said one of the investing Dragons.

The founders of FoodScrooge seeking a deal on *Dragons' Den*.

A TOP-DOWN APPROACH TO RESEARCHING YOUR MARKET

Market research can be like knowing the answers to an exam in advance, so take advantage of this wonderful opportunity to uncover the critical success factors of your market environment.

Once you have established the basic need for your product or service, put together a prototype, and discovered a profitable target audience, it's important to engage in more in-depth market research. Market research involves breaking down your market according to the business cycle (a 10,000-foot view), an industry analysis (a 5,000-foot view), the competitive landscape (a 1,000-foot view), and a target market analysis (a ground view). The four core components of a top-down approach to assessing your market are:

1. **The Business Cycle:** Where are we in the business cycle and what should I do about it? (Discussed in this chapter.)
2. **Industry Analysis:** What are the demand drivers in my industry and where are the opportunities? (See Chapter 20.)

3. **Competitive Landscape:** Who are my competitors and how will I compete against them? (See Chapter 21.)
4. **Target Market Analysis:** Who are my most profitable customers and how can I reach them? (See Chapter 22.)

By completing this four-stage market assessment, you will not only gain insight into the market dynamics that drive demand for your business but you will also uncover critical success factors that you can act on. For example, if we are in a recession, you'll know that temporary price concessions may have to be made in order to secure business. If you are operating in a counter-cyclical industry, then you may see the benefits of ramping up your advertising when the economy takes a turn for the worse. And if the basis for competition in your competitive landscape is a singular feature, you'll know how to position your product or service in relation to that feature.

THE WARM-UP: THE BUSINESS CYCLE DEFINED

The business cycle is best described as a self-correcting process that the economy goes through over time periods that can last years. When the economy becomes oversupplied with goods and services, and people have met many of their durable-goods needs, competing businesses can't all survive in their current form. This leads to a correction in the economy, called a "contraction," a time when businesses lay off employees or shut down and consumers pull back on their spending. Once the economy has fully corrected itself, and bottomed out at a point called a "trough," it is poised for a recovery. This is a time when demand picks up and businesses start to ramp up their production or service capacity to meet the new demand. Sooner or later the economy peaks and the cycle starts all over again. The process is called a "cycle" because it happens over and over again, and anyone who owns a profitable product can improve his or her overall business strategy by understanding what types of product or services sell in what market. Economists track the business cycle using the gross domestic product (GDP).

Here is a sample pattern of what could occur during the business cycle:

The Business Cycle*

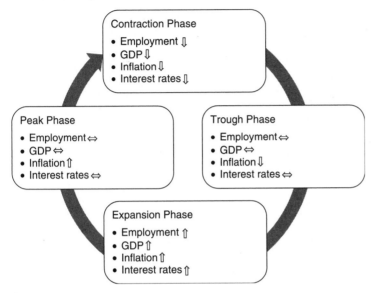

*These are sample trends, not hard-and-fast rules.

1. **Contraction Phase:** A shrinking economy with a decline in GDP; also known as "negative growth."
2. **Trough Phase:** A low point in the economy, with widespread unemployment and a bottoming out of GDP.
3. **Expansion Phase:** A growing economy, with an increase in GDP.
4. **Peak Phase:** A high point in the economy, with widespread employment and a levelling off of GDP.

Tracking the Business Cycle: What Do I Do Now?

The business cycle leaves clues. People tend to put off purchases of new homes, household appliances, new vehicles, and luxury items during an economic slowdown. They tend to purchase consumable products and services such as soap, food, and dental work irrespective of the economic environment. And they tend to buy more luxury products, travel, and durable goods such as cars and appliances in a growing economy. But you don't have to be an economist to figure out what to do when. It's just common sense. When the economy is contracting, consumers become nervous about their money, so they tend to put off discretionary purchases. When the economy is booming, consumers become more confident about their money, so they start to buy the discretionary items they were previously putting off.

You can use this information to figure out what industries to work with and when.

What Does Relatively Well During the Business Cycle?

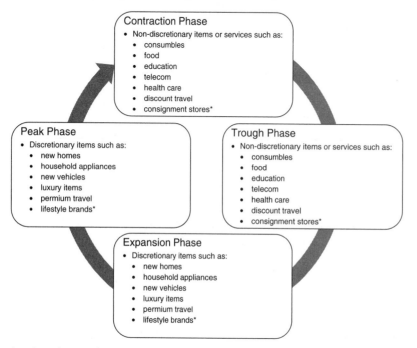

Contraction Phase
- Non-discretionary items or services such as:
  - consumbles
  - food
  - education
  - telecom
  - health care
  - discount travel
  - consignment stores*

Peak Phase
- Discretionary items such as:
  - new homes
  - household appliances
  - new vehicles
  - luxury items
  - permium travel
  - lifestyle brands*

Trough Phase
- Non-discretionary items or services such as:
  - consumbles
  - food
  - education
  - telecom
  - health care
  - discount travel
  - consignment stores*

Expansion Phase
- Discretionary items such as:
  - new homes
  - household appliances
  - new vehicles
  - luxury items
  - permium travel
  - lifestyle brands*

*And products and services that complement these categories.

The process of tracking the business cycle takes little or no time on your part. If you read the *Globe, Financial Post,* or *Wall Street Journal,* sooner or later you'll come across an article written about it. But if you want to be more proactive and dig a little deeper, there are great Web resources out there that provide quick summaries you can read over a coffee at Tim Hortons. These resources include:

- **Bank of Canada:** Canada's central bank releases a quarterly report in PDF form called the *Monetary Policy Report,* which includes information about inflation, economic growth, and an overall risk assessment of the Canadian economy. See www.bankofcanada.ca/ publications-research/periodicals/mpr/.

- **Statistics Canada:** Publishes large amounts of data daily, including whether your industry is growing or shrinking, at www40.statcan.ca/l01/cst01/gdps04a-eng.htm.
- **National Bureau of Economic Research:** Publishes core information about the U.S. economy. The United States has a huge impact on the Canadian economy because we are its largest trading partner. The bureau tracks the U.S. business cycle and publishes information about it at www.nber.org.

Dragon Lore

Start a business regardless of how the economy is doing.

Another business that has been able to capitalize on the business cycle is Gold Network Canada. Gold is a hedge that investors and savers alike turn to when market uncertainty hits the economy. And when people flock to buy gold, gold prices rise, and then more and more people look to their own internal war chest of unused jewellery and other gold items to find possessions that they are willing to part with. The entrepreneur behind Gold Network Canada visited *Dragons' Den* and showed how a market downturn can be a windfall for both gold-wielding consumers and independent retailers.

Product Snapshot: Gold Network Canada

Pitcher: Tim Wallace, Season 4, Episode 1

Gold-for-cash service that provides equipment and training to retailers who buy and sell gold at their point-of-sale.

HOW IT WORKS

Gold Network Canada supplies all the equipment and the training for existing retail outlets to buy unwanted, surplus gold from their existing customers. The company takes the jewellery or other gold products, refines it, and resells it.

THE ASK

$300,000 for 25%.

THE DEAL

$300,000 for 50% plus 7% preferred return.

KEY FEATURES

- Equipment and training is provided to retailers who collect the gold.
- An electronic tester tells the retailer exactly what carat the gold is.
- A set of scales weighs the gold.
- Retailers receive cash in return.

CORE BENEFITS

- Consumers convert their old jewellery into cash.
- Retailers who collect the gold have a new revenue source for their business.
- The business works in a bad economy when people need cash and gold prices go up.

TESTIMONIAL

"[The entrepreneur's] providing a service. It's not predatory. This is a cash flow business. This generates cash."
    —Dragon to Pitcher

Tim Wallace pitching his franchise idea, Gold Network Canada, a business for the recession.

Self-Study Workshop: The Business Cycle

Describe the stage of the business cycle we are in and how it will impact the demand for your product or service.

1. What **type of industry** are you operating in?
   - ❑ **Cyclical:** My industry-wide sales volume moves up and down with the business cycle. *Examples: Cars, houses, luxury goods.*
   - ❑ **Counter-Cyclical:** My industry-wide sales volume works in the opposite direction of the business cycle. *Example: Gold bars.*
   - ❑ **Independent:** My industry-wide sales volume is not affected by the business cycle. *Examples: Food, medical services, utilities.*

2. What **stage of the business cycle** are we in now?
   - ❑ **Contraction Stage:** Job losses are widespread and consumers are concerned about their economic futures.
   - ❑ **Trough Stage:** The economy is down in the dumps, people are tightening their belts, and there is no end in sight.
   - ❑ **Expansionary Stage:** Employers are hiring, and consumers are excited about their economic future.
   - ❑ **Peak Stage:** The economy is red hot, everybody is making money, and there is no end in sight.

3. How would you **describe** your product or service?
   - ❑ **Discretionary:** Consumers tend to put off buying it as long as possible.
   - ❑ **Non-Discretionary:** Consumers tend to buy it regardless of the economic environment.

4. How does the **current economic environment** impact the sales of your product or service?

5. What will you need to **have in place** when the next stage of the business cycle hits?

Having an understanding of the business cycle is important so that you won't receive false signals from a marketplace that may just be in the middle of a cyclical downturn. For example, if you start a business in a recession, and it fails, you might falsely conclude that you have a bad business idea, when in fact you might just have made a poor timing decision. In the next chapter, we'll move to the next level of a top-down approach to market analysis, by discussing industry analysis and how to research key market drivers.

CHAPTER 20

INDUSTRY ANALYSIS

"It's offensive to me that you would spend this much time working on a product when you've got seven competitors and you've taken no time to figure out how big the market is."

—Dragon to Pitcher

Market Assessment #2: Industry Analysis

Break your industry down into the factors that drive demand. Use these demand drivers to formulate your business strategy. Scan your industry environment on an ongoing basis.

Wayne Gretzky captured nine Hart Trophies, four Stanley Cups, and multiple scoring titles by knowing where the puck was going, not where the puck had been. He followed trends on the ice and used that information to make rapid decisions about where to skate to next, while his competitors often seemed perplexed. In business, you see this sort of thing happen all the time. The photography industry shifted toward digital imaging, while Kodak, the inventor of the technology, sat perplexed and at one point even filed for Chapter 11 bankruptcy protection. The book-buying industry shifted toward online book buying, while Borders bookstores eventually filed for Chapter 11 bankruptcy protection. The fight industry moved toward mixed martial arts and rich storylines, while the boxing world lost market share and is now dealing with a disenchanted audience. In business, industry analysis is the process of continuously monitoring market dynamics and trends to determine where the market is going, not where the market is.

No industry is more dynamic than the technology industry. Just when you start to get comfortable with a useful gadget or software program, someone comes out with a new one that makes you question your loyalty to your current brand. One such gadget, the tried-and-true computer mouse, is seemingly ripe for disruption, a conclusion that will seem obvious to you if you have ever experienced carpal tunnel syndrome. After scanning the industry for a solution to his own carpal tunnel syndrome problem, inventor Mark Bajramovic realized that the industry lacked a mouse that puts little or no strain on a user's hand and wrist. Then he took his idea, the AirMouse, to *Dragons' Den*.

Air Mouse

Pitchers: Mark Bajramovic and Dr. Oren Tessler, Season 4, Episode 14

"I think first and foremost this is a cool mouse, number one, and I think you have to market it as a cool mouse because that's why I would buy it."
—Dragon to Pitchers

PRODUCT DESCRIPTION

A computer mouse that fits like a glove.

THE ASK

$75,000 for 15%.

THE DEAL

$75,000 for 15%.

THE OUTCOME

The Pitchers pulled out a letter of intent from a manufacturer agreeing to produce the device, pending sufficient funding. The investment was to be used to refine the prototype and to move into production. After being on *Dragons' Den*, the Pitchers . . .

- Received thousands of emails from people interested in purchasing the product, including the United Parcel Service and NASA's offices in Langley, Virginia.

- Received letters of interest from several companies offering to mass produce the Air Mouse, including from Microsoft.

Pitcher Mark Bajramovic demonstrating the Air Mouse, which is designed to relieve carpal tunnel syndrome but can also be used in gaming.

THE WARM-UP: INDUSTRY ANALYSIS DEFINED

The economy can be segmented into many different **micro-economies**, each containing a collection of similar businesses. Each segment, called an "industry," reacts uniquely to the business cycle. In other words, your industry could actually be booming while the overall economy is shrinking, and vice versa. Think about how well the consignment industry, coupon advertising industry, and apartment industry work in down economies, and how they might slow down in an up economy. Or how poorly the jewellery or travel industries work during recessions, and how they might pick up in an expansion. The importance of knowing your industry dynamics cannot be overstated. Choose a growing industry and you'll have a tailwind behind you that can propel your business forward. Choose a declining industry and you might find yourself sailing into a headwind, having to fend off competitors using price concessions.

An industry analysis is an in-depth research study to uncover *factors that drive demand* for your type of product or service. The purpose of an industry analysis is to help you make better decisions about who to target, how to compete, and where your industry is going. The process of conducting an industry analysis involves research by you or someone you pay to uncover:

- **Trends:** What trends support your business concept?
- **Growth Rates:** Is your industry growing or shrinking?
- **Market Leaders:** Who are the top three market leaders?
- **Sensitivity to the Business Cycle:** How are industry-wide sales affected by the business cycle and the changing of the seasons?
- **Demand Drivers:** What is the basis for competition in your industry?

Trends: Know Where Your Industry Is Going

Trend analysis involves studying patterns that can help refine your business concept. They come in the form of:

- **Economic Trends:** In what direction is the economy moving?
- **Technology Trends:** What new technologies are being used in your product or service design?
- **Product Design Trends:** What new types of products are being used to solve customer problems?
- **Social Trends:** What type of social behaviour is influencing the industry you operate in?
- **Demographic Trends:** What is happening to the average age, income, and education of the market you are selling to?

Growth Rate: What Is the Compound Annual Growth Rate of Your Industry?

When estimating your sales forecast, it's important to use realistic growth assumptions for your business. One place to start is the growth rate of similar businesses in your industry and the industry itself. These rates can help justify your sales forecasts or forewarn you about an industry in decline. On the one hand, positive growth rates can justify your sales forecasts because a rising tide can raise all boats. On the other hand, slow or declining growth rates could signal a change in the dynamics of the industry itself.

Market Leaders: Understand the Competitive Landscape

The market leader of your industry is the company that sells the highest volume of your type of product, technology, or service. It typically controls market dynamics, such as what price levels can be charged or which features are the basis for competition. Because of its leadership position, it also endures constant attacks from savvy market followers who position themselves as solvers of the problems that the leader ignores.

Market leaders are often stuck in a fixed position, feathering their nest, so they become susceptible to attacks against their biggest weaknesses. For example, the problem with Netflix is that not everyone wants to pay a monthly subscription fee. So Redbox has 28,000 locations where you can rent movies one at a time out of a vending machine, for next to nothing per rental. The problem with Groupon is that it can't get "boots on the ground" fast enough to sign up retailers in every single local market. So new, localized deal-of-the-day websites are popping up daily all over North America. The problem with Harry & David is that its fruit baskets often arrive weeks after you place the order. So direct marketers of fruit baskets could capitalize on this problem by establishing strict delivery guidelines.

By studying market leaders, you can gain information that will help you figure out what's working and what's not in your industry before you commit resources. At the same time, you can study their strategies to figure out how you are going to create a clear contrast between your offering and theirs. Key points to pay attention to are:

- **Competitive Landscape:** Identify the top three players in your industry.
- **Market Share:** Identify how many competitors account for 50% of the industry's revenue. This information can help you determine if your industry is concentrated among a few key players or fragmented across multiple smaller industry participants.
- **Demand Drivers:** Identify the basis for competition in your industry and whether it's cost, product design, service, or some other factor.

Cyclicality: Understand How Your Business Is Affected by the Business Cycle

In some industries, the total industry-wide sales volume follows a trough-to-peak pattern that mirrors the business cycle. Having an understanding of how your industry reacts to different stages of the business cycle will help you develop a strategy for adjusting to downturns in the economy and responding to upturns. For example, if you are opening a real estate business, knowledge about the cyclicality of your industry can help you time your property investments, make more realistic sales forecasts, and improve growth-rate assumptions. If you own a restaurant, you'll know when to ramp up your advertising and use discounts, and when to conserve cash if a downturn is about to happen.

Seasonality: Understand How Your Business Is Affected by Seasonal Changes

Industry-wide sales volume can also vary up and down, based on seasons of the year. For example, some businesses generate more than 50% of their annual sales volume during the Christmas season alone. Other businesses, such as barbeque manufacturers, peak during the spring and summer. Seasonal sales-volume peaks and troughs can help you better match your advertising and sales campaigns with peaks in user demand. Understanding the seasonality of your business can also help you develop a strategy for responding to low points.

Demand Drivers: Isolate the Factors That Drive Demand in Your Industry

Every industry has demand drivers that act as the basis for purchase decisions in your industry. Personal income might be a driver for luxury goods. Monthly payment options might be a driver for at-home fitness equipment. Cutting-edge product design might be a driver for smartphones. Understanding the demand drivers in your industry can help cut down the time wasted on trial and error.

Sources of Information: Where Can I Find the Information to Conduct an Industry Analysis?

You can save years of trouble by researching your industry before you commit major resources. Each industry has a North American Industry Classification System (NAICS) code (formerly known as a SIC code), which you can use to conduct online research (or buy an industry report from a firm that has already researched your market). To get started, look up your industry's code at www.NAICS.com.

Top Three Industry Information Sources

1. **Industry Trade Associations:** The first place to start your research is with your industry's trade association. A trade association is a membership organization that's funded by companies operating in the same line of business. It holds annual conferences, conducts research among members, and publishes data it collects, available for a fee (or free sometimes). You might have to join your industry's association to access its information,

but the few hundred dollars you might pay to join for one year will definitely be worth it. And you might even find that continuing your membership on an annual basis could be good for your business.

2. **Industry Participants:** If you attend an annual conference, you can speak directly with a large number of industry vendors and participants, who are often more than willing to share information. You can also contact your local chamber of commerce, which can provide local data if you are starting a local business.

3. **Google:** The single most powerful source of data on your industry might just be Google. But be sure to cross-reference your data finds so that you know you are dealing with fresh information. The great thing about Google is that you can explore for hours and find all kinds of market information. The problem with Google is that not all of the statistics found are real, relevant, or current. By cross-referencing your data against other sources of information, you'll be able to get a handle on which data you can trust, and which data you should ignore.

Other Sources of Information

- **Statistics Canada:** You can source a boatload of demographic and economic data through www.statcan.gc.ca, or the U.S. Census Bureau online at www.census.gov if you are selling in the United States. This data can be used to support your chosen business location, assess traffic patterns for a retail outlet, and determine future business needs based on the age of the population.

- **Annual Reports:** A rich source of information is the annual reports filed by public companies. These companies are required by law to publish an annual report, which often contains an industry outlook. You can get these reports free by looking online at company websites, visiting databases that publish them (such as www.AnnualReports.com), or by contacting an investment broker. For example, if you are launching a cosmetics product, you could visit AnnualReports.com to review Revlon's annual report, which it is required by the U.S. Securities and Exchange Commission to publish, and glean information about the industry. If you are launching a chocolate company, you could review the Hershey Company's annual report and learn about the market dynamics of its business.

- **Industry Research Firms:** FirstResearch.com (run by Hoovers.com), IBISWorld.com, MarketResearch.com, and Bizminer.com can provide you with industry descriptions of just about any industry. These fee-based services provide high-level reviews of industries, so you'll have to dig down deep elsewhere if you want specific market-segment data and success factors. The cost per industry report can range from just over a hundred dollars to several thousand.

> ### Dragon Lore
>
> Uncover factors that drive demand for your type of product or service by researching your industry.

When you study the dynamics of an industry, you can uncover unique business opportunities. For example, before Q Water visited *Dragons' Den*, their research determined that restaurants lose money every time someone asks for a glass of free tap water. That's because glasses need to be washed and washing costs money. So they created an entire business model around helping businesses charge money for what would otherwise be free tap water.

Product Snapshot: Q Water

Pitchers: Paula Tekela and Stephen Beaumont, Season 5, Episode 9

Still and sparkling water filtration systems for homes, businesses, restaurants, and cottages.

HOW IT WORKS

The company installs a water filtration system in restaurants that dispenses still and sparkling water. The system is sold or rented to the establishments for a monthly fee. The restaurant then sells the filtered water to its patrons as Q Water. The revenue generated from the sale of filtered tap water more than covers the cost of washing its water glasses and it adds profit to the bottom line.

THE ASK

$250,000 for 33%.

THE DEAL

$250,000 for 50%.

KEY FEATURES

- Premium filtered water.
- Can be sold by the glass in restaurants.

CORE BENEFITS

- Eliminates the need for bottled water, the transporting of bottles, the recycling of bottles, and the inventorying of bottles.
- Profit margins for the participating restaurants are high.
- Water tastes great.

TESTIMONIAL

"What I love about this is all you've done is just taken something and looked at it from a different angle and created a whole new market opportunity. It's really smart."
  —Dragon to Pitcher

Paula Tekela and Stephen Beaumont, owners of Q Water, pitching their product to the Dragons.

Self-Study Workshop: Industry Analysis

Research your industry for the factors that drive demand.

1. What **industry** do you operate in?

2. What is your **NAICS code**? (Look it up at www.naics.com.)

3. What is the total **industry-wide sales volume** for your industry? What is the growth rate of your industry? Is it growing or shrinking?

4. Is your industry **concentrated or fragmented**?
   - ❑ **Concentrated:** A small number of firms account for 50% of total industry-wide sales volume.
   - ❑ **Fragmented:** Many firms participate in the industry and no company dominates it.

5. What **product or service lines** are sold in your industry?

6. What **trends** in your industry are currently driving demand? (Name them.)
   - ❑ Product/service design trend
   - ❑ Technology trend
   - ❑ Social trend
   - ❑ Regulatory trend
   - ❑ Other trend

7. What overriding **business-centric factor** drives demand in your industry?
   - ❑ Unique product design
   - ❑ Low price
   - ❑ Marketing
   - ❑ Support service
   - ❑ Distribution
   - ❑ Other

8. What overriding **customer-centric factor** drives demand in your industry?
   - ❑ Age
   - ❑ Income
   - ❑ Net worth
   - ❑ Education

- ❑ Occupation
- ❑ Geographic location
- ❑ Other

9. Do businesses in your industry typically have **one product or deep product or service lines?**
   - ❑ Single products
   - ❑ Deep product lines

10. How does your industry **react** to the business cycle? Pick the one that best reflects your industry, and then add a note or two to explain why your industry responds to the business cycle in that way.
    - ❑ **Cyclical:** Industry sales volume goes up and down with the business cycle.
    - ❑ **Counter-cyclical:** Industry sales volume goes up when the economy is down and vice versa.
    - ❑ The business cycle is not a factor in my business.

11. During what **season** is your sales volume the highest? Pick one that best reflects your sales volume and then add a note or two to explain why your sales volume responds so well to that season.
    - ❑ Winter
    - ❑ Spring
    - ❑ Summer
    - ❑ Fall
    - ❑ Season is not a factor

12. What are the **regulatory requirements** of your industry?

13. How do businesses **market themselves** in your industry?

14. What are the **barriers to entry?**
    - ❑ Regulations
    - ❑ Start-up requirements
    - ❑ Other

An industry analysis helps to define the mechanics of the marketplace you will be operating in, so that you take them into account when you make strategy decisions. In the next chapter you'll uncover the true basis for competition in your industry so that you can carve your niche with a sustainable competitive advantage.

CHAPTER 21

THE COMPETITIVE LANDSCAPE

"You can't justify the sales forecast. You have no revenue. Just because you have a better mousetrap, what do you think . . . the world's going to beat a path to your door?"
  —Dragon to Pitcher

> **Market Assessment #3: The Competitive Landscape**
>
> Determine the basis for competition in your industry. Decide whether to play the current game or to change the game itself.

One of the biggest factors that will drive demand for your product or service is the basis for competition in your industry. The basis for competition is called the "game," and that game might be cost, value, product design, service, distribution agreements, or some other factor that businesses use to compete against each other. Become better at playing the current game than your competitors, and you might take a large chunk of the market. Become a *game changer* through value or pricing innovation, and you put yourself in a position to rattle the competition. Think about how rattled the makers of Quicken became when Mint.com starting offering a better solution for free. Or how Kodak reacted when competitors started popping up with digital cameras that no longer required photographic film—an innovation invented by Kodak. Or how Apple's iPad team responded when Amazon.com launched the $199 Kindle Fire. If you want scalable growth, study the competitive landscape and then carve out a competitive position that changes the way the game is played.

If you determine, after studying the competitive landscape, that you're surrounded by deep competition, that's not necessarily the end of the road. For example, if you're thinking of marketing a new hand tool, a short visit to Home Depot might make you think otherwise. The market is heavily saturated with competition and most tools have already been invented. But if you dig a little deeper, like the inventor of the kelvin.23 did, you'll see that there is always room for a new innovation if you can make it cooler or more functional than current offerings on the market.

kelvin.23

Pitcher: Kevin Royes, Season 5, Episode 3

> "Sales have exploded. We've been doing home shows across Canada, Canadian Tire, we're talking with Home Depot. We expect we're going to be five times up in sales over last year."
> —Pitcher to Dragons

PRODUCT DESCRIPTION

Multi-purpose home improvement tool for the light- to medium-duty job—it's the Swiss Army knife of home-improvement tools.

THE ASK

$200,000 for 10%.

THE DEAL

$500,000 for 25%.

THE OUTCOME

After being on *Dragons' Den* . . .

- The original deal derailed in due diligence.
- A new Dragon stepped up with $400,000—double the original ask.
- Product sold on The Shopping Channel.

In his first appearance in the Den (Season 4, Episode 12), Kevin Royes uses his kelvin.23 to hang a picture for the Dragons and special guest Debbie Travis.

THE WARM-UP: THE COMPETITIVE LANDSCAPE DEFINED

The competitive landscape consists of all the businesses and other factors that are competing for your customers' money and attention. The purpose of competitive analysis is to figure out how to position your business against your competitors' weaknesses, just like a giant game of Rock, Paper, Scissors. If you strategize correctly, you'll effectively turn your competition into a backdrop against which your offering will stand out. A competitive analysis involves research into your:

- Sources of competition
- Competitor SWOTs (strengths, weaknesses, opportunities, and threats)
- Competitor strategies
- Competitor advantages

Sources of Competition

Any number of entities are competing for the wallets of your customers on a daily basis. Soy milk competes with dairy milk, chocolate bars compete with fruit, planes compete with trains. Competition is everywhere. There may be brand-name competitors; other forms of the same service or product that you sell; or other ways to solve the same problem your product, technology, or service solves. Or maybe it's that potential customers have other budgetary priorities and so are forgoing buying from you right now. Keep in mind that if potential customers are not buying from you, they may not be buying from anyone else either—they might be solving the problem themselves.

With so many forms of competition, it's important to stay focused on executing and controlling your own game plan, and not reacting to someone else's. That's why the majority of your business concept development efforts should be spent honing your value proposition. The two general categories of competition are:

- **Direct Competition:** Most people understand direct competition because it is the most obvious. These are other producers or providers of the same products and services that you sell. They can be a rich source of information, especially with the Internet—many of their strategies can be gleaned from websites or online interviews with their owners. Or you can learn about them just by buying their products and analyzing them yourself.
- **Indirect Competition:** A less obvious source of competition is other types of products, technologies, or services that are capable of satisfying the same needs as yours. A laptop Internet connection competes with a cellphone Internet connection. Home cooking competes with that of a restaurant. Online news competes with newspapers. Financial magazines compete with financial advisors. Indirect competition can help you refine your value proposition because it can uncover the weaknesses in your business concept.

Competitor SWOTs

Once you have made a list of all possible direct and indirect competitors, the next step is to jot down the strengths, weaknesses, opportunities, and known threats to each. You can't compete with Revlon head-on when you first start your business because you won't have the marketing dollars or brand power behind you. But you can compete against its weaknesses, such as its lack of desire to serve certain markets or to sell through in-home marketing parties.

Gauging your competition means you'll be better equipped to understand their limitations and pressure points. You'll also know who not to get into a price war with, who has the resources to out-innovate you, how to position your products and services against their weaknesses, and what their capabilities and limitations are.

Competitor Strategy

A simple way to understand your competitors' strategies is by visiting their stores, buying their products, using their services, or talking to their customers. Of course, this is not always possible and may not be ethical in your specific industry. But in order to compete in any market space, you need to know your competitors' strategies so that you can figure out your own. Here's what you should be looking for:

- **Feature Highlights:** What product or service features are proprietary, and which ones stand out?
- **Price Range:** What are your competitors' price ranges, and what type of discount strategies do they follow? Do they offer weekly discounts, as grocery stores do, or month-long discounts, as the department store J.C. Penney does? Are their price discounts offered at certain times of the year, or do they have a no-discount policy? Are their price levels in line with industry standards?
- **Distribution Strategies:** Where are their products and services available for sale? Do they use intermediaries and agents, or do they sell direct?
- **Marketing Matters:** How do they market themselves, and what are their unique selling points? What types of marketing materials do they put out there, and what kind of messages do they use?

Competitive Advantage

A competitive advantage is a double-edged sword. On the one hand, it can keep copycats at bay. On the other hand, it leaves the market leader open to attack by feature-driven innovative entrepreneurs. Here is how it works: Businesses that dominate their market spaces usually commit to a singular direction that is based on a hard-to-replicate competitive advantage. But on any given day, they are open to attack. Walmart commits to everyday low prices, while Target attacks it daily with a more upscale, service-oriented environment. Starbucks commits to a variety of blended coffees, while Tim Hortons attacks it daily with coffee that everyone can afford. Coca-Cola commits to great-tasting cola, while Red Bull Cola attacks it daily with more caffeine per millilitre in each can. Market leaders can be beaten on any given day if you see the competitive landscape as a giant game of Rock, Paper, Scissors:

- **Feature Advantage (Rock):** Innovative features can beat low-price competitors by appealing to feature-driven consumers who just want the best product, no matter how much it costs.
- **Service Advantages (Paper):** Support services can beat innovative-feature advantages by appealing to consumers who place more value on outside assistance than they do on the product itself.
- **Price Advantage (Scissors):** Low-price competitors can beat service-driven competitors by appealing to price-conscious consumers who don't care about service but just want the lowest price.

Of course, these examples can be picked apart if you look at them closely, but they do illustrate that customers, not businesses, own the competitive landscape. And once you realize that, you are free to out-innovate any current market leader using a feature-, price-, or service-driven strategy.

Dragon Lore

Research your competitive landscape to uncover the basis for competition in your industry.

Another industry you might choose not to compete in, after a little research, is the tea industry. The market is saturated with competition because the tea market has been around for centuries. But the key to competing effectively is to see your competition as the forest, not the trees. In other words, lump all your competition together and then figure out a way to change the basis of competition. For example, Domo Tea could have chosen to go to market with another bagged tea format for their organic teas, but instead they chose to launch their tea in an instant, tea-powder format. A simple strategy decision, tea powder instead of tea bags, enables them to capture a niche market looking for an instant-tea formula that doesn't take time to steep.

Product Snapshot: Domo Tea

Pitchers: Anne Yeo and Tammy Olssen, Season 5, Episode 5

Authentic organic green, rooibos, and chai teas enhanced with all-natural flavours, sold as instant tea powder.

HOW IT WORKS

A collection of instant tea powders sold through retailers. A new entrant in a very crowded, competitive market.

THE ASK

$50,000 for 20%.

THE DEAL

$50,000 for 50%.

KEY FEATURES

- Tea comes in powder form.
- Instant-tea format.
- All the nutrients are contained in tea leaves, and Domo Tea retains those nutrients.

CORE BENEFITS

- It's an immune-boosting, feel-better tea when you have a cold coming on or when you're feeling hungover.
- Powder form means it's easy to make.
- Appeals to health-conscious consumers.

TESTIMONIAL

> "I'm crying. This is good stuff. I like it. It's the cayenne in there."
> —Dragon to Pitcher

Anne Yeo and Tammy Olssen presenting their Domo Tea products to the Dragons.

Self-Study Workshop: The Competitive Landscape

Research your competition to figure out how to compete against them.

1. What is the **basis for competition** in your industry?
   - ❏ Price
   - ❏ Product design
   - ❏ Service
   - ❏ Distribution
   - ❏ Branding
   - ❏ Other

2. Who are your **direct and indirect competitors**?
   - ❏ Similar offerings (e.g., Tim Hortons vs. Dunkin Donuts)
   - ❏ Form competitors (e.g., bikes vs. cars)
   - ❏ Priorities (e.g., work vs. play)

3. For each of your main competitors, identify their **strengths, weaknesses, opportunities, and threats**.
   - ❏ **Strengths:** On what basis does this competitor compete?
     Examples: Product advantage, service, price, brand awareness.

❑ **Weaknesses:** What are its weaknesses?

Examples: Product voids, markets neglected.

❑ **Opportunities:** What market opportunities does this competitor currently have available?

Examples: New strategic partnerships, shelf space at a major retailer.

❑ **Threats:** What challenges is this competitor currently facing?

Examples: Sudden market shift, financial pressures, outdated product line.

4. What is your **competitive advantage** vis-à-vis your direct or indirect competitors?

❑ Cost

❑ Value

❑ Product design features

❑ Service

❑ Distribution agreements

At this point of your market analysis, you should have a clear picture of the business cycle in which you are operating, the demand drivers of your industry, and the competitive landscape you are trying to compete in. In the next chapter you'll build a clear definition of your target customers so that you can find and communicate with them more effectively.

CHAPTER 22

TARGET MARKET ANALYSIS

"Until you prove revenue, until you get someone to actually believe and cut you a cheque, you're worth nothing."
—Dragon to Pitcher

Market Assessment #4: Target Market Analysis

Define your target market. Refine your product or service to appeal to their motives. Look for new markets along the way.

Every year we hear countless stories of real problem-solving businesses like restaurants, retail outlets, and highly functional inventions that never quite got off the ground. Yet we live in a world where seemingly crazy ideas like the Chia Pet, Pet Rock, Sea-Monkeys, and Star Trek conventions achieved enormous success by *finding a market*. The difference lies in target marketing. It doesn't matter how useful or seemingly useless your business idea seems—if you can find a paying customer, you have the basis for a growing business. However, if you fail to define your target customers in a way that allows you to locate them, appeal to them, and profit from them, your business will shut down. Once you define those customers, don't become too attached, because serendipity might lead you to an even bigger market. Just like when you're hunting for your lost keys, you find 10 things you weren't looking for along the way. So be sure to keep your eyes and ears open while searching for your ideal customer, because you might just uncover a much bigger market opportunity.

When you start the process of defining your ideal target customer, your gut instinct might tell you to use a broad definition that includes as many customers as possible. But that type of logic will require that you water down your offering with as few customizations as possible because you won't want to alienate anyone. And the customers who do buy from you won't be as satisfied as they could have been, because you won't have added the deep feature customizations that would have made them happy. When the founders of Anivac visited *Dragons' Den*, they showed that narrowing their focus on the horse-only market might just be a sound business strategy for everyone.

Anivac

Pitcher: David Hachey, Season 2, Episode 4

"You better know your business. You better know your numbers. You better know the market. And be able to speak on it well."
—Pitcher to Dragons

PRODUCT DESCRIPTION

A vacuum bathing system for horses.

THE ASK

$150,000 for 20% equity.

THE DEAL

$0.

THE OUTCOME

After being on *Dragons' Den,* Pitcher David Hachey . . .

- Stuck to the target horse market segment and didn't venture into the bigger pet market segment, as suggested by the Dragon.
- Scored $150,000 from another investor.
- Secured funding and a distribution agreement in 36 countries.
- Is on track for $500,000 in revenue.

David Hachey about to demonstrate Anivac, a cleaning system for horses, on his dog, Bailey.

THE WARM-UP: TARGET MARKET ANALYSIS DEFINED

Target market analysis is not an exact science because data is not always neatly packaged in the format that you need it in. What matters most is that your research uncovers where your most profitable customers can be found, so that you can reach them and serve them profitably. For example, the market for restaurant food in Canada is $60 billion; Chipotle targets the $20.4-billion quick-service market segment of that larger market.[1] The fitness industry in Canada may be $2.2 billion in size,[2] but you might target only the home-equipment segment with your new home-equipment gadget. The process of defining your target market involves:

- **Market Segmentation:** Segment your overall market into homogeneous clusters of similar customers.
- **Market Size Analysis:** Put a dollar value on the size of each market segment.
- **Market Dynamics:** Describe what drives demand in your industry and the basis for competition.
- **Market Needs Analysis:** Identify the singular pain point in each market segment.
- **Target Market Definition:** Separate your target customers into primary, secondary, and tertiary market segments.

Market Segmentation

A market is a group of people who have the same need or problem. A **market segment,** on the other hand, is a cluster of people within that group that might choose your type of product or service to solve that problem. For example, we all have a need for fitness because we all need exercise to stay healthy. But that need can be solved by any number of fitness solutions. Some people solve their fitness problem with running, others with a technical sport like tennis, and still others with an exercise program such as step aerobics. Whichever market segment you choose to target, you will need to research where that segment shops, how it prefers the delivery of a product or service, and what print and online publications it reads—all of which will inform you as to how you're going to reach that segment.

Definable Market Segments

If you have not completed an industry analysis, go back to Chapter 20 and complete one now. The results of your industry analysis should give you a general breakdown of how your market is segmented. You can use this general breakdown to further define your ideal market segments by:

- **Geographic Profile (Where They Are):** If your ideal customers were dots on a map, where would you find clusters of them? Identify where they live, work, network, and socialize.
- **Demographic Profile (Who They Are):** If you were describing your ideal customers to a stranger, what demographic traits would you use to describe them? Is there an average age, income, education level, household size, or occupation of your ideal customer, or a certain gender? Demographic information is readily available through Statistics Canada, so deciding on a profile in advance can help you find typical customers.
- **Psychographic Profile (How They Are):** If you were describing your ideal customers to a stranger, what personality traits would they have? Are they aggressive, optimistic, cynical, or recognizable by some other personality trait?
- **Behavioural Profile (What They Do):** If you were describing your ideal customers by their habits, what type of work, sports, or hobbies would they have?

Market Dynamics

After completing your industry analysis, you should have a clearer picture of what drives demand in your industry, what is the basis for competition, and where the growth opportunities lie. One way to categorize these growth opportunities is by using a simple tool known as Ansoff's growth matrix to break down your growth opportunities into goals you can aim for. The four components of Ansoff's growth matrix are:

- Sell more of your current products to current markets.
- Sell current products to new markets.
- Sell new products to current markets.
- Sell new products to new markets.

Market Needs Analysis

One critical goal of target market analysis is to uncover the events that lead a customer to make a call, visit, or a decision to make a purchase from you. If you understand what triggers a purchase, you can put your product or service in the right place at the right time with a marketing campaign that appeals to that customer's underlying buying motives. These motives can be broken down into consumer motives and business-to-business motives (B2B):

Consumer Market Motives
- The customers' **rational** buying motives. (***Example:*** *I need a coffee to help me wake up.*)
- The **function** your product or service performs. (***Example:*** *I need a coffee maker to make coffee.*)
- The **unique application** the customer may have for your product or service. (***Example:*** *I need a coffee maker to filter tea leaves.*)
- The **practical appeal** of your product or service. (***Example:*** *I need a coffee maker to keep me from paying for coffee at Tim Hortons.*)
- How your product or service appeals to your customer's **emotions**. (***Example:*** *I need a coffee maker that looks good in my kitchen.*)
- The **social benefits** that your product or service offers. (***Example:*** *I need a coffee maker that doesn't use filters that harm the environment.*)

Business Market Motives
- Cut costs by X%.
- Reduce inventory by X%.
- Increase productivity by X%.
- Increase revenue by X%.
- Improve profit margins by X%.
- Improve [_____] by X%.

Target Market Definition

Scalable-growth companies grow quickly by having a clearly defined customer. A clearly defined customer is the basis for a highly efficient marketing campaign; a highly customized product or service; and a highly efficient, repeatable business process. Dell Computers achieved astonishing growth in the second full year of business by targeting direct-mail buyers with low-cost, customizable PCs. Five Guys burgers and fries grew from one location in Virginia to more than 600 locations across North America by targeting fast-casual-category customers with a simple menu of fries, drinks, and customizable burgers. Tapout grew from being a T-shirt vendor selling out of the back of a car to a company with more than $200 million in revenue by targeting mixed martial arts fans at mixed martial arts sporting events across North America.

Of course, the last thing you want to do is say no to somebody who is willing to pay you for your product or service when you are just starting out and need the cash. But being decisive early on about who you can serve most profitably will help you become a magnet for customers. You'll be able to improve your:

- **Product/Service Focus:** You can customize your product or service around the needs of one customer type.
- **Operational Efficiency:** You can systemize your business around the needs of one customer type.
- **Marketing Efficiency:** You can build marketing programs around the needs of one customer type.

Keeping an open mind is a critical part of target marketing success. While your primary target market is your Plan A, always have a secondary market (Plan B) and tertiary market (Plan C) waiting in the wings in case things don't work out. As a starting point for defining who your most profitable customers might be, here are two simple templates that you can modify to fit your needs:

Template #1: The Consumer Market

People who *[live/work/travel to/can be found]* in *[neighbourhood/city/county/region/ province or state/nation/other]* who are *[describe quantifiable variables such as age, income, education level, household size, occupation, or gender]* and whose lifestyles include *[describe using relevant lifestyle variables such as clothing choices, entertainment choices, family situation, food habits, hobbies, home choice, leisure habits, social habits, sports, vacation habits, or work habits].*

Template #2: The Business Market

[State/name the job title/presidents/vice-presidents/marketers/managers/other decision makers] of *[businesses/resellers/governments/institutions/industrial users/other]* in *[neighbourhood/city/county/region/province or state/nation/other]* that have *[average sales volume/product type/number of employees/number of years in business/other].*

Dragon Lore

Don't be afraid to narrow your target market definition in a way that seems to alienate some types of customers. You'll allow yourself the freedom to add features that meet the needs of a specific group of customers.

Another company that visited *Dragons' Den*, a company that clearly understands the power of target marketing, is Barrier 2 Go. By specifically targeting the mining industry, the company is able to add deep customizations to its offering which leads to a deeper level of satisfaction for their mining industry customers. And their target market definition also allows them to focus their marketing resources on one single market instead of spreading it thinly over multiple markets.

Product Snapshot: Barrier 2 Go

Pitchers: Guy and Janelle Courchesne and David Lalancette, Season 6, Episode 15

Safety signs for the mining industry.

HOW IT WORKS

The Pitchers developed a simple yet effective signage system for the mining industry to indicate danger areas. The signs come in a bag to make them portable, with ropes that are adjustable to the size of the area of danger, as well as alternative notations that set out the specific danger. This makes the situation much more visible for the next worker and reduces risk. It's a very particular product to meet specific needs in a clearly defined market segment.

THE ASK

$275,000 for 15%.

THE DEAL

$275,000 for 25%.

KEY FEATURES

- A kit that is carried in a portable bag.
- Contains signs, rope, fasteners, and tape.
- Slogans are interchangeable.
- Simple system that is adjustable to surround the area that needs to be demarcated.
- Portable in an easy-to-carry bag.

CORE BENEFITS

- Clear signage saves lives.
- Improves safety in mines.
- Clarity in terms of identifying the nature of the risk.

TESTIMONIAL

"I very much respect what you have built. You should be very proud."
—Dragon to Pitcher

The perils of not using Barrier 2 Go are demonstrated to the Dragons.

Self-Study Workshop: Target Market Analysis

Define your target market in a way that makes them easy to find. Then narrow that definition as much as possible until you have identified one group of customers with a common set of needs.

MARKET DYNAMICS

1. What **drives demand** in your industry?
2. What is the **basis for competition** in your industry?
3. **How often** will your ideal customers buy from you?
   - ❑ One time
   - ❑ Several times
   - ❑ Other

4. Is your product or service a **must-have** item or a **discretionary** purchase?
   - ❑ Discretionary
   - ❑ Non-discretionary

5. What are the common **behavioural traits** of your ideal customers?
   - ❑ Association memberships
   - ❑ Club memberships
   - ❑ Events attended
   - ❑ Group memberships
   - ❑ Hobbies
   - ❑ Magazines read
   - ❑ Newspapers read
   - ❑ Network memberships
   - ❑ Online stores visited
   - ❑ Retail stores visited
   - ❑ Social media used
   - ❑ Sports played
   - ❑ Other

6. What **type of marketing** do your ideal customers respond to?

MARKET NEEDS

1. What **functional motives** drive purchase decisions in your product or service category?
   Example: Our service provides an electrical fence that protects your house while you sleep.

2. What **rational motives** drive purchase decisions in your product or service category?
   Example: Our product saves you $75 a month in security service costs.

3. What **emotional (and social) motives** drive purchase decisions in your product or service category?
   Example: Our product gives you the peace of mind that your family is protected while you sleep.

TARGET MARKET DEFINITION

1. Demographic Profile
   Age/income/education level/ household size/occupation/gender

2. Geographic Profile
   Neighbourhood/city/county/region/province or state/nation/other

3. Psychographic Profile
   Interests/attitudes/lifestyle

4. Behavioural Profile
   Associations/memberships/purchase habits

5. Link the four profile descriptions into a single statement

---

A market assessment helps to give you a clear understanding of the market landscape in which you are operating and a clear definition of who you are selling to. The next part of this book, Part V: Go-to-Market Strategy, is where the rubber meets the road. In this final section you'll establish a launch strategy for your business by taking action in four key areas.

PART V

GO-TO-MARKET STRATEGY

Launch your business now by taking action in four key areas: select traditional channels, build strategic relationships, launch a marketing program, and implement a sales process. Then track your market, technical, and financial results to prove that your business concept works.

CHAPTER 23

HOW DO YOU PLAN TO LAUNCH YOUR BUSINESS?

"It looks like you made the right move. You've gone away, you've proven the model. It was the right move."
    —Dragon to Pitcher

Creating a Go-to-Market Strategy

Build a go-to-market strategy. Complete a limited market pilot test. Validate your business concept by gathering market, technical, and financial proof. Create a full-scale business plan based on your initial success.

It's 1945 and the Second World War is ending. Three enterprising entrepreneurs, Harold Mattson and Elliot and Ruth Handler, decide that the world needs more picture-frame products. So they combine their names and start producing and marketing them *out of their garage*. Little did they know that their **go-to-market strategy** would seed the world's largest toy company, Mattel, Inc. Soon they would repurpose their picture-frame scraps into dollhouse furniture for kids, launching what would become a toy empire.[1]

Nineteen years later, it's 1964, just months before the Summer Olympics in Tokyo. Phil Knight finds a need for high-quality running shoes and establishes a partnership with track coach Bill Bowerman. They team up to distribute and sell Tiger brand running shoes. But they need a go-to-market strategy. So Knight starts selling the first 300 pairs of shoes *out of the back of his car* at any track meet he can get to.[2] Soon after, they develop their own shoe products, planting the seed for what would become Nike, Inc.

Fast-forward to the year 2000. The world is recovering from massive preparation for a Y2K computer disaster that never happened. Budding entrepreneur Sara Blakely launches what will become an undergarment empire after deciding to cut off the legs of a pair of pantyhose and turning them into her first prototype for Spanx—a line of body-shaping undergarments. After approaching several manufacturers in North Carolina, she finally persuades one to manufacture her product. With product in hand, she launches her go-to-market strategy by contacting buyers at department stores *by telephone.* After a convincing demo in the ladies' room, she lands shelf space at Neiman Marcus.[3] Today she finds herself on the latest world list of billionaires put out by *Forbes* magazine.

All three of these success stories highlight the fact that getting your concept off the ground, no matter what go-to-market strategy works for you, is the key to long-term success. Most entrepreneurs who visit *Dragons' Den* figure this out pretty quickly, because they end up having to discuss their go-to-market strategy with the Dragons, as was the case when the founder of Tail Wags Helmet Covers visited *Dragons' Den.*

Go-to-Market Snapshot: Tail Wags Helmet Covers

Pitcher: Karyn Climans, Season 6, Episode 12

GO-TO-MARKET

Tail Wags Helmet Covers, which previously entered the Dragons' Den in Season 4, make it fun for kids to wear their safety helmets. The Pitcher's go-to-market strategy is focused on selling at trade shows and through boutique stores.

THE ASK

$100,000 for 20% equity on her second visit to the Den.

COMPANY VALUATION

$500,000.

THE DEAL

$100,000 for 30% equity plus 5% royalty on sales.

PROOF-OF-CONCEPT

- Interest from Canadian Tire for 10,000 units in the fall.*
- One of the Dragons is a customer.

*As of show participation on Season 6, Episode 12.

TESTIMONIAL

> "The entire ordering experience from her was fantastic. The stuff arrived on time. It was very high quality."
> —Dragon to Pitcher

Karyn Climans revisiting the Dragons' Den, explaining what's changed since she first entered the Den in Season 4, Episode 14.

THE WARM-UP: GO-TO-MARKET DEFINED

A go-to-market strategy is a set of actions you need to take in four key areas to launch your business and monetize your concept. These four areas are distribution channels, strategic relationships, marketing programs, and sales process. A go-to-market strategy is not an in-depth marketing plan—that will come later, once you have proof that your business model works. The companion guide to this book, *The Dragons' Den Guide to Investor-Ready Business Plans,* will help you create such a plan. For your purpose now of assessing your business concept and its market, you need a *market entry* strategy, not a costly marketing plan. Consider a go-to-market strategy to be a mini-marketing plan designed to help you gain a foothold for your new product or service before you risk valuable resources on a full-scale plan that may or may not work. The purpose of a go-to-market strategy is to generate initial sales volume, called "market traction."

The go-to-market process involves:

- **Market Entry Strategy:** Intensity and channel conflict.
- **Market Entry Channels:** Traditional channels vs. strategic relationships.
- **Market Entry Programs:** Sales push vs. marketing pull.

Market Entry Strategy: Intensity and Channel Conflict

Intensity refers to the number of direct and indirect channels that you use to market your products and services. Each participant in the channel that helps you sell your product or service, such as a retail outlet or distributor, is called a channel partner. Use too few outlets and your sales may trickle in over time, leaving your business starved for cash. Use too many outlets and your channel partners may start competing against each other on price. Use outlets that don't reflect your brand (such as selling jewellery at a convenience store) and you may do more damage than good to your brand image. Ideally, most businesses should follow a *selective* strategy, unless there is an unbeatable deal on the table with guaranteed non-refundable cash up front. The remainder of this book discusses how to map out the channels that will work for you. Once you make a decision, make sure that you minimize any conflict among your channel partners. For example, if you sign an agreement with a distributor, you should have internal pricing rules in place so that you don't end up undercutting the distributor on your website.

Don't saturate a geographic territory by being available in too many outlets there. And if you sell a premium product or service, it shouldn't start showing up in lower-quality outlets such as dollar stores.

Intensive	Selective	Exclusive
Selling through as many outlets as possible, including directly by phone, mail order, or website; through distributors and retailers; and through channel partners, with complete disregard for channel conflict. Works with ultra-short sales cycle *commodity* products and services that won't be harmed by the image of the sales outlet—for instance, industrial supplies and consumable products.	Selling through a select few outlets that reflect your brand, such as boutique stores, regional outlets, or national retailers. In exchange for limiting distribution to a select few, your intermediaries should agree to some sort of minimum price and volume guarantees. Works well for *most* products and services that people shop for over time, such as clothing, gadgets, and sports equipment.	Sign exclusive relationships in each geographic territory. Works well with *premium* products and services that people spend time shopping for and where serious harm to the brand's image might occur if the channel or outlet doesn't reflect the brand. Helps to appease an outlet that can give you broad market exposure while enhancing your brand image by creating a feeling of scarcity.

Market Entry Channels: Direct vs. Indirect Market Entry Points

If you want to avoid the hassle of trying to find intermediaries to help you distribute, market, and sell your products or services, you can put out a shingle tomorrow and start hawking your wares instantly. This **direct path** to the customer may involve mail order, teleselling, a website, a sales force, or opening up your own retail outlet if you can find a cost-effective location. But don't be fooled into thinking that this is the fastest path to the market. Since you're bypassing all intermediaries, you won't benefit from the established ecosystem that a relevant intermediary may already have in place. You won't benefit from its marketing and sales expertise. And you won't be able to reach remote markets as easily as an established intermediary will be able to. Consider a direct channel strategy if you have a high-priced product or service, are a first mover with something unique that can get a lot of press, or if you are just trying to get some traction in the market and are willing to do the legwork required for direct sales.

However, if you're willing to do a little more up-front work, give up a piece of the per unit pie, and possibly save more time in the long run, you can seek out relationships with channel partners who already have access to your ideal customers. In exchange, you'll have to pitch a clear revenue opportunity for them, complete with an acceptable profit margin. These **intermediaries** include agents, distributors, and retailers. Getting connected to your customers through the links of an already-established channel can lead to a constant stream of business for you. So it is well worth the effort if you have a compelling revenue opportunity that a willing channel partner will be attracted to. Indirect selling works best for low-priced items that are sold in small quantities, though it can work for high priced items, too. When contacting intermediaries, make sure you know your numbers (discussed in chapters 13 and 18) and be sure to mention any relationships you have already established, the rationale for your choices, and any profit potential involved.

The various channel options that you will read about in the upcoming chapters are:

Traditional Channels	Strategic Relationships
• Mail order	• Private labelling
• Teleselling	• Co-branding
• Website	• Licensing
• Sales force	• Franchising
• Agents	• Joint venture
• Distributors	• Bundling
• Retailers	

Dragon Lore

One of the most common questions that entrepreneurs get asked by investors is "What's your go-to-market strategy?" Be prepared to answer that question without hesitation if you ever seek capital from an investor.

When it comes to entering a market with a sound go-to-market strategy, sometimes the outlet you sell through becomes the product itself. That is the case for Woofstock, a festival for dogs that is held at various venues throughout Canada. It took them two visits to the Den to actually secure investor capital but two times was the charm.

Go-to-Market: Woofstock

Pitchers: Marlene Cook and partner Jamie, Season 6, Episode 12

THE BUSINESS

Woofstock is a festival for dogs.

GO-TO-MARKET

Its go-to-market strategy is focused on securing venues to hold summer and winter festivals for dogs, and deriving revenue from sponsors and event participants who want to reach the attendees.

SALES PITCH

"The idea of the show is a show that you can bring your dog [to]. We're back because we did what we said we were going to do without the Dragons."

TESTIMONIAL

"You're going for the big times here. And I think that's cool. I've seen how crazy dog people can be. I'm very simple to understand. I love dogs, but I love money more."
—Dragon to Pitchers

PROOF-OF-CONCEPT

- $500,000 from a summer show and a winter show.
- $150,000 profit after personal salaries.
- Summer show doubled the sponsorships.
- Have been approached about doing shows in Chicago, New York City, and Miami.

THE ASK

$200,000 for 30%.

THE DEAL

$200,000 for a 50% stake.

Marlene Cook and partner Jamie revisiting the Dragons' Den, explaining the success they've had since they first entered the Den back in Season 4, Episode 9.

Market Entry Programs: Push vs. Pull

If you are trying to convince intermediaries to work with you, you can use either a push or a pull strategy. Sales "push" means contacting an intermediary directly and selling your product or service as a revenue opportunity for them. Marketing "pull" means advertising or publicizing to the end user of your product or service, to create so much public awareness that the end user starts requesting your product or service through intermediaries (who in turn contact you). If you think this doesn't happen, think again. Most infomercial products that end up at big box retailers like Walmart are there because people get so used to seeing them on TV that they start requesting them. Many fashion lines are launched when the budding designers convince celebrities to wear their fashion lines. Independent single-store retailers use requests as a way to shop for new inventory. You can replicate this method locally yourself by asking for free media coverage in the local newspaper or TV news.

Marketing Pull	Sales Push
Drawing attention to your product or service through advertising, publicity, word-of-mouth marketing, or viral marketing campaigns so that consumers start requesting your product or service at retail outlets or retail buyers start requesting your products from distributors.	Picking up the phone and calling potential intermediaries such as distributors or national, regional, and local retailers to persuade them to carry your product or service line.

Self-Study Workshop: Go-to-Market Strategy

Look for market entry points that reflect customer behaviour and your revenue goals, timing, and budgetary constraints.

1. What **product or service** will you go to market with?
2. What **target market** will you enter? Describe it geographically.
3. What **price point** will you charge, and what volume price breaks will you give to:
   - Customers
   - Distributors (e.g., X% off manufacturer's suggested retail price)
   - Retailers (e.g., X% off manufacturer's suggested retail price)
4. How do products and services like yours typically **reach your target market**?

Direct Channels
- ❑ Mail order
- ❑ Teleselling
- ❑ Websites
- ❑ Sales force
- ❑ Other

Indirect Channels
- ❑ Agents
- ❑ Distributors
- ❑ Retailers
- ❑ Strategic partners

❑ A chain of all of the above

❑ Other

5. What is the **most effective action** you can take to achieve success in your business in each of the following areas? Limit your answer to one action and one sentence for each category.

    Example Go-to-Market Strategy

    Traditional Channels: Call a buyer at Costco and ask if the company will carry your product.

    Strategic Relationship: Call up a company that sells a complementary product to yours that is on the shelf at Walmart and show them how bundling your product with theirs will improve their sales.

    Marketing (Pull): Get free local media exposure by calling local newspapers and news outlets, so that people start asking for your product by name at local boutiques.

    Sales (Push): Call on a local boutique and show the owners how carrying your product on their shelves will be profitable for them.

    Now try it yourself. Remember, this is a high-level discussion that you will delve into more deeply in the upcoming chapters. So limit your answers to one sentence and one action for each of the four components of your go-to-market strategy.

    My Ideal Go-to-Market Strategy

    ❑ The traditional channel I would like to sell through.

    ❑ The strategic relationship I would like to establish.

    ❑ The marketing activity I will launch this month.

    ❑ The sales call I will make today.

As you can see, developing a go-to-market strategy is not a one-size-fits-all approach for launching a business. Every business is different, and you'll need to use the results of the market research that you did earlier in this book to guide your strategy decisions. The most important takeaway of this chapter is *that you have* a go-to-market strategy because it's not only good business but every investor you ever speak to will ask you for one. In the next chapter, you'll start creating your go-to-market strategy by coming up with a sales channel.

CHAPTER 24

WHERE WILL YOU SELL YOUR PRODUCTS AND SERVICES?

"I love how genuine you are. I think great businesses are built when people are passionate about their product, and I admire that."
  —Dragon to Pitcher

Go-to-Market Step #1: Research Traditional Distribution Channels

Make a list of every intermediary type that is currently being used to distribute your product or service type to the final consumer. Choose the channel that can help you go to market rapidly and cost effectively.

Before there were Facebook, Twitter, and LinkedIn, there was the home party plan. This in-home sales event disguised as a social event was made famous by Tupperware sales innovator Brownie Wise. Brownie knew more than anyone that the key to sales is a *captive environment* or, in her case, a party—not just a sales pitch. Once you get your product or service in front of a prospective customer, then you can put on a demonstration.

Today the home party plan is still in action at Tupperware and has even been used to launch other companies like the Pampered Chef. Now, the practice doesn't work for every type of product or service, but it does demonstrate one simple rule: Make your product or service available to prospective customers through distribution channels that already have access to them. A distribution channel is a chain of intermediaries, with each link in the chain giving you access to a pre-established group of customers. Without them, we would never have tasted Tim Hortons coffee, never have put on a Roots sweatshirt, or ever have played the game Trivial

Pursuit. All you have to do is figure out the quickest path to your ideal customer and then strike a deal with the link in the chain that can get you to market the quickest.

Now some businesses are more dependent on intermediaries than others. Low-cost, high-volume products like food or jewellery will usually do better when sold through intermediaries than through a direct sales approach. That's what Julia Kirouac, founder of *Nud Fud* (pronounced "nude food"), determined before visiting *Dragons' Den*, and her product is now sold in 70 stores as of this writing.

Go-to-Market Snapshot: Nud Fud

Pitcher: Julia Kirouac, Season 6, Episode 6

GO-TO-MARKET

Nud Fud produces organic, raw, vegan, gluten-free snack foods. The go-to-market strategy of Nud Fud is focused on fostering relationships with grocery managers in retail stores.

THE ASK

$100,000 for 33% equity.

COMPANY VALUATION

$300,000.

THE DEAL

$100,000 for 35% equity plus 2% royalty.

PROOF-OF-CONCEPT

- Already selling in several stores in Toronto.
- $20,000 in sales ($4,000 this month).*

*As of the show participation.

TESTIMONIAL

"I love the packaging, I love the name. I love the idea."
— Dragon to Dragons

Pitcher Julia Kirouac from Nud Fud counter-offering the Dragons' initial deal.

THE WARM-UP: DISTRIBUTION CHANNELS DEFINED

A distribution channel is a chain of intermediaries between you and your customer, each reselling (and/or passing) your product or service to the next person in the chain, until it finally reaches your customer. The purpose of a channel is twofold. First, it allows you to get connected to ideal customers wherever they are located, using a series of links to them. Second, it allows you to make your product or service available for sale in a place that's *convenient to your customers*. Distribution channel language varies by industry, but the three general categories are:

- **Direct Sales:** Sell directly to another individual—with no middlemen in between. Examples include selling through a website, by direct mail, or door-to-door.
- **Distributors:** Sell to wholesalers, who in turn resell to retail buyers.
- **Retailers:** Sell to buyers that work for retailers, who in turn resell to your ideal customers.

Direct Sales: Selling Directly to Another Individual—with No Intermediary

Direct sales involves selling your products or services directly to consumers through telephone calls, door-to-door sales, home parties, in-person sales calls, direct mail, or a website. A direct sales campaign can be a low-cost way to go to market because all you need is a phone, a sales pitch, and a sample or demonstration. The process involves one or more of the following techniques:

- **Teleselling:** This method involves cold-calling prospective customers or intermediaries by telephone. The process can work well for getting face-to-face meetings with business owners and intermediaries, but this is not the best approach for calling on consumers, since it is deeply frowned upon by most. The fact is most consumers hate receiving cold calls from telemarketers. Plus telemarketers who violate the rules of the National Do Not Call List (or Registry in the United States), by calling people who have asked not to be called, could end up with steep penalties. For more information visit www.lnnte-dncl.gc.ca/verins-chkreg-eng.
- **Door-to-Door Sales:** One of the oldest methods of direct selling is door-to-door sales. This process involves knocking on doors in target neighbourhoods, business districts, or industrial parks and pitching your products or services on the spot. The practice is still popular with people selling anything from financial services to advertising for businesses to chocolate bars for charitable causes. But there are laws in place that require that you follow certain protocols, so be sure to do your homework so you don't end up violating any regulations.
- **Home Party Plans:** At these parties, trained sales people sell their products or services to party attendees as part of a social event in the home. The party host receives a reward for bringing the event together, such as free product or a percentage of revenue.
- **Sales Calls:** This method requires you to set up appointments to get in front of potential buyers. Salespeople meet everywhere, including in homes, at places of business, and even in coffee shops (the "third place," as Starbucks calls it). The key to a one-on-one sales meeting is to have a short pitch book in hand, complete with product samples, testimonials from clients, any press coverage you have received, and references whom prospective customers can contact if they need a slight nudge to move forward.
- **Direct Mail:** This method involves sending out mailers to targeted mailing lists. The process requires significant capital outlay and testing, and should be supplemented by Web sales in the early stages of any direct-selling effort.
- **Website:** This method involves securing a domain name (www.yourcompany?.ca) for your business and then setting up an online shopping cart and store so people can start buying from you directly online.

Always seek legal advice to make sure that your sales methods adhere to the Direct Sellers Act of your province and the ethical sales methods of your industry.

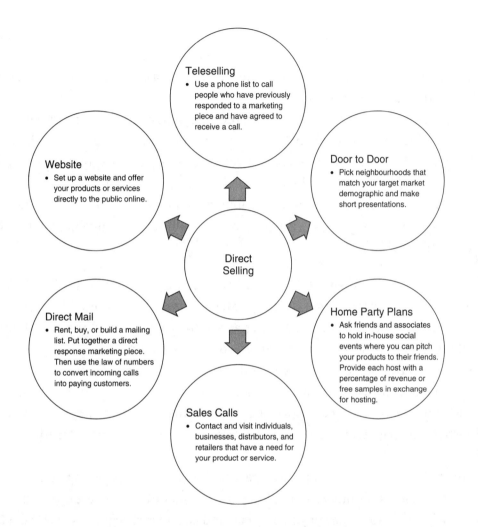

Distributors: Intermediaries That Warehouse, Sell, and Deliver Your Product to Retailers

Most industries have a vibrant ecosystem of intermediaries that buy goods at wholesale from manufacturers and suppliers, and then resell them to retailers. These middlemen, also known as distributors, are the channel of choice for millions of established brands in the marketplace. Once they take control of your product, they are responsible for warehousing it, protecting it, and delivering it to retailers to meet even the smallest order volume.

To find a distributor that is connected in your industry, start by shopping local retailers that carry your type of product and ask the managers who their distributors are. Talk to industry participants at industry trade shows and conferences to find out who the main players are. Or even do a Google search. Try to establish pricing specifics such as standard mark-ups, volume discounts, and payment terms. Then make contact with the distributors themselves and give them your sales pitch.

Remember, distributors are interested in revenue opportunities, not just better mousetraps. Be prepared in advance with answers to questions regarding your estimated sales volume, current shelf space at independent retailers, and standard mark-ups. If you have proof that your product is already being carried and sold by several local retailers, that will help. If you are lucky enough to find a distributor willing to take on your product, always speak to a lawyer before signing anything. Here are some general agreement issues that you should be familiar with:

- **Exclusive vs. Non-Exclusive:** If you are asked to give exclusivity to one distributor, try to limit that exclusivity to a single geographic territory. You need to establish the real reach (i.e., the number of customers they have access to) your distributor has and find other distributors that can service other markets for your product better.
- **FOB:** In many transactions, your wholesale price to the intermediary will include free on board pricing, known as FOB, which means your pricing includes the cost of shipping to the distributor. But this is not always the case. Be sure to understand who pays for shipping when you negotiate pricing; in most cases, you'll have to pay for transportation, but it can be negotiable.
- **Payment Terms:** The most important part of the sales cycle is getting paid. If you don't receive cash for six months, you might be forced out of business even though you have sales. Look for 30- to 60-day payment cycles and consider charging late payment charges such as 1.5% of the balance due.
- **Termination Clause:** Look for distribution agreements that have a limited term with clear conditions for ending the relationship, in addition to a clear understanding of how your product is to be displayed.

Retailers: Selling through an Intermediary That Sells to Consumers

Finding a national or regional multi-department retailer like Walmart, Canadian Tire, or The Bay to agree to stock your product is a tall task. If you don't have a compelling value proposition or a deep sales history through another channel, you won't have a platform to convince the retailer. A more strategic route for most is to establish shelf space at local independent retailers first. Independent retailers can make quick decisions because they don't have the same buying protocols as the larger branded retailers. You might even be able to get "on the shelf" in weeks or even days if you can convince them that you have a good product that fills a gap in their line. Once you achieve success on a small level, you can leverage that success to establish a foothold in the larger branded retailers.

National and regional retail buyers, and most independent store owners, will have their own retail agreement documentation. Be sure to seek legal advice so you don't end up giving up exclusivity or getting poor pricing terms unnecessarily. Some retail agreement issues to be aware of in advance include:

- **Exclusive vs. Non-Exclusive Territory:** Don't give out exclusivity unnecessarily. You don't want to lose the opportunity early on to expand into branded national or regional retailers. If you have to give up exclusivity, limit it to a geographic territory for a limited term if necessary.
- **Minimum Order Volume:** Try to establish a minimum order volume so retailers realize that you are serious about your product.
- **Pricing:** Do your homework and understand what percentage off manufacturer's suggested retail price (MSRP) to charge the retailer. Research pricing through industry magazines or by talking to prospective retailers or industry participants.
- **Finance Charges:** Consider charging finance charges for payments received over 30 days so cash receipts aren't open-ended.
- **Product Information:** Be prepared to provide product information, samples, images for marketing, and in-store training and demonstrations when possible.
- **Negotiating:** Be prepared to buy back inventory that is not sold or to replace inventory that is damaged or broken.

Your Own Retail Location

If you are serious about opening a retail location, I strongly recommend that you pick up the companion guide to this book, *The Dragons' Den Guide to Investor-Ready Business Plans,* in which retail-outlet planning is discussed in more detail. Many people seek riches by opening up their own retail outlets but end up with the equivalent of a job and little or nothing left over to pay their salaries.

The process involves picking a theme or specialty for your store and sourcing products from wholesalers and producers that reflect that theme. You'll need to do demographic research in the locations you are looking at, to make sure that the foot traffic matches your target market profile. Sam Walton was known for flying over locations in his twin-engine Cessna to study traffic patterns for future Walmarts. Here are some tips:

- **Mock-Up Store:** Consider setting up a downsized mock-up or prototype location of your store in a warehouse, empty space, or garage so that you can actually map out your store concept *before* signing your first lease.
- **Cash Reserve:** Ideally, you should have six months of cash flow in the bank before opening (which you can plan in your business plan). This topic is discussed in more detail in Chapter 4.
- **Market Research:** By now, you should have a clear definition of your target market, but you'll still need to do demographic research in the area you are planning to locate. Visit the area and monitor the traffic on weekends and weekdays. Talk to other retailers in the area to find out when their busiest times are. And if you get the chance, the best market research you could do might just be to work in a retail store like yours (preferably in a geographic territory where you won't be competing).
- **Foot Traffic:** Although you may rely on foot traffic as a large part of your marketing program, don't count on it. Just because you open a retail outlet doesn't mean people will shop there. Merchandising is a key skill, so be sure to take some courses through the Learning Annex or find a course through your industry trade association as part of your business planning.
- **Store Promotion:** In addition to merchandising (how you display your goods), it's important to have a promotional plan in place that includes seasonal pricing, periodic sales promotions, a "store opening" through your local chamber of commerce to garner press attention, and ongoing direct mail communication with your customers, depending on the type of retail outlet that you open.

> **Dragon Lore**
>
> The shortest distance between you and your customer is often through an established chain of intermediaries. While selling directly out of a garage is admirable, it's not always the most efficient route.

One company that succeeded in the retail market space, well *before* visiting *Dragons' Den*, is Balzac's Coffee Roasters. Founder Diane Olsen proved that you actually can compete against big brands, even when it comes to a seemingly commodity-type retail outlet like a coffee shop.

Go-to-Market: Balzac's Coffee Roasters

Pitcher: Diana Olsen, Season 6, Episode 1

THE BUSINESS

Balzac's Coffee Roasters is a small chain of company-owned cafés, currently in business, that appeals to customers looking for alternatives to Tim Hortons or Starbucks.

GO-TO-MARKET

It currently has five company-owned retail locations in place, and recently won two competitive bids for two additional high-profile retail locations in Toronto.

SALES PITCH

"In order for you to get the full experience of Balzac's Coffee, it would be necessary to bring you to one of our five cafés. But since we can't do that here, we've decided that we would bring a little bit of a café to you. We've decided that we would bring a miniature version to you. When you go into one of those coffee companies [our competitors] . . . you see prefabricated laminated countertops, you see a lot of merchandise, you see backlit menus. We don't do any of that. We want it to look like it did 100 years ago. I would like a strategic partner. I would like someone that I could go to for advice who can help me figure out where I am taking this company."

TESTIMONIAL

"They are right beside me in the Distillery district. It's my go-to place. I go there every day."
—Dragon to Dragon

PROOF-OF-CONCEPT

- Has five retail locations in southern Ontario and may soon add two more.
- Has been in business for 10 years.
- Total sales for 2011 is $3.2 million.

THE ASK

$350,000 for a 20% stake.

THE DEAL

$350,000 for a 20% stake.

Pitcher Diana Olsen of Balzac's Coffee Roasters standing in front of a miniature version of one of her retail coffee outlets.

Self-Study Workshop: Identify the Sales Channels You Will Use

Describe where your products or services will be made available to your customers.

1. What **traditional channels** are typically used in your industry to reach your ideal customers?

    Direct Sales Channels
    - ❑ Teleselling
    - ❑ Door-to-door sales
    - ❑ Home party plans
    - ❑ Sales calls
    - ❑ Direct mail
    - ❑ Website
    - ❑ Other

    Distributors (name them if possible)
    - ❑ Wholesalers
    - ❑ Distributors
    - ❑ Manufacturer's agents
    - ❑ Other

    Retailers
    - ❑ Independent stores
    - ❑ Regional stores
    - ❑ National stores
    - ❑ Other

2. What **types of retailers** (if any) sell your category of product or service?

3. Which **local independent retailers** stock your category of product or offer your type of service?

4. Which **regional retailers** stock your category of product or offer your type of service?
5. Which **national retailers** stock your category of product or offer your type of service?
6. If you are selling a product, what are your **mark-ups for retailers**? What are your **mark-ups for distributors**?

Now that you've figured out where to sell your product or service, it's important to delve deeper into Success Factor #7: Collaborate with Strategic Partners, which you learned in Chapter 7. In the next chapter, you'll learn creative ways of partnering with other businesses including private labelling, co-branding, and bundling.

CHAPTER 25

WHAT PARTNERS CAN HELP YOU GO-TO-MARKET FASTER?

"That million-dollar idea [is] absolutely worth zero until you can prove revenue."
—Dragon to Pitchers

Go-to-Market Step #2: Build Strategic Relationships

Make a list of businesses, products, or services that can help you achieve your marketing, distribution, and production goals. Look for a strategic relationship that works for your type of product or service. Make contact with potential partners and try to structure a deal.

The proverbial garage start-up that evolves into a million-dollar enterprise is the dream of many. In fact, one company, Hewlett-Packard, is so proud of its heritage as a garage start-up that it even restored the original garage that was used to launch the computer and printing behemoth it has become.[1] But the reality is that for every Hewlett-Packard, there are thousands of great ideas that never get out of the garage. While setting up a business in a garage and selling your wares is certainly admirable, without a timely go-to-market strategy your idea may end up going nowhere. Sometimes traditional channels are so congested with other products or services that your path to market can be less than smooth. When you run into channel friction like this, it's important to start thinking outside the traditional box. Look for complementary products, services, or businesses that you can team up with to achieve your go-to-market goals.

One market space where go-to-market creativity is key, is water (as we saw earlier with Q water). Since most people can find a free source of drinking water, they really don't have to buy it unless there is a compelling reason to do so. Event Water Solutions (a very descriptive yet less-than-memorable business name) figured out that event managers need a way to hydrate their attendees—especially when those events are held in a field in the middle of nowhere.

Go-to-Market Snapshot: Event Water Solutions

Pitchers: Paul Baker and Marilyn Berrys, Season 6, Episode 1

GO-TO-MARKET

A portable, stainless-steel water refill station the company transports to festivals and events across North America. The company's go-to-market is through attendance at festivals and events.

THE ASK

$100,000 for 20% equity.

COMPANY VALUATION

$500,000.

THE DEAL

$100,000 for 20% equity.

PROOF-OF-CONCEPT

- 24 water stations operating in Ontario, California, and Texas.
- $125,000 in revenue last year.
- This year revenue booked so far is $250,000, excluding bottle revenue.*
- The company's phone rings every day with inquiries from event organizers.

*As of show participation.

Paul Baker, Marilyn Berrys, and an associate from Event Water Solutions pitching their product to the Dragons.

THE WARM-UP: STRATEGIC RELATIONSHIPS DEFINED

A strategic relationship is an alliance with another business to achieve a specific marketing or business goal. The purpose of a strategic relationship is to get you to market quicker than you could get there on your own. The process involves teaming up with a complementary business, product, or service that can add value to your business through its established customer base or manufacturing infrastructure. It's important to be creative here, but don't discount the better-known types of strategic relationships either:

- **Private Labelling:** Branding your product or service with someone else's business name *instead of yours,* so you can *reach* their customer base.
- **Co-Branding:** Branding your product or service with someone else's business name *in addition* to yours, so you can *attract* their customer base.
- **Licensing:** Permitting another business to produce your product or deliver your service in exchange for an ongoing royalty.
- **Franchising:** Permitting another business to use your business model, brand name, and operating process in exchange for an ongoing royalty.

- **Joint Venture:** Establishing a business entity separate from your own that is co-owned with another business.
- **Bundling:** Persuading another product manufacturer or service provider to sell your product or service as an add-on to its own.

Private Labelling: Sell Your Product at Wholesale with Someone Else's Brand on It

Many adults in Canada remember seeing commercials of Dave Nichol aggressively promoting the bright yellow No Name brand of Loblaws. His campaign has been one of the most successful examples of private labelling in Canadian history. Private labelling involves selling your product to another business, to put their brand name on it instead of yours. For example, if you make scented candles, you could sell your product at wholesale cost to local gift shops. The gift shop can then market your product under its name. Or you might even charge it a set-up fee to add its logo to your product.

There is a downside to private labelling: you won't be establishing your brand name with the final customer. But the upside is that you'll be able to sell your product to many businesses if you structure your agreement correctly. Continuing with the example of scented candles, you could sell your product to many gift shops across the country. The revenue you generate would come from set-up charges (for branding the other business's logo on your product) plus the wholesale cost you charge for the product itself (such as 50% off the manufacturer's suggested retail price). Alternatively, if you want to sell a product or service that someone else makes, you could find a company that allows you to put your brand name on *its* product or service.

Co-Branding: Two Logos Brand One Product or Service

Another strategic relationship that involves putting another business's name on your product or service is called co-branding. Co-branding involves combining your product or service with complementary products or services and then sharing the label space and marketing costs. For example, a local ice-cream shop could use Starbucks coffee in its mocha-flavoured ice cream to attract Starbucks lovers. Or if you have invented a multi-purpose tool like the kelvin.23, you could allow a home-improvement television show to sell its own co-branded version of your tool on the program. Even this book is co-branded with *Dragons' Den* and the author's name.

Alternatively, you could develop a shared retail environment where two business's products or services are offered. For example, Cold Stone Creamery has a co-branding relationship with Tim Hortons. Several of its franchisees now have co-branded locations where both Cold Stone Creamery offerings and Tim Hortons products are available.[2] The benefit of co-branding relationships is that each brand attracts its respective audiences to the other's brand. A deal can be struck using whatever terms you want, but one way is to charge a commission or share a percentage of revenues for each unit sold.

Licensing: Permitting a Manufacturer to Produce and Distribute Your Product or Service under a Limited-Term Licence

Sometimes it's more cost-effective to stay out of the manufacturing business altogether and let someone else take over the manufacturing and distribution of your product. You can even license your service model. Licensing can be an attractive option if you have a compelling value proposition and a unique product or service that can bring profit to an already established company.

Here's how it works. You license your invention to a manufacturer that produces and distributes it, with your permission, and the licensee pays you a royalty fee as a percentage of all sales. Consider licensing as a way of renting your idea to someone else, since you are allowing another business to make money off your concept for a limited period. For example, if you invent a new type of shoe, you could license your concept to a major manufacturer in exchange for a percentage of its sales of your product. If you own a popular restaurant for kids, you could sign a licensing agreement with a toy company to produce and distribute toys based on your restaurant's theme.

Deal structures vary but, ideally, you'll receive a percentage of ongoing gross sales (say 5% to 15%), with a minimum annual royalty payment structured into the deal. You might even receive an upfront royalty or advance. Because your licensee will incur all costs of manufacturing, distribution, and sales, this can be a relatively easy go-to-market strategy.

One of the more successful Canadian examples of licensing occurred when Selchow & Righter licensed the game Trivial Pursuit from its creators for a limited term. Today, a different company, Hasbro, owns the game outright. So what started out as a licensing deal ended up leading to a complete buyout for the licensor.

> **Dragon Lore**
>
> Try to team up with another business that complements your own. Use a limited-term relationship so that you can test the waters first before committing long term.

Partnering opportunities are critical for many entrepreneurs, especially when you have invented something that's never been sold before. One major element of an effective go-to-market strategy is to find strategic partners who have already made contact with your target audience. Then brainstorm ways to share revenue with those partners, in exchange for distribution and marketing exposure. KickSpike, a popular visitor to *Dragons' Den* because of the bidding frenzy they generated, learned that partnering with all five Dragons can be as helpful as finding a manufacturer to license your product.

Go-to-Market: KickSpike Retractable Metal Spike Golf Shoe

Pitchers: Darrell and Colleen Bachmann, Season 3, Episode 1

THE BUSINESS

KickSpike is the world's first retractable metal spike golf shoe.

GO-TO-MARKET

The go-to-market strategy is focused on licensing the idea to a manufacturer and collecting royalties.

SALES PITCH

"If you guys are golfers, I'm sure you've witnessed the soft spike damage at the end of the day. So we've come up with a new revolution and it's called KickSpike. This is the shoe. The world's first retractable metal spike golf shoe."

TESTIMONIAL

"I actually think this thing could go."
    —Dragon to Dragon

PROOF-OF-CONCEPT

- The president of the U.S. Golf Association called it the best idea since the sand wedge.
- A preliminary meeting with a major shoe manufacturer.
- A potential three-year licensing agreement worth $4 to $7 million.

THE ASK

$1,000,000 for 10% equity.

THE DEAL

$1,000,000 for a 30% stake plus the collective expertise of all five Dragons.

Pitchers Darrell and Colleen Bachmann demonstrating the KickSpike retractable metal spike golf shoe.

Franchising: License Your Repeatable Business Model to Another Business Owner

The most successful franchise system in history is McDonald's because its team has managed to systemize everything, including how customers place an order (using value meals), what time those customers eat breakfast (before 10:30 a.m. in many regions), and even how often they return, through timely sales promotions. But just having a systematic way of doing business that others can follow under a franchise agreement in their own geographic market may not be enough. The truth is, franchising a new business model can be very difficult to set up. It is a heavily regulated process that is designed to protect the franchisee from false expectations and mistreatment.

Here's how it works. You license your business model to another business owner, called a franchisee. In exchange for an initial franchise fee upfront and an ongoing royalty paid to you (such as 6% to 8% of gross sales), you provide a business model, equipment, training, operations manuals, the right to use your trademark, and ongoing support. In many cases, you also set up an advertising fund (by charging the franchisee 2% to 4% or some other percentage of gross monthly sales) that you use to promote all franchisees. In some cases, you might even help the franchisee secure financing. Of course, the deal can be structured based on your needs, but the help of a franchising lawyer is a must to ensure you achieve your goals.

Joint Venture: Limited-Term Shared Ownership of a Joint Business Venture

It can be very difficult to establish a foothold in some markets because of established players entrenched there. At the same time, permanently merging your business with another business might limit your business options or leave you with less control to move forward. This is where joint ventures come in.

Here's how it works. You form a separate business entity with another business to market and develop your product or service. All revenues and costs are shared according to an agreed formula, based on investment dollars put into the venture and other factors. This method works when you need to enter markets that you otherwise would have little or no access to or understanding of—for instance, China—without having to share equity in your main business. If you have invented a product or service that might sell in China, it could take you years to navigate the regulations and cultural environment there. But if you partner with an established business in that market, where you bring skills and competencies that that business doesn't have, then you can enter that market much more quickly than you could on your own. The key to all strategic relationships, including joint ventures, is to have a honeymoon period or limited term. That way, if you don't like your strategic partner, you can sever the relationship and find another one.

Famous joint ventures include:

- **Dow Corning:** An ongoing joint venture, which has been in place since 1942, between Dow Chemical and Corning Glass to develop and supply silicones. The companies, Dow Chemical and Corning Glass, continue to operate as separate businesses.
- **MillerCoors:** An ongoing joint venture between Molson Coors and SABMiller with the purpose of combining their U.S. and Puerto Rico operations in an entity called MillerCoors while leaving their own businesses intact as separate entities. This type of relationship works when you want to enter a new market where a joint venture partner already has access to an established market but needs your marketing or manufacturing resources to do the job.
- **Starbucks Ice Cream:** Started out as a joint venture with Dreyer's ice cream. Changed into an exclusive licensing agreement with a different company, Unilever. Starbucks also has licensing agreements with Unilever and PepsiCo for marketing and distributing Tazo Tea. Pepsi provides Starbucks with ready-to-drink (i.e., bottling) expertise and Unilever has an established history selling tea with its ownership of Lipton tea. Pepsi has previously worked with Unilever to market Lipton tea.

Bundling: Include Your Product or Service as a Component of Another Business's Product

You could strike a deal to have another business put your product into its own as an ingredient, or sell your product or service as an add-on to its own. This type of relationship is called bundling and has the same benefits as co-branding. Sometimes it's done to strengthen the image of one brand by adding the ingredients and brand of a second brand. For example, if you have a boxed software product that you are trying to sell through retail stores in addition to an online download mechanism, you could partner with a company that is already on the shelf and structure a deal to add your product to its line. If you have invented a new type of tea strainer, you could approach Starbucks or a tea manufacturer like the Tazo Tea Company and try to have your product bundled with theirs during the holiday season. Or if you sell premium chocolate, you could try to get on the radar of an international gift company like Harry & David, to strike a deal to have your product included in its gift baskets. Bundling is as effective a go-to-market strategy as they come.

Self-Study Workshop: Build Strategic Relationships

Businesses that complement your business, product, or service, are potential strategic partners. Develop a list of businesses, products, or services that complement yours. Then brainstorm ways to partner with them.

1. What types of businesses **sell** your product category? Try to name 10.

2. What types of businesses **complement** your product or service? Try to name 10.

3. What specific **manufacturers** build your type of product? Try to name 10.

4. In what **regions** of the province or country would your business model work well? If you find opportunities in other markets, you could potentially license your concept to another business or even franchise it.

5. What types of products could you **bundle** yours with? Try to name 10.

6. Review your answers to the above questions, and try to **set up a meeting** with one or more strategic partners who can help you reach your goals. In the blank lines below, summarize the outcomes that you expect from each relationship.

Having channels in place to sell your product or service will certainly prepare you to generate revenue. But if no one has heard about your business, then they'll have no reason to buy from you or partner with you. In the next chapter you'll create an efficient marketing program to help get the word out about your business.

CHAPTER 26

HOW WILL YOU GET THE WORD OUT?

"You taught everyone at home a lesson today, which is: It's rarely about the product; it's about the individual."
— Dragon to Pitcher

Go-to-Market Step #3: Create Your Marketing Program

Develop a consistent marketing message. Design low-cost, high-quality sales collateral and marketing pieces to communicate that marketing message. Implement your plan with a cost-effective marketing program.

If you have to "light your hair on fire" (to quote U.S. presidential candidate Mitt Romney in the 2012 primaries) to draw attention to your product or service, there might be something seriously wrong with your business concept. At the same time, if you want to monetize your business concept, you have to draw attention to it. Richard Branson draws attention to his Virgin brand products and services using PR stunts such as his record-breaking hot-air-balloon rides around the world. Mary Kay Ash, while alive, drew attention to her cosmetics line sales force using unique performance incentives such as pink Cadillacs. Donald Trump routinely draws attention to his Trump brand properties, television show, and other business ventures just by showing up on the morning news to comment on some event or other. Now that you have refined your business concept and have a commercial product or service ready, it's time to share it with the world. Start with a marketing communications strategy and then get that message out with a consistent, focused marketing program.

You don't need a billboard advertising campaign to draw attention to your business. But you do need a clear, consistent marketing message when you visit Dragons' Den. Ken Moscovitz of Eco-Freez Premium Coolants fortunately had a pretty straightforward message to fall back on—his premium line of coolants comes from recycled anti-freeze. And even though the Dragons weren't buying it on the entrepreneur's first visit to Dragons' Den, the company has a successful marketing campaign that has enabled it to stay in business since 1994.

Go-to-Market Snapshot: Eco-Freez Premium Coolants

Pitcher: Ken Moscovitz, Season 6, Episode 3

GO-TO-MARKET

Eco-Freez collects and processes waste anti-freeze and turns it into a premium line of coolants. The go-to-market strategy is focused on fostering relationships with auto maintenance and oil change providers like Mr. Lube.

THE ASK

$600,000 to expand the model into Ontario.

COMPANY VALUATION

There is no company valuation because the pitchers didn't mention the equity they were willing to give up.

THE DEAL

$0.

PROOF-OF-CONCEPT

- $800,000 in revenue in previous markets.
- $200,000 in profit in previous markets.*

*As of show participation.

TESTIMONIAL

"I think you've got a good product. The numbers are great."
—Dragon to Pitcher

A vacuum distillation unit used by Eco-Freez to help process waste anti-freeze into premium coolant.

THE WARM-UP: MARKETING PROGRAM DEFINED

A marketing program is a limited-term marketing activity or event such as advertising, a sales promotion, or a publicity stunt. During the initial start-up phase, limit your efforts to low-cost, rapid-response programs instead of long, drawn-out, expensive brand-building campaigns. The purpose of a marketing program is to draw attention to your product or service and generate leads for your sales efforts. The process of building a marketing program involves:

- **Marketing Communications:** A clear, consistent marketing message and collateral materials that will support your sales effort.
- **Marketing Programs:** Limited-term, one-to-many programs such as advertising, publicity, and social media campaigns that engage your prospective customer using Twitter and blogs; and one-to-one programs and tools such as face-to-face or online networking or word-of-mouth marketing on Facebook and LinkedIn (both can be one-to-many tools too). As a percentage of sales, consider spending no more than 5% to 10% of projected revenues, if that, as long as your projected revenues are based on credible assumptions.

Marketing Communications

Positioning

If you've ever been to a Starbucks in the United States in the morning, you'll notice lines going out the door while nearby mom-and-pop coffee shops struggle to get customers. That's because Starbucks has a competitive advantage and value proposition that, when combined with social proof (Americans line up for it as much as we line up for Tim Hortons), makes it very difficult to compete against. The truth is that most mom-and-pop coffee shops in the United States have no advantage at all, so they end up trying to copy Starbucks coffee with new names and then try to compete on price. Unfortunately, you can't out-Starbucks Starbucks or out-Tim Hortons Tim Hortons.

The downfall for most new businesses that try—but fail—to compete against established brands is poor positioning. Positioning is the process of labelling yourself as "the expert" in providing a specific type of product or service benefit. Consumer products companies like Johnson & Johnson are masters at it. For example, for one type of customer, J&J chooses to highlight the whitening power of its Listerine mouthwash by creating a variation that has foaming action. It calls this product, which looks and works like mouthwash, "whitening rinse." For another type of customer, it chooses to highlight the breath-freshening power of the mouthwash by creating a variation that has bacteria-killing powers. For this version it keeps the category label "mouthwash."

Taking on an identity, and then backing up that identity with real product or service features that customers value, is the art of positioning. So, going back to the mom-and-pop coffee shop example, instead of competing head-to-head with Starbucks, you'd be better served by trying to position yourself against Starbucks. For example, become the tea expert instead. First, stop serving coffee. Offer a high tea early in the evening, with a meal, and a low tea late in the afternoon with snacks. Private-label the tea of high-quality tea suppliers under your brand name and sell it to your clientele with other tea products. And design an environment that makes customers feel as if they are in England sitting with the queen. Just do something other than trying to copy Starbucks or Tim Hortons. Make a strong choice and run with it or you'll get crushed in the marketplace by established players.

The concept of positioning as a way of differentiating your product or service offering has been refined for decades by many experts, including Al Ries, Jack Trout, and Geoffrey Moore, so read their books if you want to become an expert. Once you've established your positioning, which can change your entire product or service design strategy, it's time to build a message.

Message Platform

Building a marketing message is both an art and a science. It's an art because you never know which precise message will resonate with your audience. It's a science because it's based on several definable product, service, business, or customer attributes, including:

- **Buying Motive:** The trigger event that leads to a typical customer seeking out your product or service.
- **Competitive Advantage:** The feature advantage, cost advantage, or support services advantage that your business can sustain over the long term.
- **Key Selling Feature (Unique Selling Proposition):** The distinctive feature of your product or service that prospective customers will be attracted to.
- **The Appeal:** What the key selling feature means to the customer you are targeting.

You should have a minimum of two basic messages in your arsenal at all times: one for advertising and one for sales.

Advertising Message	Sales Message
Unique Selling Proposition	**Elevator Pitch**
A unique feature, attribute, or benefit that you choose to highlight in an advertising campaign based on the market segment you are targeting.	A short 30- to 60-second statement that describes what your product or service is, what it does, why it's valuable, and what proof you have that it's successful.

Sales Collateral

If you are looking to present your product or service to others, including channel partners, alliances, or customers, it's a good idea to have marketing materials in hand that can be used to back up your demonstration. These materials, called "sales collateral," include:

- **Website:** Can be the most cost-effective in the long run because you can change the message without incurring any print charges. A website is perfect for over-the-phone sales presentations because you can ask your prospective customer to get online while you are on the phone with them. You can guide them through your website over the phone, showing them images and product descriptions that you are discussing with them.

- **Presentation Binder:** You can buy presentation binders at any office supply store, to hold product or service pictures, press clippings, written testimonials, and order forms.
- **Brochures:** For brochures to look good, they should be designed and printed professionally. The ones printed on your own printer usually hurt your image more than they help. The problem with having them professionally designed and printed is that it can cost thousands of dollars, and if you have to change to revise and refine your message, you'll incur repeat printing charges.
- **DVD:** When visiting trade shows, handing out a DVD that includes a demo to a prospective customer or potential intermediary can simplify their decision-making process.
- **Contracts, Order Forms, and Price Lists:** Anything you need to get the order and sign on the customer should be preprinted.

Marketing Programs: One-to-Many Programs

Advertising

Advertising is a one-to-many method of persuading targeted groups of people to take an interest in your product or service. It can serve many objectives, including supporting your sales team's efforts on the ground, creating awareness for a sales promotion, and generating phone leads to be followed up later by your sales force.

Don't confuse advertising with marketing. Marketing is an all-inclusive strategy that includes pricing strategy, channel strategy, and promotional strategy. Advertising is a type of marketing, the purpose of which is to inform people about your product or service, persuade them to buy it, and remind them to purchase it again.

There are many types of advertising, which you will explore if you put together a comprehensive business plan as explained in the companion guide to this book, *The Dragons' Den Guide to Investor-Ready Business Plans*. These include:

- Online advertising
- Television advertising
- Radio advertising
- Outdoor advertising
- Newspaper advertising
- Magazine advertising

Publicity

Publicity is an event or activity for which you receive free media coverage. It's any free one-to-many method you use to draw attention to your business, product, or service. Because it's free, you don't control the message as much as you do with paid advertising. But it can be the equivalent of "setting your hair on fire" if the stunt is big enough and fits your brand message. Editors and media personnel are always looking for newsworthy items to write or talk about, so give them something. You can also get on their radar by buying advertising through their publications or by contacting them during the year with story ideas that relate to your product or service category.

Publicity-generating techniques include:

- **Publicity Stunts:** Holding out-of-the-ordinary (legal, of course) events in public places and notifying the press beforehand.
- **Press Releases:** Sending out newsworthy announcements about items of interest such as product or service breakthroughs.
- **Articles of Interest or White Papers:** Writing articles of interest that focus on unique problem-solving methodologies.
- **Media Invitations:** Sending out invitations to media outlets to view demonstrations of your product or service (only works for true game-changing innovations).
- **Newsletters:** Publishing newsletters that focus on informing your current and prospective customers about news of the month.
- **Social Media:** Tweeting or posting on Facebook campaigns that focus on giveaways and contests, with the hope that they go viral (an example of word-of-mouth publicity).

Some of the most valuable brands in the world are driven by publicity. Again, think of the Virgin brand. Richard Branson goes on and also funds around-the-world hot-air-balloon trips that draw huge attention to his Virgin brand. Facebook is constantly being reported about online and on television, and all of this exposure doesn't cost it a dime. *Forbes* magazine reports on the best websites, and those websites receive completely free advertising if they are fortunate enough to be named. But the free advertising that publicity gives you is useless if you don't have a good product or service to sell.

> **Dragon Lore**
>
> No amount of advertising will help to sell a product or service that isn't any good. Make sure you have a product or service that people are willing to pay you for before you start investing valuable resources on a marketing program.

If you want to see publicity campaigns in action, look no further than the barbeque sauce industry, where entering and winning awards can mean the difference between winning customers and leaving your business hungry for more. But even if don't you live in North Carolina or the heart of Missouri (two places that each claim to be the "barbeque capital of the world"), you can still get great barbeque. Look no further than *Dragons' Den*, where Canadian company Buster Rhino's Southern BBQ sauce was put to the test.

Go-to-Market: Buster Rhino's Southern BBQ Sauce

Pitchers: Darrell and Beth Koster, Season 3, Episode 3

THE BUSINESS

Buster Rhino's makes award-winning barbeque sauces, barbeque rubs, spice rubs, and prepackaged prepared meat.

GO-TO-MARKET

The go-to-market strategy is focused on winning barbeque sauce contests and using the resulting credibility to establish relationships with wholesalers and retailers like Costco.

SALES PITCH

We are a Southern barbeque company. We make barbeque sauces, barbeque rubs, spices, and prepackaged meat for the wholesale and retail industry.

TESTIMONIAL

"Of all the sauce guys who have come in here, I think you're the best."
—Dragon to Pitcher

PROOF-OF-CONCEPT

- Award-winning barbeque sauce driven by word-of-mouth marketing.
- $536,000 in sales last year.
- On track to do more than $800,000 in sales this year.
- Their major purchaser is Costco, and they also sell through mom-and-pop retail locations.

THE ASK

$200,000 for 25% of the company.

THE DEAL

$200,000 for a 51% stake.

Pitchers Darryl and Beth Koster from Buster Rhino's Barbeque Sauce discussing the deal they just accepted from two Dragons.

Word-of-Mouth Marketing

You certainly don't have to pay for advertising to get the word out. If you have absolutely zero budget, you can start by making a list of 100 to 250 people you know. Then you can spread the word about your product or service by picking up the phone and letting them know that you have a novel idea. Just think twice about trying to sell them your product or service because you might end up losing them. Instead, see them as a resource and ask them to mention your new venture to anyone who might benefit from it. You can even contact news outlets and ask them to cover your new business. And you can hand out free samples to people with influence (such as local celebrities), to give people something to talk about.

Trade Shows

A trade show is a demonstration event where products and services can be tested or distribution agreements can be signed. Your core goals at a trade show are to come in contact with industry decision makers, customers, and colleagues and to build a list of interested prospects that you can follow up with after the event. It is one of the few places where you can come in contact with a large number of targeted people at one time and in one place.

Keep in mind that you don't need a booth to gain from attending a trade show. You can visit to see what your competitors are up to, to network with attendees and exhibitors, and to generate new ideas for your own products and services. For a list of trade shows in your industry, contact your industry association.

Social Media

Online social networking can be a boon to your business or a horrendous waste of time, so make sure that your campaign is purpose-driven. The purpose of social networking is to link up with people with whom you can share resources or contacts. Ideally, the connections you make will lead to distribution, marketing, or sales opportunities. Here are some tips:

Facebook Tips

- Use it to network with people with whom you can share resources and/or make connections.
- Try to build a list of 100 Facebook friends you actually know. Then use that core base to connect with people you have never met before.
- Announce events on a free Facebook fan page (a one-to-many strategy).
- Engage your friends for advice, contacts, and feedback.
- Use wall posts, status updates, or comments on other posts to make it a one-to-many program.

LinkedIn Tips

- Use it to stay in touch with people who are connected to others who can help you build your business.
- Try to connect with 100 people and join 10 or more interest groups.
- Use recommendations to build your credibility.
- Engage your colleagues for advice, contacts, and feedback.

Twitter Tips

- Use it to announce events, contests, blog posts, industry-specific news, and newsworthy items.
- Try to build a critical mass of 1,000 followers by following people who tweet about your product or service category.
- Listen to feedback from your followers.

Blogging Tips

- Open a free blog account at WordPress.com or Blogger.com.
- Use it to blog in short paragraphs about topics that relate to product- or service-specific problem solving, industry innovations, and newsworthy items.
- Build a following and broadcast your blog posts on Twitter and Facebook.

Sales Promotion: When a Sales Pitch Isn't Enough

Sometimes advertising isn't enough to persuade a prospective customer to try your products or services, especially if what you are selling is unfamiliar to your market. For a variety of reasons, including the state of the economy, people may put off a purchase until another time. To motivate someone to buy now instead of later, you can use a sales promotion as an external incentive—for instance, free samples, bonus rewards, temporary discounts, or rebates. To maintain their effectiveness, sales promotions should be timely and used sparingly.

Self-Study Workshop: Create Your Marketing Program

Focus on cost-effective marketing activities that draw the most attention for the least amount of money.

1. What is your **unique selling proposition**?
2. What is your **elevator pitch**? (Read Chapter 27 if you don't have one.)
3. What types of **marketing tools** can you put together cost-effectively?
   - ❑ Website
   - ❑ Presentation binder
   - ❑ Brochure
   - ❑ DVD
   - ❑ Contract
   - ❑ Order form
   - ❑ Price list
   - ❑ Other
4. Which **newspapers** do your ideal customers read?
5. Which **magazines** do your ideal customers read?
6. What **percentage of projected sales** do businesses in your industry typically spend on advertising?
7. What is **newsworthy** about your product or service?
8. Which **media outlets** reach your typical customer?
9. What can you do to gain **free media coverage** for your product or service?

Once your customers start contacting you, it's important to be able to close sales. If you're able to make your phone ring off the wall, but you can't convince people to place an order, then your marketing efforts will be wasted. Just go through a local drive-through where you can't hear the person speaking through the microphone and you'll know what I'm talking about. In the next chapter, you'll put together a sales pitch, strategize about possible customer objections, and list and develop order processing materials.

CHAPTER 27

HOW WILL YOU GENERATE SALES?

"The DNA of a business is to make profit for its shareholders."
   —Dragon to Pitcher

> ## Go-to-Market Step #4: Develop Your Sales Process
>
> Identify the length of your sales cycle. Choose a transactional or consultative sales model. Get commitments from your customers over time.

Marketing's job is to lead the horse to water. The job of sales is to persuade the horse to drink. How you do that is up to you, but history provides us with many successful models to draw from. For example, for years, the Encyclopedia Britannica was sold door to door. Sales reps walked through targeted neighbourhoods and developed nerves of steel by repeating the same sales pitch over and over until they got an answer of yes. They knew their goal was not to avoid no's but to seek them out. Because behind every 10 or 20 no's was a yes. Plus, the more doors they knocked on, the better their sales pitches got as they learned to deal with objections. This process, though frowned upon today, has been used to sell vacuums, encyclopedias, chocolate bars, pens, and many other products.

But whether you're knocking on doors, calling on distributors, selling through a website, or networking at a party, the premise is the same: If you're not failing, then you're not talking to enough prospective customers. Sara Blakely, the youngest female billionaire according to *Forbes* magazine, and founder of the Spanx empire, sees failure as a big part of an entrepreneur's success. In many interviews she talks about how her father would ask her, "What did you fail at today?" She learned early on in life that failure happens because you're getting out of your comfort zone and trying new things, and with those risks you're going to fail from time to time. So embrace it. The sales process involves getting a series of commitments from a prospective customer, distributor, or retail buyer over time. These commitments come in the form of an agreement to meet for an appointment, to follow up, to accept a sample or view a demo, and hopefully to sign a contract or place an order. Each commitment moves the customer closer to agreeing to buy from you.

Keep in mind that your sales pitch should vary depending on whether you are targeting direct consumers of your product, intermediaries, or investors. Each of the three groups requires a different sales pitch. For example, if you're the owner of B.K.H. Jerky, a visitor to *Dragons' Den* in Season 6, then consumers will want to know whether your jerky is great tasting. Intermediaries will want to hear about the revenue opportunity you are bringing them. And investors will want to know the return on investment that an investment in your business will bring them. The reason why B.K.H. Jerky was successful when they visited *Dragons' Den* is that, after finishing a successful taste test of their product, they refocused their selling efforts on their current audience: the Dragons.

Go-to-Market Snapshot: B.K.H. Jerky

Pitchers: Scott and Raymond Lim, Season 6, Episode 2

GO-TO-MARKET

B.K.H. Jerky produces Singapore-style beef and pork jerky that contains less salt, fat, and MSG than the competition's. B.K.H. Jerky plans to sell through distributors and retailers and is in talks with Urban Fare, Costco, Vancouver International Airport, and B.C. Ferries.*

*As of show participation.

THE ASK

$150,000 for 25% equity.

COMPANY VALUATION

$600,000.

THE DEAL

$150,000 for 50% equity.

PROOF-OF-CONCEPT

- Family-owned business for over 25 years.
- $485,000 in direct sales.
- $160,000 net profit.

TESTIMONIAL

"The best jerky I've ever had. The product's very good. It's all distribution."
   —Dragon to Dragons

Scott and Raymond Lim pitching B.K.H. Jerky.

THE WARM-UP: SALES PROCESS DEFINED

A sales process consists of a series of steps, each designed to get a small commitment from a prospective customer in order to move that customer closer to agreeing to buy from you. The purpose of a sales process is to build trust over time, rather than pressuring someone to say yes or no after a quick sales pitch. The good news is that you don't have to reinvent the wheel, because there is a formal sales process you can follow and/or modify to meet your needs. Three important aspects of this sales process are:

- **The Sales Cycle:** A series of events that a customer goes through between the time he or she first contacts you and the time he or she commits to buy from you.
- **The Sales Model:** A strategy for sales consisting of either a transactional model or a consultative model.
- **The Sales Pitch:** A repeatable sales pitch that can be 60 seconds or 60 minutes, depending on how complex your product or service is.

The Sales Cycle

Drawing attention to your product or service is one thing. Converting interested prospects into paying customers is another. The time it takes to get an order from a customer after you have made your initial contact with him or her is referred to as the sales cycle. You can do all the preparation in the world that you want, but if you don't master the sales cycle of your business, your business won't survive. Most sales cycles follow a pattern that can be repeated over and over. Your first contact with a prospective customer is the beginning of the sales process. The importance of understanding the sales cycle cannot be overstated, because the longer it takes to close a sale, the longer it takes for you to get paid. Although each sales model can be unique, yours may evolve from the generic phases that many sales go through before an order is made.

Length of the Sales Cycle: How Long Does It Take to Convert an Interested Buyer into a Paying Customer?

The length of your sales cycle depends on the complexity of your product or service and the amount of buyer education and customization required. Your sales cycle can be measured in seconds, hours, days, months, or even years. For example, the chocolate-bar-buying sales cycle is short—it might take seconds in a line-up at the grocery store. But the car-buying sales cycle might be six months because the buyer might shop around. Over time, you'll want to shorten the sales cycle by qualifying customers in advance for financing or by doing a better job at marketing.

Phases of the Typical Sales Cycle

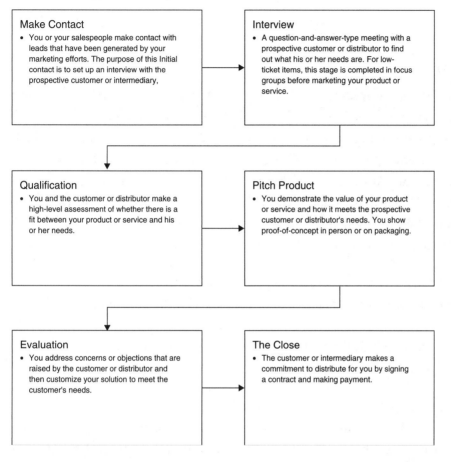

Make Contact
- You or your salespeople make contact with leads that have been generated by your marketing efforts. The purpose of this Initial contact is to set up an interview with the prospective customer or intermediary,

Interview
- A question-and-answer-type meeting with a prospective customer or distributor to find out what his or her needs are. For low-ticket items, this stage is completed in focus groups before marketing your product or service.

Qualification
- You and the customer or distributor make a high-level assessment of whether there is a fit between your product or service and his or her needs.

Pitch Product
- You demonstrate the value of your product or service and how it meets the prospective customer or distributor's needs. You show proof-of-concept in person or on packaging.

Evaluation
- You address concerns or objections that are raised by the customer or distributor and then customize your solution to meet the customer's needs.

The Close
- The customer or intermediary makes a commitment to distribute for you by signing a contract and making payment.

The Sales Model

Consultative Sales Model: Higher-Priced Items

In an ideal world where time and money aren't an issue, you'd speak to every individual customer, one by one; ask what his or her needs are; and then customize your product or service to fit those specific needs. Of course, this is not always possible, but it is the heart of the consultative sales model. Using a consultative sales model, it may take days, weeks, months, or even years to persuade the customer, distributor, or retailer to buy from you. Some attributes of the model to consider are that it:

- Works with higher-priced items (e.g., landscaping services, professional services, car sales) because of the cost of spending time with each customer.

- Requires phone, Web, or face-to-face contact with the customer.
- Requires a longer sales cycle.
- Requires a customer-training process in some cases.

Transactional Sales Model: Low-Ticket items

The core function of the sales process is to determine the customer's needs and then offer a product or service as a solution. But when you're selling a relatively lower-priced product or service, this can't always happen on the spot. You have to do some work in advance, through focus groups, and then come up with a solution that requires little or no customization or education at the point of sale. At the heart of the transactional sales model is the exchange between you and the customer that should require little or no customization on your part. Customers do their own homework in advance, before they buy from you, based on marketing you have done. Some attributes of the model to consider are that it:

- Works with lower-priced items (chocolate bars, gadgets, perfume, cosmetics).
- Requires little or no phone, Web, or face-to-face contact with the customer.
- Involves a shorter sales cycle.
- Involves little or no customer training, though an online demo or support manual might support the sales process.

The Hybrid Sales Model

If you are marketing a low-ticket item, you would still use a consultative model when speaking with intermediaries. The sale to the final consumer would then depend on a transactional model.

The 60-Second Sales Pitch

Imagine that you have 60 seconds or less to convince a customer or intermediary that you have a product or service that it should order. What are you going to say?

1. What problem does your product or service solve or what need does it fill?
2. How does your product or service uniquely solve that problem or meet that need?
3. How do you charge? (Refer to the discussion on revenue models in Chapter 4, to define how you charge.)

4. What proof/demo/sample do you currently have that proves that the customer should need or want your product or service?

5. How do you want the customer to place his or her order?

Dragon Lore

Try to get smaller commitments over time from the person you are trying to sell to, such as an agreement to meet in person, to follow up, or to view a demo.

What triggers a sale is not always what you think. Some businesses that visit *Dragons' Den* make money by selling water, while others make money by helping to eliminate the need for it. When GoClean Waterless Carwash visited *Dragons' Den*, it wasn't until pitcher Sunny Yashpal mentioned that it's illegal to wash your car with water in Toronto, that all of the Dragons started to finally pay attention to his business.

Go-to-Market: GoClean Waterless Carwash

Pitcher: Sunny Yashpal, Season 6, Episode 5

THE BUSINESS

GoClean Waterless Carwash lets you wash, wax, polish, and protect your car with one solution.

GO-TO-MARKET

Sold through retailers, including Canadian Tire, and direct through a website.

SALES PITCH

"In Toronto, it's actually illegal to wash your car with water . . . GoClean Waterless Carwash is Canada's best and first to market waterless carwash . . . It is a proprietary mix of polymers, lubricants, organic surfactants, and natural soaps. It's a biodegradable product. It lifts the dirt off the surface of the car and it lubricates the surface of the car. So it's actually not hurting the car. One bottle actually gives you 10 car washes."

TESTIMONIAL

"I've got to tell you, it's pretty amazing."
—Dragon to Pitcher

PROOF-OF-CONCEPT

- Sold 3,000 units in Canadian Tire, at $15 apiece.
- 500 stores will carry it.
- For each bottle sold, a donation is made to the African Well Fund to build wells in Africa.

THE ASK

$35,000 for a 10% stake.

THE DEAL

$35,000 for a 10% stake.

Pitcher Sunny Yashpal pitching GoClean Waterless Carwash to the Dragons.

Self-Study Workshop: The Sales Process

Structure your sales pitch in a way that makes it repeatable and effective. Be prepared to make slight modifications to your pitch, based on the type of person you are selling to.

Step 1: Your **sales pitch**

1. What **problem** does your product or service solve? What need does it fill?
2. What is your product or service and how does your product or service **uniquely solve that problem** or meet that need?
3. How much do you **charge**?
4. What **proof/demo/sample** do you currently have that proves that the customer should need or want your product or service?
5. How do you want the customer to **place his or her order** (over the phone, in person, by fax, or over the Web?)
6. Link each of the last four responses into a single **60-second pitch**.
7. Pick up the phone today and **test your pitch** on 10 people you know. Keep a list of who you spoke with and how they responded.

Step- 2: Where is the **first contact** with a customer made?

- ❑ Website
- ❑ Phone-in
- ❑ Face to face
- ❑ A store
- ❑ Other

Step 3: How is the first **question-and-answer interview** with a customer completed?

- ❑ Online form
- ❑ Person to person
- ❑ Other
- ❑ Prospective customers aren't interviewed.

Step 4: How is a prospective customer **qualified** once they contact you?

Step 5: What can you do to **demonstrate** your product or service to a prospective customer?

Step 6: What types of **objections** might a prospective customer have about your product or service?

Step 7: What is **required** to process an order?

- ❑ Contract
- ❑ Order form
- ❑ Credit card
- ❑ Cash payment
- ❑ Other

One goal of any business should be to become more proficient over time at doing what you do. When it comes to proficiency, nothing is more valuable than shortening the time it takes to close a sale, by improving your sales pitch. To make your sales job even easier, the final chapter of this book provides you with a framework for developing proof points that you can use to convince both customers and even investors that your offering is right for them.

CHAPTER 28

WHAT PROOF DO YOU HAVE THAT YOUR BUSINESS MODEL WORKS?

"This guy will not have any trouble raising $150,000 in another room down the street. This guy is one of the best salesmen. He understands his business, his numbers."
—Dragon to Dragons

Go-to-Market Step #5: Getting to Proof-of-Concept

Prove your concept technically using prototypes. Establish market proof using a limited market pilot test. Establish financial proof by generating profitable revenue.

Business concepts that can be proven early have the potential to spread like a virus. We go to see new movies because everyone else raves about them. We frequent new restaurants because someone else tells us how great they are. We buy new gadgets because somebody told us about a problem they were able to solve. We buy from soon-to-be successful businesses because those companies solve burning problems that we previously have been unable to solve. Karl Elsener proved his *product concept* for a multipurpose rust-resistant knife when he got an order from the Swiss Army back in the 1890s. John Schnatter proved his *service concept* for a pizza delivery service called Papa John's Pizza by selling pizzas out of a former broom closet in the back of his father's tavern. Chip Wilson proved his *retail concept* for a healthy living hub when he opened his first store in Kitsilano, British Columbia, back in 2000, selling Lululemon Athletica yoga clothes and running gear. In order to prove that your business idea has the potential for the kind of growth you are seeking, prove your concept before investing heavily by using prototypes, limited market tests that can be extrapolated, and testimonials from early customers, distributors, and retailers in the field.

Proof-of-concept is such a critical part of the launch of any business that many businesses will appear to be completely pie-in-the sky until you actually achieve it. For example, if you tell someone you are going to start a high-end designer jewellery business from the ground up, most people will think you're crazy because the business sector can require an expensive, high-risk branding campaign. But when Rachel Mielke of Hillberg & Berk visited *Dragons' Den*, she showed how a high-quality product, backed by a creative marketing campaign, can lead to results with both customers and Dragons alike.

Go-to-Market Snapshot: Hillberg & Berk

Pitcher: Rachel Mielke, Season 3, Episode 3

GO-TO-MARKET

Hillberg & Berk design, manufacture, wholesale, and retail high-end designer jewellery. The go-to-market strategy is focused on designing collections and fostering relationships with retailers. It also uses innovative PR, including giving out the jewellery to celebrities.

THE ASK

$200,000 for 20%.

THE DEAL

$200,000 for 33%.

PROOF-OF-CONCEPT

- $110,000 in revenue over the last year.*
- Distributing to about 20 stores in western Canada.*
- Deidre Hall from *Days of Our Lives* has worn pieces from the collection on the soap opera.

*As of show participation.

TESTIMONIAL

"It's really, really, very nice."
—Dragon to Pitcher

Rachel Mielke (left) from Hillberg & Berk showing off her high-end designer jewellery collection.

THE WARM-UP: PROOF-OF-CONCEPT DEFINED

Proof-of-concept refers to a stage in your business when you have technical, market, and financial evidence that proves you have a business model that works. It's important to prove that your business is technically viable, market feasible, and financially viable *before* you invest heavily. The process of achieving proof-of-concept involves achieving three types of milestones, called "proof points." Definitions vary by industry, but the components are the same:

- **Technical Milestones:** A working product or service prototype, and method of scaling the prototype to higher volumes.
- **Market Milestones:** Consists of a revenue-generating pilot test, letters of intent, testimonials, and case studies.
- **Financial Milestones:** Profitable revenue (i.e., monetization), investor funding targets, and other financial results for your business concept.

Proof points are the single most powerful way to grip investors. Once you have gathered a list of proof points, you can use them to build your business plan (see *The Dragons' Den Guide to Investor-Ready Business Plans,* the companion guide to this book, for more on building a business plan) and even to seek investment capital. After all, if you can't convince a test group of people to rave about your product or service, why would an investor believe that you have a good business idea? Once you have established proof-of-concept through proof-point milestones, you have the basis for a full-scale business—or for an investor-ready business plan, if you need to seek outside capital.

Technical Milestones

The biggest problem with many back-of-the-napkin business ideas is that they become a solution looking for a problem. You invent something that sounds exciting to your immediate circle of friends, family, and maybe fools, but when you ask them to buy it from you, they give you a blank stare. That's because many opinions from people close to you are clouded by the excitement they have for making you feel good about your decision to launch a business. But unless you ground your decision in real facts, you may be stuck with a garage full of inventory. To achieve technical proof-of-concept you'll need a:

- **Working Prototype:** A prototype product or service that works and allows you to give live demonstrations.
- **Commercial Version:** A market-ready version of your product or service that can be sold.
- **Operational Model:** A repeatable method of producing your product or delivering your service.
- **Intellectual Property Protection:** A patent, trademark, domain name, copyright, or other form of intellectual property protection that shows you have something proprietary.

Dragon Lore

You don't have a business if you don't have revenue. And if you want that business to be sustainable, then you need to make sure that your revenue is profitable.

Proof-of-concept milestones are particularly important when you are trying to unseat an industry norm. For example, EcoTraction, producers of an all-natural road salt replacement, most likely had its hands full when it first tried to compete against road salt. But by targeting individual business consumers of road salt one at a time, the business slowly established enough market proof to convince big brand name consumers of road salt, such as Starbucks and Pharmasave, to sample and use their solution in their parking lots.

Go-to-Market: EcoTraction

Pitchers: Mark Watson and Marc Appleby, Season 3, Episode 5

THE BUSINESS

EcoTraction is an all-natural, highly porous volcanic mineral that can be used in place of road salt.

GO-TO-MARKET

The company's go-to-market strategy is focused on establishing relationships with national retailers and gas stations that use EcoTraction in their parking lots, and with retailers that sell EcoTraction on their shelves.

SALES PITCH

"About three years ago, my dog, Grover, suddenly died from cancer. After going to the oncologist, they suggested there was a toxin in the environment and it may have been the road salt. This led me to look for an eco-friendly alternative to road salt. EcoTraction is basically an all-natural volcanic mineral. It's a highly porous, naturally occurring stone that basically absorbs the thin layer of water on the surface of ice, embeds itself almost like Velcro, creating a sandpaper effect. So rather than actually melting the ice, it creates a safe traction zone so that you don't slip and fall."

TESTIMONIAL

"I think this is a great product, and I think they have something very, very on-target."
—Dragon to Dragons

PROOF-OF-CONCEPT

- On track to sell $500,000.
- Starbucks, Pharmasave, pet shops, and gas stations across the country.
- Exclusive mining rights for all of North America so long as they reach their sales quota.

THE ASK

$150,000 for 5% stake or $300,000 for 10%.

THE DEAL

$500,000 for a 25% stake.

Pitchers Mark Watson and Marc Appleby of EcoTraction leaving the Dark after the Dragons finished structuring an offer.

Market Milestones

Most people like knowing that someone else has already tried something before they go ahead and try it themselves. What proof do you have that your business concept works? Have you field-tested your products or services? Do you have revenue or testimonials from a test pilot? Do you have customer evangelists who just love talking about how great your product or service idea is? It's important to listen to what the market is telling you because the ultimate judge of your business model is a continuous stream of paying customers—or lack thereof. And until you have them, your business idea is nothing more than a hypothesis that could fail miserably. To prove your concept in the market, you'll need to gather proof that real customers are buying from you. This proof comes in the form of case studies and testimonials.

Case Studies: Real-World Success Stories

The single most important factor in the success of any new business concept is a paying customer who faces a challenge that you can help overcome. There is nothing more valuable than a customer who has achieved success with your product or service and is willing to talk about it. Customers have their own unique motivations for buying your product or service; a case study describes a specific customer's motivation and successful use of it. Not to be confused with a user story, which is an aspirational story about what a customer would like to do if a product or service like yours existed, a case study is an actual example of your product or service in use. To build case studies for actual customer types, include these three components in each:

- **Trigger Event:** The event or circumstances that led to the customer purchasing your product or service.
- **Customer Challenge:** The specific problem or obstacle a customer was looking to overcome before he or she used your product or service.
- **Customer Solution:** The unique way that your product or service was used to address the customer's challenge.

Testimonials: A Written Endorsement

People who are satisfied with your product or service are usually more than happy to provide you with a statement about their positive experience. These statements, preferably written, can be used to convince distributors, retailers, investors, and prospective customers that your product or service is as good as you say it is. You can use a testimonial from a retailer that carries your line to persuade another retailer to give you some shelf space. You can use a testimonial from a supplier to convince a manufacturer to work with you. You can even use a testimonial to convince a potential advisor to join your advisory board. Just be sure to follow the specific ethical and regulatory protocols of your industry.

Financial Milestones

Being an entrepreneur is about taking risk and executing. It involves trial-and-error execution that can lead to big wins and big losses. To build a sustainable business you have to establish financial proof (a.k.a. market traction) early and often that your product or service concept will actually work. It doesn't mean you have to start generating $50,000 in revenue per month a few short months after you open the doors. But you do have to see some indication that you're not betting the farm on an unviable idea. And that means generating revenue. If you're on the wrong track, and no one is paying you, have the wherewithal to change direction or cut your losses fast. Here are some simple financial indicators to look for:

- **Revenue Milestones:** Financial targets that cover your expenses and/or your salary.
- **Top-Line Growth:** Revenue is increasing.
- **Bottom-Line Growth:** Profit is increasing.

Self-Study Workshop: Prove That Your Business Model Works

Proof-of-concept consists of mini-milestones that you achieve early on in your business venture. Proof points, or lack of them, show you whether you should continue to invest in your business model.

1. Build a **working prototype**.
   Produce a working version or mock-up of your product or service in the next 7 to 30 days. It must be a visual representation of what you plan to sell, and can be a paper prototype if necessary. Note any takeaways or observations from the process.

2. Set up a **live demo**.
   Set up a method for conducting a live demo of your product or service to show a prospective customer how it works to solve a burning problem. Note any takeaways or observations from the process.

3. Acquire **intellectual property protection**.
   Acquire a patent, trademark, copyright, domain name, or other form of intellectual property protection that shows you have something proprietary. Note any takeaways or observations from the process.

4. Hold a **pilot test**.
   Conduct a limited market test with 10 to 100 paying customers. Pilot tests help to test the logistics of your business concept so you can work out the kinks before you invest in a full-scale business plan. Note any takeaways or observations from the process.

5. Get **testimonials**.
   Get 5 to 10 written statements from users of your working prototype that indicate satisfaction with your product or service concept. Note any takeaways or observations from the process.

6. Collect **case studies**.
   Write up case studies that describe actual scenarios from real users of your product or service. Include the event that triggered interest in your product or service, the challenge or problem the customer was looking to overcome, and how your product or service was used to solve that real problem. Follow the ethical guidelines for your industry, get permission from anyone whose name you use, and keep the case studies short. Note any takeaways or observations from the process.

7. Build a **customer list**.
   Keep track of customers and prospective customers. Note any takeaways or observations from the process.

8. Get **commitment from potential employees and advisory board members** who you have on board or will bring on board once revenue milestones have been achieved. Note any takeaways or observations from the process.
   Name them.

9. Continue to build **market traction**.
   Achieve one or more revenue milestones that have been outlined in your sales projections.
   Name them.

10. Write a **mini-business plan**.
    Put together a 10- to 15-slide PowerPoint presentation that explains your business. Note any takeaways or observations from the process.

Proof-of-concept is the Holy Grail of a business start-up. It gives you something called "social proof" that can be used to convince more customers and prospective investors to take an interest or even a stake in your business. Now that you have completed, and hopefully enjoyed the process, it's time to recap what you've learned and figure out next steps.

CONCLUSION

THE DRAGONS' DEN PLAYBOOK

THE 10 DRAGONS' DEN SUCCESS FACTORS IN REVIEW & NEXT STEPS

"Get a good idea and stay with it. Dog it, and work it until it's done and done right."

—Walt Disney

> **The Dragons' Den Playbook**
>
> Inject your business concept with the 10 Dragons' Den Success Factors. Then create a business plan around that business model.

Where would we be without Google, the Swiss Army knife, Apple, Facebook, or Twitter? These ventures all started with a vision of how to solve a problem or meet a market need. Google came about when Sergey Brin and Larry Page figured how to use backlinks to improve search results on a Web page. The Swiss Army knife came about after a request from the Swiss Army for a multi-purpose tool that could be used in battle. Facebook came about when Mark Zuckerberg figured out how to help students find, contact, and update each other through an online website. And Twitter came about when Jack Dorsey figured out how to share a text message with a small group of people at one time.

The Dragons' Den Playbook: The 10 Dragons' Den Success Factors in Review

The most important ingredient in all of these businesses wasn't a business plan. It was the problem their products or services originally solved, the team behind them, and their speed to market. If a business plan was the *only* ingredient for dominating a market, then Microsoft's Bing would have crushed Google's search engine by now, Palm would be crushing Apple's iPhone, and MySpace would never have let Facebook get off the ground. All of these businesses put the customer first and then built a business model and business plan around that customer. Here's a recap of the 10 Dragons' Den Success Factors that can help you do just that:

SUCCESS FACTOR #1: FOCUS ON A SINGULAR PAIN POINT

Solve a yet-to-be solved burning problem that no other solution on the market currently addresses, or addresses poorly.

SUCCESS FACTOR #2: BUILD A PROTOTYPE

Put a rudimentary version of your product or service idea together as fast and as cheaply as possible.

SUCCESS FACTOR #3: DEFINE YOUR VALUE PROPOSITION

Figure out why the world is better off with your product or service than without it.

SUCCESS FACTOR #4: ESTABLISH A REPEAT REVENUE MODEL

Charge a price point that will generate the highest number of repeat profitable customers in the shortest amount of time.

SUCCESS FACTOR #5: TARGET A DISRUPTABLE MARKET

Target an addressable market segment, preferably one that is fraught with dissatisfaction.

SUCCESS FACTOR #6: BUILD A LEAN FEATURE SET

Stand out in a sea of competition by eliminating as many unnecessary features from your prototype as you can, so that the important features have a chance to stand out.

SUCCESS FACTOR #7: COLLABORATE WITH STRATEGIC PARTNERS

Collaborate with advisors, staff, outsourced service providers, and other businesses that can help you achieve your goals faster than you can achieve them on your own.

SUCCESS FACTOR #8: FIND A CATALYST FOR GROWTH

Find a person, action, or event that can trigger a rapid increase in sales that you otherwise wouldn't have achieved on your own.

SUCCESS FACTOR #9: SCALABILITY

Establish a repeatable internal operating process that can handle sudden increases in customer volume without being constrained by staff or financial resource limitations.

SUCCESS FACTOR #10: DEVELOP A BUSINESS MODEL

Establish a sustainable money-making system that describes your product/service sold, the customer served, and your repeat revenue model.

Summarize your business concept

1. **Focus on a Singular Pain Point**: "The customer problem that my business concept solves is . . ."
2. **Build a Prototype**: "The next action I need to take to create or improve my prototype is . . ."
3. **Define Your Value Proposition**: "The world is better off with my business idea than without it because . . ."
4. **Establish a Repeat Revenue Model**: "The revenue streams of my business are . . ."
5. **Target a Disruptable Market**: "My most profitable customer can be described as . . ."
6. **Build a Lean Feature Set**: "The three most important features of my product/service are . . ."
7. **Collaborate with Strategic Partners**: "Three businesses I can partner with to reach my goals faster are . . ."
8. **Find a Catalyst for Growth**: "An event or action I can take to achieve a sudden increase in sales is . . ."
9. **Scalability**: "My business can handle a sudden increase in customer volume because . . ."
10. **Develop a Business Model**: "My sustainable money-making system can be described as . . ."

NEXT STEPS: CREATING YOUR BUSINESS PLAN

Whether you like it or not, your business has to have a plan. If you take control of that plan by documenting it and refining it, your business concept has the chance to impact your life beyond your wildest dreams. But if you don't, you may regret that you ever let the idea of a business creep into your life. Customers will disappear. Your team may lose interest. Unsold inventory will sit unsold. And funding will dry up. That's why this book has focused on helping you assess the most important aspect of every business: a revenue-generating business concept. Once you have completed the 28 workshops in this book and have concluded that you should go forward with your business, the next step is to create a business plan. At the same time, once you have proven that your business concept works, it's time to add structure, in the form of a 10- to 40-page business plan.

If you are ready to plan your business in more detail, then I invite you to take this information and structure your business using the companion guide to this book, *The Dragons' Den Guide to Investor-Ready Business Plans*. In it you'll learn the investor courting process, structure an elevator pitch, design a PowerPoint pitch deck, put together an executive summary, and create an investor-ready, bank-ready, or operational business plan. Plus you'll learn how to set up a management structure, financial roadmap, and an operations plan to reach your business goals . . . all using the same *workshop-driven approach* that you have become accustomed to in this book.

If you have enjoyed this book or want to learn more, please visit the book's website, www.FastGrowthDNA.com.

Good luck!

Glossary

100 People You Know A list of 100 people you could call up tomorrow, with whom you have rapport at some level.

Account Receivable A promise made by a customer to pay you cash at a later date.

Advertising A sales pitch that can be sent to multiple people at once.

Advisory Board A team of people you know who agree to provide periodic advice, support, and connections in exchange for being involved with your venture.

Attributes An intangible characteristic of your product or service.

B2B Business-to-business sales efforts.

Beginner's Mind Once you think you know everything, you'll stop learning. Operating with a beginner's mind means you are open to switching your business direction on a dime if the market shifts, or if the right opportunity presents itself.

Behavioural Profile A description of your ideal customer in terms of his/her habits.

Behaviouristic The shared hobbies, sports or other activities of your ideal customer.

Benefit Why each of your product or service features is important.

Bootstrapping Funding a business startup using your own funds.

Boundaries A personal set of limits that you have in place.

Brand Experience The set of customer interactions that you will use to tell your brand story.

Brand Messaging What you would like your product or service to be known for.

Brand Story Everything about your product's or service's history that makes it interesting.

Brand What your business is known for.

Breakeven The number of units that you have to sell in order to cover your fixed costs.

Bundling Convincing another product manufacturer or service provider to sell your product or service as an add-on to theirs.

Business Case The summary of details that justify your business both financially and non-financially.

Business Model A sustainable money-making system that describes your product/service sold, the customer served, and your repeat revenue model.

CAGR The compound annual growth rate of your industry.

Case Studies Real-world success stories from paying customers.

Cash Flow Timing When you receive your cash, which could be upfront, over periods of time, or after a service is performed.

Cash Flow A snapshot of the difference between the cash coming into your business minus the cash going out of your business.

Catalyst A person, action or event that can give you access to an immediate increase in sales revenue.

Channel A method used to reach your customers.

Channel Conflict Arises where different distribution channels are at cross purposes in terms of pricing, territory, or other factors.

Closing Getting an order from a paying customer.

Co-Brand Allowing another business to put its name on your product, in addition to yours.

Collaboration Working toward a common goal with people and partners who want to work with you.

Competitive Advantage An operational or feature advantage that makes your business, product or service more attractive than your competitors'.

Consultative Sales Model A problem-solving method of selling in which the customer is probed for problems, and then a solution is applied to that problem.

Copyright Protection for authored work such as a drawing, a software program, a book, music, or an article.

Core Purpose The mission behind your business.

Cross-Functional Support A group of functional experts from multiple disciplines, whom you can assemble periodically to complete projects that require multiple skill sets.

Cyclicality How industry sales volume reacts during various stages of the business cycle.

Demand Drivers Factors that affect purchasing decisions in your industry.

Demographic Profile A description of your ideal customer in terms of ideal age, income, education, occupation, and gender.

Demographic Describes your typical customer's age, income, and education.

Direct Channels Making your product or service available directly to consumers. Includes door-to-door sales, teleselling, and ecommerce.

Direct Competition Competitors that sell a product or service that is similar to yours.

Direct Sales Selling directly to another individual, with no intermediary.

Distributors Intermediaries who carry your product and resell it to retailers.

Domain Expert Someone who is skilled in a specific industry or market space.

Elevator Statement A brief personal sales pitch that describes what your product or service is, why it is valuable, and what proof you have that it's worth the price.

Emotional Value Describes how your product or service makes the customer feel.

Environment A description of the environment in which your product or service will be used.

Exclusions Features people might expect your product or service to include, that you are purposely excluding from your offering.

Exclusive Distribution Making your product or service available through one intermediary per geographic region.

Feasibility Study The process of thinking through a business idea and documenting it on paper to determine whether to go ahead with it or not.

Feature Set A set of functions or attributes of your product or service that your ideal customers value.

Feature A component of your product that is uniquely valuable.

Financial Feasibility Testing Assessing whether your potential revenue and profit are enough to support your business goals.

Financial Milestones Profitable revenue.

Fixed Cost A sunk cost that doesn't change regardless of how much volume your business does.

Franchise Giving another business the legal right to use your business model, brand name, and operating process, in exchange for an ongoing royalty.

Functional Value Describes why your product or service is useful.

Geographic Profile A description of your ideal customer in terms of where that customer can be found (in a specific province, city, home environment, work environment, etc.).

Geographic Where your ideal customers are located.

Go-to-Market A strategy for bringing your product or service to market.

Gross Domestic Product (GDP) The total value of all goods and services produced in Canada at any point in time. This is a term that most countries use to measure the size of their economies.

Gross Profit The amount of profit you generate on product and service sales, after cost of goods sold, and before selling, general, and administrative expenses are factored in.

Growth Rate The percentage increase in total industry-wide sales volume, year over year.

Highest-and-Best-Use The ideal purpose for which your product or service is meant.

Home Party Plans In-home social events made famous by Tupperware, where products are sold.

Identity The visual look and feel of your product or service, including the name, logo, colour scheme, and overall design.

Indirect Channels Making your product or service available through intermediaries. Includes distributors, retailers, and strategic relationships.

Indirect Competition Products and services that fill the same need that yours does.

Industrial Design The form (look and feel) and function (quality, aesthetics, etc.) of your product, or the steps involved in your service.

Innovation A novel approach to solving a customer's problem.

Intensity Refers to the number of locations or channels through which your product or service is made available.

Joint Venture Establishing a business entity separate from your own, that is co-owned by another business.

Kano Model A framework for categorizing product or service features as either must-haves, nice-to-haves, or "wow" factors.

License Giving another business the legal right to produce your product or deliver your service, in exchange for an ongoing royalty.

Licensing Model A business model that you choose to let others use, in exchange for an ongoing licensing fee.

Line Extension An add-on product that appeals to a new market segment.

Market Demand The industry-wide sales that a product or service category generates per year.

Market Feasibility Testing Assessing the proposed market to quantify if it is large enough to support your business goals.

Market Leader A company that sells more of your product or service than any other business in the industry.

Market Milestones A successful pilot test, letters of intent, testimonials, and case studies.

Market Size Analysis A framework for breaking a market down into available, serviceable, and obtainable markets so you can more accurately project revenue going forward.

Marketing Pull Advertising to the end user of your product or service, to create public awareness, so the end user starts requesting your product or service.

Message Platform A set of basic selling points you communicate through your marketing efforts.

Mock-up A representative version of your product or service that is made out of paper or modelling clay.

Monetary Value Describes how your product or service makes or saves the customer money.

MSRP Manufacturer's suggested retail price.

Non-Compete Agreement Protection from employees in the form of a contract or contract clause, to keep them from setting up a rival business and stealing your customers.

Operating Profit The amount of profit you generate on your business, after factoring in cost of goods sold and selling, general, and administrative expenses.

Operational Concept A bird's-eye view of how your product or service works.

Outcomes Personal results you expect out of launching your business concept.

Output The product you produce, or the tangible result of your service.

Owner/Operator Model A business model that you choose to run yourself, instead of licensing it to someone else.

Pain Point A pain point is a yet-to-be solved problem that your product or service addresses.

Partnering Working with other organizations, at arm's length, toward a common goal.

Patent Protection for inventions such as equipment or processes.

Personal Selling One-to-one selling between you and a customer or intermediary.

Piggyback Marketing Piggyback marketing is a go-to-market strategy that uses channels that are already in place, to sell your product or service.

Planned Obsolescence Building a product or service that will need to be replaced in the future.

Point of Differentiation The features, attributes, and benefits that are unique to your business.

Positioning One of many different personalities or identities that your product or service takes on in the eyes of the public.

Private Labelling Allowing another business to put their name, instead of yours, on your product.

Problem Statement A single declarative statement of the void your product or service fills in the marketplace.

Process A series of steps taken to produce a product or perform a service.

Product Category A product or service type such as dry cleaning services, dog walking services, or smartphones.

Product Environment The place where your product or service is used.

Product Lifecycle A lifelike pattern of sales growth for a product or service type.

Product or Service What customers get in exchange for payment.

Product Roadmap A release schedule for new features and versions of your product or service.

Product A tangible good or intangible service.

Product-Centric Process Finding a market for a product that you have already come up with.

Proof-of-Concept Technical, market, and financial proof that your business works.

Prototype Review A walk-through of your product or service with a real potential customer.

Prototype A partial or fully functional version of your product or service that is used to elicit feedback from potential customers.

Psychographic Profile A description of your ideal customer in terms of how that customer thinks and makes decisions.

Psychographic The attitudes of your ideal customers.

Publicity Free advertising.

Rapid Prototyping A process used to produce a three-dimensional throwaway model of your tangible product, in a very short period of time for a very low cost.

Recession Two straight quarters of declining GDP (also known as negative growth).

Resellers Intermediaries who buy and sell someone else's product or service.

Retailers Specialty stores and multi-department stores that carry your product or allow you to offer your service.

Return on Investment What an investor receives in return for the amount invested, usually expressed as a percentage of the amount invested. This can be a complicated calculation because it is based on a series of net cash flows over time that may be uneven.

Revenue Model How you charge for your product or service.

Revenue Sources What your business does to generate revenues.

Role Model A successful business that uses a business model that you would like to emulate.

Sale Collateral A set of marketing pieces that a sales rep can show to potential customers or intermediaries.

Sale Process A strategy for sales involving a short sales transaction or a long problem-solving process.

Sales Calls In-person appointments where you pitch your product or service using a live demonstration, or free sample.

Sales Cycle A series of stages that a customer goes through before he or she commits to buying your product or service.

Sales Push Contacting an intermediary directly and selling your product or service as a revenue opportunity for them.

SAM Total available market that is serviceable by any competitor, including you.

Scalability Scalability is the ability of a business system to handle sudden increases in customer volume without slowing to a crawl.

Scalable Growth The ability to adapt to growing volume in sales without your business systems slowing to a crawl.

Seasonality The seasonal highs and lows of market demand for your type of product or service.

Selective Distribution Making your product or service available through a select number of intermediaries or outlets per geographic region.

Self-Assessment A personality assessment that is an introspective look at the mindset you have going in.

Service Prototyping Creating a storyboard of sticky notes, with each note representing a step in your service process. Or setting up a small-scale pilot test of your service.

SOM Total available market that is both serviceable and obtainable by you.

Sourcing Screening suppliers, vendors, and manufacturers.

Stakeholders Customers, investors, partners and others who have a vested interest in the successful launch of your business.

Standardized A predictable quality level.

Supplier A source of raw materials, components, or ingredients for your product or service.

Survey Techniques Methods of discovering problems that people have with current products and services available on the market.

Sustainable Competitive Advantage Cost or feature advantages that are difficult to replicate.

SWOT An analysis of the strengths, weaknesses, opportunities and threats that your competitors have or are facing.

Synergy When two separate entities are more valuable together than they are worth on their own.

TAM Total available market.

Technical Feasibility Testing Assessing whether your product or service works, as promised, and if it can be produced at a volume scale that is required to support your business goals.

Technical Milestones Evidence that your product or service works.

Teleselling Calling customers, distributors, or retailers to convince them to buy or carry your product or service.

Testimonials A written endorsement from a paying customer.

The Business Cycle A trackable cycle of up-and-down patterns in economic activity (a.k.a. GDP) in Canada and other countries. The business cycle can be like a tidal wave that influences unemployment, inflation, interest rates, and consumer confidence.

Touchpoint A point of contact that your customer makes with your product or service.

Trade Association An organization that provides support to a product or service category.

Trade Secret Protection for a formula or process that you keep a secret.

Trade Show A place where intermediaries go to find products and services to resell.

Trademark Protection for symbols, names, and a logo that you use to identify your product or service.

Trade-off Swapping out one expensive component for a lower-cost alternative.

Transaction Model A method of selling in which the customers make quick purchase decisions.

Trends Economic, technology, design, social, and demographic patterns in your industry.

Trigger Events The events that lead to people seeking out your product or service.

Unique Selling Proposition A unique feature, attribute, or benefit that you highlight in your advertising campaign.

Use Case A sequence of steps that someone would follow to solve a problem.

User Story A user story is a single sentence statement of what a customer would like to be able to do with a product or service like yours if given total design freedom.

Validation Acknowledgement that your product or service does something that a real customer would be willing to pay for.

Value Proposition What superior outcome can customers expect by using your product or service, instead of their current solution?

Variable Cost A cost per unit of product or service.

Verification Verify that your product or service works to solve the problem.

Waste Elimination Eliminating unnecessary components of your product or service.

Endnotes

CHAPTER 1

1. For more on this subject, I recommend that you read Mike Cohn, *User Stories Applied* (Boston: Addison-Wesley, 2004).
2. CBC Digital Archives, "Tim Hortons: 'Ron Joyce has a story to tell,'" accessed June 6, 2012, http://www.cbc.ca/archives/categories/economy-business/consumer-goods/tim-hortons-coffee-crullers-and-canadiana/ron-joyce-has-a-story-to-tell.html.
3. Ibid.
4. Tim Hortons, "The History of Tim Hortons," accessed May 14, 2012, http://www.tim-hortons.com/us/pdf/en_media_kit.pdf.
5. Ibid.

CHAPTER 2

1. For more on this subject, I recommend that you read Nassim Nicholas Taleb, *The Black Swan: The Impact of the Highly Improbable* (New York: Random House, 2010).
2. BPG Werks, "BPG Werks > Home of the DPV Shredder," accessed June 25, 2012, http://bpgwerks.com.
3. Marcia Froelke Coburn, "On Groupon and Its Founder, Andrew Mason," Chicagomag.com, August 2010, accessed June 6, 2012, http://www.chicagomag.com/Chicago-Magazine/August-2010/On-Groupon-and-its-founder-Andrew-Mason.
4. Christopher Steiner, "Meet the Fastest Growing Company Ever," Forbes.com, August 12, 2010, http://www.forbes.com/forbes/2010/0830/entrepreneurs-groupon-facebook-twitter-next-web-phenom.html accessed June 6, 2012.
5. Groupon.com, "About Us," accessed May 14, 2012, http://www.groupon.com/about.

CHAPTER 3

1. Dinesh D'Souza, Ronald Reagan: How an Ordinary Man Became an Extraordinary Leader (New York, Free Press: 1999).
2. Clayton Christensen, a professor at Harvard Business School, pioneered the concept of disruptive innovation. See: Larissa MacFarquhar, "When Giants Fail," *The New Yorker*, May 14, 2012, p. 84.
3. Eleanor Beaton, "Born to Make a Giant Leap," *Profit Magazine*, August 28, 2011, accessed June 6, 2012. http://www.profitguide.com/manage-grow/sales-marketing/born-to-make-a-giant-leap-30203.
4. Reed Hastings, as told to Amy Zipkin, "Office Space: The Boss; Out of Africa, onto the Web," *New York Times*, December 17, 2006, accessed June 25, 2012, http://query.nytimes.com/gst/fullpage.html?res=9B0CE2D91231F934A25751C1A9609C8B63.
5. Netflix is the world's leading Internet subscription service for movies and TV shows, with over 23 million subscribers. See: Netflix, "Investor Relations," July, 2011, accessed June 25, 2012, http://ir.netflix.com.
6. Steve Lohr, "And the Winner of the $1 Million Netflix Prize (Probably) Is. . .," *New York Times*, June 26, 2009, accessed June 25, 2012, http://bits.blogs.nytimes.com/2009/06/26/and-the-winner-of-the-1-million-netflix-prize-probably-is.

CHAPTER 4

1. BBC News Berkshire, "Groupon vouchers decision cost Berkshire business thousands," November 18, 2011, accessed May 14, 2012, http://www.bbc.co.uk/news/uk-england-berkshire-15791507.
2. Re/Max Corporate Information, History of Re/Max, accessed May 14, 2012, http://www.remax.com/national-corp/history/index.aspx.
3. Re/Max Corporate Information, Board of Managers and Officer Biographies, Dave Liniger, accessed May 14, 2012, http://www.remax.com/national-corp/biographies/dave_liniger.aspx.

CHAPTER 5

1. Rod Canion, *The Compaq Story*, 1982, accessed May 14, 2012, http://www.youtube.com/watch?v=t3qI5kAjh4M.
2. The Computer History Museum, "Compaq Portable," accessed May 14, 2012, http://www.computerhistory.org/revolution/mobile-computing/18/316/1195.
3. IBM, "The PC: Personal Computing Comes of Age," accessed May 14, 2012, http://www.ibm.com/ibm100/us/en/icons/personalcomputer/breakthroughs/.

CHAPTER 6

1. *The New Encyclopedia Britannica,* 15th edition, 1992, s.v. "Ockham's razor."
2. Noriaki Kano, "Attractive Quality and Must-Be Quality," *Journal of the Japanese Society for Quality Control,* 1989, 14(2), pp.39–48.
3. Apple, "Apple Reports Fourth-Quarter Results," October 18, 2010, accessed June 25, 2012, http://www.apple.com/pr/library/2010/10/18Apple-Reports-Fourth-Quarter-Results.html.
4. AppleGazette.com, "Apple Prototypes: 5 Products We Never Saw," accessed June 6, 2012, http://www.applegazette.com/mac/httpwwwapplegazettecomwp-adminpostphpac-tioneditpost272.
5. StrategyAnalytics.com, "90% of Apple iPad Buyers Will Be Existing Apple Owners," August, 23 2010, accessed June 25, 2012, http://www.strategyanalytics.com/default.aspx?mod=pressreleaseviewer&a0=4944.

CHAPTER 7

1. Peter J. Boyer, "The Deliverer," *The New Yorker*, February, 2007, accessed June 6, 2012, http://www.newyorker.com/reporting/2007/02/19/070219fa_fact_boyer.
2. Dominosbiz.com, "Making pizza since 1960," accessed May 14, 2012, http://www.dominosbiz.com/Biz-Public-EN/Site+Content/Secondary/About+Dominos/History/.
3. National Association of Pizza Operators qtd. in Chris Nichols, "Today in Food Finance: Domino's to Let You Go Gluten-Free," *Yahoo! Finance*, May 7, 2012, accessed June 25, 2012, http://finance.yahoo.com/blogs/the-exchange/domino-let-gluten-free-160438224.html.
4. Dominosbiz.com.
5. Ibid.

CHAPTER 8

1. Holy Crap, "We're Dragons' Den biggest success story," March 14, 2012, accessed May 14, 2012, http://holycrap.ca/news/holy-crap-were-dragons-den-biggest-success-story.
2. Background information provided by Amy Federman, Director, Corporate Communications, Bacardi Limited.

CHAPTER 9

1. Inc.com, "How This Kid Made $170 Million in Two Years," accessed May 14, 2012, http://www.inc.com/ss/aaron-patzer-made-170-million#1.
2. Serkan Toto, "Mint is Yodlee's YouTube," *TechCrunch*, September, 2009, accessed June 6, 2012, http://techcrunch.com/2009/09/18/mint-is-yodlees-youtube.
3. Ibid.
4. Jason Putorti, "How Mint.com Acquired 1.5M+ Users," *Jasonputorti.com*, March 25, 2010, accessed June 25, 2012, http://putorti.tumblr.com/post/472866002/how-mint-com-acquired-1-5m-users.

CHAPTER 10

1. Mary Theresa Bitti, "Running on Empties." *Financial Post*, October 10, 2011. Accessed May 14, 2012, http://business.financialpost.com/2011/10/11/running-on-empties/#more-99356.
2. Research In Motion, "Introduction," accessed May 14, 2012, http://www.blackberry.com/select/get_the_facts/pdfs/rim/rim_history.pdf.
3. Ibid.

CHAPTER 11

1. The 5 Whys was conceived by Sakichi Toyoda prior to his death and was used to solve problems at the Toyota Motor Co. See: José Rodríguez Pérez, *CAPA for the FDA-Regulated Industry*, Milwaukee, WI: ASQ Quality Press, 2010.
2. Times Colonist, "Into the Dragons' Den," September, 23, 2008. http://www.canada.com/victoriatimescolonist/news/arts/story.html?id=f8e20e5b-a810-485e-b638-92be-83be01a8.

CHAPTER 12

1. Essentia, "Message from Jack," accessed May 14, 2012, http://www.myessentia.com/message.

CHAPTER 15

1. Chipotle Mexican Grill, "Chipotle Story—How It All Started," accessed May 14, 2012, http://www.Chipotle.com/en-US/chipotle_story.
2. Nike, Inc., "History & Heritage," accessed May 14, 2012, http://nikeinc.com/pages/history-heritage.
3. Starbucks, "The Starbucks Company Timeline," accessed May 14, 2012, http://www.starbucks.com/assets/aboutustimelinefinal72811.pdf.

CHAPTER 19

1. Tiffany & Co., "History," accessed May 14, 2012, http://press.tiffany.com/Local/en-US/Doc/Tiffany_&_Co_History.pdf.
2. Martin Van Buren, accessed May 14, 2012, http://www.whitehouse.gov/about/presidents/martinvanburen.
3. P&G, "A Company History 1837—Today," accessed June 6, 2012, http://www.pg.com/translations/history_pdf/english_history.pdf.

CHAPTER 22

1. Canadian Restaurant and Foodservices Association, "Research," accessed June 6, 2012, http://www.crfa.ca/research.
2. Fitness Industry Council of Canada, "Canadian Fitness Industry Statistics," accessed June 6, 2012, http://www.english.ficdn.ca/canadian-fitness-industry-statistics.

CHAPTER 23

1. Mattel, "Mattel History," accessed May 14, 2012, http://corporate.mattel.com/about-us/history/default.aspx.
2. Nike, Inc., "History & Heritage," accessed May 14, 2012, http://nikeinc.com/pages/history-heritage#tab2-tab.

3. Spanx, "Sara's Story," accessed May 14, 2012, http://www.spanx.com/corp/index.jsp?page=sarasStory&clickId=sarasstory_aboutsara_text.

CHAPTER 25

1. Hewlett-Packard, "Rebuilding HP's Garage," accessed May 14, 2012, http://www8.hp.com/us/en/hp-information/about-hp/history/hp-garage/hp-garage.html.
2. Cold Stone Creamery, "The Cold Stone Creamery Story," accessed May 14, 2012, http://www.coldstonecreamery.com/about/cold_stone_story.html/.

Acknowledgements

Thank you for buying this book, because the real catalyst for this book is you—an entrepreneur who has decided to take action on a business idea, with the hope of changing your life for the better. Everyone who watches *Dragons' Den* loves it—not just because it's entertaining, but because it shows every person in this country that an idea can be turned into a business that will change their life and the community around them.

There are many people who need to be thanked for putting this book together:

The team at the CBC *Dragons' Den*, including Marc Thompson, Sandra Kleinfeld, Tracie Tighe, Keri Snider, and Karen Bower, with specific thanks to Molly Duignan, producer of CBC *Dragons' Den* and resident expert on the show, and to Dianne Buckner, host of *Dragons' Den*, for contributing the foreword. Thanks also go to Lisa O'Connell and Lindsay Pearl at Sony/2WayTraffic for making the project possible.

The team at Wiley, with a special call-out to Jeremy Hanson-Finger, production editor, and Jane Withey, developmental editor, as well as the copyeditors, Judy Philips and Nicole Langlois.

Several others who also need to be thanked include James Murphy, a personal development expert and executive coach at Evolution for Success, who added insight and technical value to the Self-Assessment section of this book, as well as Luc Hekman, Jean-Marc Poirier, Raj Ananthanpillai, David Lester, Brien Fraser, Lars Bodenheimer, and Raj Narasimhan, who provided support through the writing process.

Personal thanks go to my wife's cousin, author Marilyn Picard, for connecting me to Wiley; my entrepreneurial father-in-law, John Milne, Sr.; my mother-in-law, for her constant support and quiet strength; and my parents John & Annette Vyge, for their support and inspiration. And, finally, my wife and partner in life, Sandy, for her support, and our two children, Trinity and Whitney, who helped me think through many of the words on these pages during our routine "monster walks" through the parks and fields around our home. Your passion for learning new things continues to inspire me every day.

About the Author

John Vyge is a Certified Financial Planner™ professional and business plan analyst who advises entrepreneurs and investors on how to create investor-ready business plans around winning business concepts. He researches fast-growth companies to develop insight for his recommendations. John is the author of *Model Marketing Kit,* is a contributing author for *Investing in an Uncertain Economy for Dummies,* and was a technical reviewer for *76 Tips for Investing in an Uncertain Economy for Canadians for Dummies.* He has been quoted in various publications including *The Washington Post, Business Week* online, *Investment News Magazine,* BankRate.com, and *Insurance & Advisor* magazine.

Index

Looking for More?

VISIT WWW.JOHNVYGE.COM

Share your success story
Talk to the author online
Share your brand story
Download worksheets
and more . . .

Bring these concepts into your business through training initiatives,
consulting engagements, and keynote addresses.